More Praise for

"What is the future of Meth⸺⸺⸺⸺⸺⸺⸺⸺⸺⸺⸺⸺⸺⸺
tion on this difficult question and suggests an answer: we find its future in
the margins of the church. To live into this future, Nashville and London
must learn to sing together with Seoul, Latin America, and Africa."
    —Pablo R. Andiñach, PhD, Professor of the Hebrew Bible, Instituto
Teológico Santo Domingo; Universidad Católica Argentina; Seminario
Rabínico Latinoamericano

"In *The People Called Metodista*, Edgardo Colón-Emeric has mined trea-
sures that have been hidden to many of us, particular in the North American and European expressions of Methodism. If Methodism is a renewal
movement, voices speaking to us from the margins will lead us to new
insight and to holy living. Through the translation of doctrine, worship
and mission into a language that surfaces new accents and engages a wider
community of conversation partners, Colón-Emeric has broken new
ground that will hopefully enlarge our vision for who we are in the present moment."
    —Ken Carter, Bishop, Florida and Western North Carolina Confer-
ences, The United Methodist Church

"The Holy Spirit, who blows wherever it wishes, continues to give life
around the world. Across this book, Dr. Colón-Emeric helps us open our
eyes to see and enjoy God's new creation in and through the people called
metodista. He reminds us of how the Spirit continues to create something
new amid chaos. This book will renew your hope and inspire you to join
God's move!"
    —Eric A. Hernández López, DMin, Chair of the Board of Directors,
Evangelical Seminary of Puerto Rico

"The Wesleyan tradition—as a piety, a community in mission, and a theology—took rise within and has found repeated renewal through engagement with those on the fringes of the reigning 'powers.' At its best, it has
nurtured deep respect for its foundation in Scripture and earlier Christian

witness, while cultivating openness to new understandings and expressions of 'faith working by love.' Colón-Emeric's study exemplifies Wesleyanism at its best, probing the witness of Hispanic streams of Methodism for insights addressing the entire movement, much of which suffers from malaise and morbidity. Highly recommended."

—Randy L. Maddox, PhD, William Kellon Quick Emeritus Professor of Wesleyan and Methodist Studies, Duke Divinity School

"Gratitude to God for this winsome, faithful, encouraging resource for the people of God in every place. Edgardo Colón-Emeric refreshes and deepens the powerful gospel summons to attentiveness at the margins. Let us go with him to the edge, where our strangely warmed hearts become hearts afire, corazones ardientes."

—Hope Morgan Ward, Retired Bishop, North Carolina Conference, The United Methodist Church

More about the Author

Edgardo A. Colón-Emeric is dean of Duke Divinity School, Irene and William McCutchen Associate Professor of Reconciliation and Theology, and director of the Center for Reconciliation. His work aims to reconcile Christian traditions by attending to the concrete intersections of Wesleyan and Latin American forms of Christianity and engaging classic and contemporary theological sources from the margins. Born and raised in Puerto Rico, Colón-Emeric was the first Latino to be ordained as an elder in the North Carolina Conference of The United Methodist Church and was founding pastor of Cristo Vive UMC in Durham, North Carolina. His award-winning books include *Wesley, Aquinas, and Christian Perfection: An Ecumenical Dialogue* (Baylor University Press, 2009) and *Óscar Romero's Theological Vision: Liberation and the Transfiguration of the Poor* (Notre Dame University Press, 2018).

Edgardo Colón-Emeric

To Paul,
With deep gratitude for your support
and friendship.

Edgardo

THE PEOPLE CALLED
METODISTA

Renewing Doctrine, Worship, and Mission from the Margins

 Abingdon Press™

Nashville

THE PEOPLE CALLED METODISTA:
RENEWING DOCTRINE, WORSHIP, AND MISSION FROM THE MARGINS

Copyright © 2022 by Abingdon Press

LCCN: 2022939329

ISBN: 9781791024000

Unless noted otherwise, Scripture quotations are from the New Revised Standard Version Bible, copyright © 1989 National Council of the Churches of Christ in the United States of America. Used by permission. All rights reserved worldwide. http://nrsvbibles.org/

"Chapter 2: Jesus Was Born in Guatemala: Towards a Latinx Wesleyan Christology" was previously published as Edgardo Colón-Emeric, "Jesús was born in Guatemala: Towards a Latinx Wesleyan Christology," *Wesleyan Theological Journal* 54.2 (2019), reprinted with permission of the *Wesleyan Theological Journal*, in association with the Wesleyan Theological Society (https://wtsociety.com/wesleyan-theological-journal).

"Chapter 3: Medellín through Methodist Eyes" was previously published as Edgardo Colón-Emeric, "Medellín through Methodist Eyes," *Journal of Ecumenical Studies* 54.3, 2019, reprinted by permission of the publisher (University of Pennsylvania Press, a.k.a. Penn Press, https://jes.pennpress.org/home).

Chapter 5, "Wesleyans and Guadalupans: A Theological Reflection," was previously published as Edgardo Colón-Emeric, "Wesleyans and Guadalupans: A Theological Reflection" in *American Magnificat: Protestants Reflect on the Virgin of Guadalupe*, edited by Maxwell Johnson, Liturgical Press, copyright (2010) by Order of Saint Benedict, Collegeville, Minnesota. Permission granted by Liturgical Press.

Chapter 6, "Singing Wesley in Spanish," was previously published as Edgardo Colón-Emeric, "Singing Wesley in Spanish," *Liturgy* 25.2 (January 2010), reprinted by permission of the publisher (Taylor & Francis Ltd, http://www.tandfonline.com).

Chapter 8, "The Word of Reconciliation: A Wesleyan Perspective on Public Theology," was previously published as Edgardo Colón-Emeric, "The Word of Reconciliation: A Wesleyan Perspective on Public Theology" in *Exploring a Wesleyan Political Theology*, edited by Ryan Danker, Wesley's Foundery Press, 2020, in association with the General Board of Higher Education and Ministry of the United Methodist Church.

The lyrics on pages 59–60 are from Federico Pagura, "Tenemos esperanza" ("We have hope"), *Mil voces para celebrar* (Nashville, TN: United Methodist Publishing House, 1996), Hymn 129. The translation into English is my own. Used by permission.

The lyrics on page 224 are from Federico Pagura, "Hemos cubierto la tierra," *Un cántico nuevo*, ed. Jorge Maldonado (Quito, Ecuador: Eirene, 1989), 192. Used by permission.

Unless otherwise noted, all translations are the author's.

MANUFACTURED IN THE UNITED STATES OF AMERICA

Contents

Contents

Foreword

It would be very difficult to deny what seems to be one of the starting points of this book: Methodism is in crisis. A crisis may not always be bad, but it is always painful and unsettling. The reason is obvious: a crisis forces us to look at what we have always taken for granted, and (even more) a crisis often lays bare insidious compromises of which we were not aware.

Part of the crisis that Dr. Colón-Emeric so clearly describes is the result of the very success of Methodism. What began at Oxford as a group of young men seeking to be more faithful to their calling is now a worldwide movement with millions of followers, many of whom are not even aware that they are heirs of Wesley. Today, the Methodist movement has more spiritual heirs in Latin America than it does in the United States, and the people actually "called Methodist" show greater vitality in Africa, Asia, Latin America, and the islands of the Pacific than they do in the North Atlantic.

At the heart of the present crisis is a new polycentric reality, so that no longer can North-Atlantic Methodism be considered normative. While in some matters the centers may still be in the North-Atlantic, in others new centers have emerged—centers in Korea, Zimbabwe, Brazil, and the Philippines, to name just a few. These centers see the world from their own perspectives: they read the Bible with their own questions, and they seek to worship in their own style and within their own contexts. As their faith and their Methodist heritage become more and more enculturated, they tend to think that their way of seeing and doing things is the only proper way, and that the old center from which they first received their faith is abandoning that faith. At the same time, those in the old centers are unable to see to what degree their faith has been compromised by their own enculturation. For this reason, they cannot understand why others no longer accept the notion that their understanding and practice of Christianity should be normative.

Such a crisis should not necessarily lead to a lack of love and understanding that Wesley would deem catastrophic. It could well become a fruitful crisis, leading to new experiences of faith, to new acts of love, to new gleams of hope. However, this cannot be done unless we all, each looking at our own situation, acknowledge the degree to which our own experience of faith, our practice of love, and our action in mission are limited by our own captivity to the compromises we and our ancestors have made with prevailing cultural trends.

In my own case, I can illustrate this using two examples from two traditions within Methodism that I deeply love, that have shaped me, that could be mutually enriching, and yet are so committed to their own way of doing and seeing things that it is very difficult for either one of them to learn from the other.

Let me begin with the North American church. My first awareness of the captivity of most Methodists in the United States to its socioeconomic environment came some seventy years ago. My older brother was a seminary student and told me stories about how in the late Middle Ages corruption in the church was such that the people could buy ecclesiastical offices, a practice called "simony." We were at our home in Cuba, and our dinner guest was the bishop of Florida, who at that time was also the bishop of Cuba. In the after-dinner conversation he told us that he had to hurry home because it was time to decide on appointments, and he had to take into consideration the salary level of each appointment because the churches with larger budgets expected to receive the best preachers. I was puzzled because in our annual conference all salaries were equal, no matter the size of a church. My immediate comment—with a lack of discretion typical of a teenager—was: "My brother has been telling me about how in the Middle Ages people would buy positions in the church. What is the difference between pastors buying churches and churches buying pastors?" My shin still hurts from the kick I received under the table!

As I now remember that event, what I find most disturbing is that the bishop did not even understand the enormity of what I was saying—or rather, the enormity of what the entire church was doing. He just kept on going about the beauty of the appointment system.

Some time later, the same bishop called my brother and told him, "You are one of our best pastors. We have a very difficult church, divided, bankrupt, and full of immorality. I am sending you there, not as a punishment, but because I believe you can do what is needed there."

I am now convinced that in this latter instance he was being more faithful to the true *ethos* of Methodism—and of Christianity—than in the former case. In that former case, he was tied to the traditional center. He was so tied to it that he could not see how far it had deviated from traditional Christianity. I am immediately reminded of Wesley's nostalgic comments about the time when most Methodists were poorer, and therefore better.

Then there is another face of Methodism that I cherish just as much as I cherish its North American face. This is the Methodism in which I grew up and the Methodist heritage of which I partake when I visit many a Methodist or Pentecostal church either in Latin America or in a North American Latino barrio. It is a face of joy. It is a form of worship that is a true fiesta to the glory of God. It is an evangelism that is truly good news to those without hope. It is a church constantly pouring itself out in service to neighbor. And yet, it still has much to learn from that other North Atlantic Methodism that I experience daily and love dearly.

This too I could illustrate with many anecdotes and experiences. I remember visiting a church that called itself Methodist and, when I asked how often they celebrated communion, I was told that they never did, for communion was "Popish." I remember the anguish and anger of a classmate who was also a member of one of our churches, trying to deal with a pastor who insisted that he shouldn't go on with his studies because faith was enough, and if he studied too much he would lose his faith. That pastor, a respected leader in our annual conference, even tried to pressure my friend's parents to pull him out of school!

Thankfully, much of that has changed. But there is still in some Latin American Christian circles a tendency to what Wesley would despairingly call "enthusiasm"—by which he meant a faith with much emotion but no content, with much joy but little knowledge, and rejoicing in that condition as if it were the will of God.

We are all captive of what we take for granted. Now in the United States I constantly experience what I saw in the bishop's comments in our dining room and would now call the "socioeconomic captivity" of Methodism—and of much of the rest of the church. Liberation from such captivity will not come primarily from within but by listening to the witness and experience of the church catholic—of the church in Brazil, in Nigeria, and in Fiji. On the other hand, all too often, both in Latin America and in the Latinx community in this country, I find people who are subject to the "spiritualistic captivity" of the church. This is a captivity—in some Methodist circles as well as in other branches of the church—to a view of Christianity that seems to believe that the best way to be suited for the coming world is to ignore the present, and that self-righteousness trumps love. This branch of the church cannot liberate itself from its captivity without listening to the witness and experience of the church catholic—including First United Methodist Church of Wherever in the North Atlantic.

In many ways, in this book Colón-Emeric presents numerous cogent arguments for, and examples of, such dialogues—not just among people called *metodista*, nor even only among heirs of the Wesleyan tradition, but throughout all the church catholic. Significantly, he is inviting us to share in the experiences and views of a Methodist church in a small Latin American village, of the Conference of Catholic Bishops meeting in Medellín, of Archbishop Óscar Romero, and of many others of the great cloud of witnesses covering the earth.

May we listen to what he says, and through this listening may we also hear the voice of God, calling us to face the present crises, not with belligerence, but with love; not with platitudes, but with justice; not in despair, but in hope!

Justo L. González
Decatur, GA
Lent, 2022

Acknowledgments

This book on Methodist doctrine, worship, and mission has its origins in pastoral ministry. It was as a young pastor starting a new Hispanic congregation in Durham, North Carolina, that I first began to reflect on the gift of Spanish-speaking Methodists for the church as a whole. Thus, when I think of giving credit where credit is due, I begin with thanking the congregation of Cristo Vive, which I served for five years, and the people who accompanied me and supported me then. There was the intellectual support of Justo González, who graciously agreed to write a foreword to this book; the pastoral accompaniment of pastors like Hector Millán; and the prayers and patience of many parishioners. On the latter, I need to mention my wife Cathleen, who served as our chief church musician, and my sons Nate and Ben, who accompanied me to many Bible studies.

After entering full-time service at Duke University, I have been introduced to Methodist communities in Latin America that have powerfully formed my vision of the gospel and understanding of my intellectual vocation as a Christian theologian. In particular, I am grateful for the Methodist churches in El Salvador, Guatemala, Honduras, Nicaragua, Puerto Rico, Perú, Cuba, and Argentina for opening their doors to me as a teacher and learner.

Hispanic/Latinx theologians underscore the importance of working en conjunto (together), and this book is no exception. I am grateful to Abingdon Press for publishing this work and for the mentorship and guidance of colleagues at Duke Divinity School like Greg Jones and Kavin Rowe.

I owe special thanks to support from the Provost's office for securing the assistance of Jacki Price-Linnartz as a research editor. I cannot overestimate the significance of Jacki's contribution to this project. Amidst the many competing demands for my time, she helped keep me on schedule and elevated the quality of my work through her diligent research, coordination of conversations with publishers, and stellar editing work. ¡Gracias!

Finally, I am thankful to God for calling me to ministry in, for, and from the Methodist church. It has now been around forty years since I answered that call affirmatively. The journey has been long; the road conditions have been difficult at times. However, the company has been good, and as John Wesley said, "The best of all is, God is with us."

Edgardo Colón-Emeric
Easter, 2022

Note on Wesley Works

When possible, the following work relies on *The Bicentennial Edition of the Works of John Wesley*, General editors Frank Baker and Richard P. Heitzenrater (Nashville, TN: Abingdon Press, 1984–).

Volumes cited include:

Vol. 1: *Sermons I: 1–33*, edited by Albert C. Outler, 1984.

Vol. 2: *Sermons II: 34–70*, edited by Outler, 1985.

Vol. 3: *Sermons III: 71–114*, edited by Outler, 1986.

Vol. 4: *Sermons IV: 115–151*, edited by Outler, 1987.

Vol. 7: *A Collection of Hymns for the Use of the People Called Methodist*, edited by Franz Hildebrandt and Oliver A. Beckerlegge, with the assistance of James Dale, 1983.

Vol. 9: *The Methodist Societies: History, Nature, and Design*, edited by Rupert E. Davies, 1989.

Vol. 10: *The Methodist Societies: The Minutes of the Conference*, edited by Henry D. Rack, 2011.

Vol. 11: *The Appeals to Men of Reason and Religion and Certain Related Open Letters*, edited by Gerald R. Cragg, 1989.

Vol. 18: *Journals and Diaries I (1735–1738)*, edited by W. Reginald Ward and Richard P. Heitzenrater, 1988.

Vol. 19: *Journal and Diaries II (1738–1743)*, edited by Ward and Heitzenrater, 1990.

Vol. 20: *Journal and Diaries III (1743–1754)*, edited by Ward and Heitzenrater, 1991.

Vol. 21: *Journal and Diaries IV (1755–1765)*, edited by Ward and Heitzenrater, 1992.

Vol. 22: *Journal and Diaries V (1765–1775)*, edited by Ward and Heitzenrater, 1993.

Vol. 24: *Journal and Diaries VII (1787–1791)*, edited by Ward and Heitzenrater, 2003.

Vol. 25: *Letters I (1721–1739)*, edited by Frank Baker, 1980.

Vol. 26: *Letters II (1740–1755)*, edited by Baker, 1982.

Introduction

Renewing the Methodist House

The Future of Methodism

"Pour the streaming deity on all thy church below."[1] These words from a hymn by Charles Wesley for Pentecost Sunday express a simple truth: the church lives by the Spirit. The presence and power of the Holy Spirit constitute the church as more than a social gathering, making it the body of Christ and the people of God. Spirit and church belong together. Irenaeus of Lyons expresses this connection in a memorable statement: "For where the church is, there is the Spirit of God; and where the Spirit of God is, there is the church, and every kind of grace."[2] No Pentecost; no church. The early Methodists lived into the Pentecostal reality of the church with such intensity that it startled observers, even evoking charges of heresy from those who confined the work of the Spirit to the apostolic

---

1. Charles Wesley, Hymn 14, *Hymns for Whitsunday* (Bristol: Felix Farley, 1746), https://divinity.duke.edu/sites/divinity.duke.edu/files/documents/cswt/37_Whitsunday_Hymns_%281746%29_mod.pdf.

2. Irenaeus, *Against Heresies*, III.24.1, https://www.newadvent.org/fathers/0103324.htm.

1

age.[3] The parallels between Pentecost and the Methodist revival testified to the "streaming deity" in their midst and to the future of Methodism as a reform and renewal movement.

When I think of the future of Methodism, two stories come to mind. The first happened during a visit to Huitzapula, a village deep in the mountains of central Mexico. I went there in May 2008 with a group of pastors, lay persons, and seminary students from Duke Divinity School. Our Methodist hosts fed and sheltered us in their main sanctuary, a structure with a dirt floor, reed walls, and a sheet metal roof. Despite the humble setting, this congregation had three missionary outposts. One was a building made of adobe with no doors and a half-crumbled wall. We were not expecting to meet anyone. It was, after all, a Thursday afternoon, but soon after we arrived, people started coming to the church to greet us. We soon realized they expected to worship and that one of the visitors should preach. A friend of mine reluctantly volunteered but only felt comfortable preaching in English. The members of the Methodist congregation in Huitzapula belonged to the Tlapaneco people, and while some spoke Spanish, most were more comfortable in their Indigenous language. So as my friend preached in English, I translated to Spanish, and one of the lay leaders of the Methodist church of Huitzapula translated to Tlapaneco. I do not recall our words, but I vividly remember how it sounded: it sounded like Pentecost.

My second story regarding the future of Methodism happened during the General Conference of The United Methodist Church (UMC) that met in St. Louis, Missouri, in February 2019. Against the backdrop of persistent and acute divisions on inclusion of LGBTQ persons, over a thousand United Methodists from around the world gathered in a convention center to pray, discuss, and vote on various proposals for a way

---

3. In a 1760 sermon, James Clark states, "In a word, there seems to be a very great affinity between the spirit of Montanism, at its first appearance, and the spirit of Methodism. They both went upon the same plan and with the same view and design of raising the Christian religion to a greater height of perfection and spirituality than it was before and both oblige their disciples to much more frequent and severe acts of mortification, fasting, and self-denial, than the Catholic Church ever thought fit or necessary to oblige her sons to, or require from them." James Clark, *Montanus Redivivus: Or, Montanism Revived, in the Principles and Disciplines of the Methodists* (Dublin: H. Saunders, 1760), 16.

forward. The delegates and attendees only agreed on one point—that it was a painful gathering. As a delegate in attendance, I felt the nadir of the meeting on its final afternoon. By then, most delegates had voted to uphold a version of what was known as the traditional plan, and many delegates, particularly from the United States, were deeply frustrated with the process and hurt by the results. After coming back from a long recess, the presiding bishop called us to order by asking the musicians to lead the assembly in song. As voices rose singing "Spirit of the Living God, fall afresh on me," a group stood and shouted "No!" The clash of words and sounds was jarring and continuous: "Melt me." "No!" "Mold me." "No!" "Fill me." "No!" "Use me." "No!" I am not here criticizing the singing or the protest. Rather, my point is that the cacophonous overlap of song and shout did not sound like Pentecost. It sounded like Babel, and it did not bode well for the future of the UMC.

What is the future of Methodism?[4] This is not a new question. In 1786, five years before his death, John Wesley expressed his concern: "I am not afraid that the people called Methodists should ever cease to exist either in Europe or America. But I am afraid lest they should only exist as a dead sect, having the form of religion without the power."[5] There are signs Wesley's fears have come to pass. One need look no further than the aforementioned 2019 General Conference of the UMC. But that is not the whole story. There is also the story of the Pentecost in Huitzapula.

Is there a future for Methodism? I am neither a forecaster nor a gambler—I dare not guess the fate of the UMC, global Methodism, or Christianity itself. I am, for better or worse, a theologian. Thus, when I think of the future of Methodism, I begin not with the current struggles but with the end. John Wesley believed God raised the Methodist people "to reform the nation, and in particular the Church, to spread scriptural

---

4.   I addressed this topic in a *Circuit Rider* piece in 2020 following the publication of the "Protocol of Reconciliation and Grace through Separation." See Edgardo Colón-Emeric, "The Future of Methodism Is not Methodism," *Circuit Rider* (February 2020): 50–52.

5.   John Wesley, "Thoughts upon Methodism," ¶1, in *The Methodist Societies: History, Nature, and Design*, ed. Rupert E. Davies, vol. 9 of *The Bicentennial Edition of the Works of John Wesley* (hereafter *Works*) (Nashville, TN: Abingdon, 1984–), 527.

holiness over the land."[6] The end of Methodism was not to create and sustain a powerhouse denomination; its purpose was ever-sharable, ever-growing, holy love. At heart, Methodism remains a reform, renewal, and revival movement that makes disciples of Jesus Christ (not simply disciples of John Wesley) for the transformation of the world (not simply for congregational growth).[7]

Is there a future for Methodism? Yes, but the future of Methodism is not North American Methodism. Church affiliation has declined significantly in the United States.[8] Faced with an aging (and dying) church population, mainline denominations like the UMC have been warned of what Lovett Weems calls a "death tsunami" sweeping through their lands, causing untold damage to congregations and communities.[9] Meanwhile, Methodism—like Christianity in general—is booming in regions of the world associated with the Global South. In *The Next Christendom*, Philip Jenkins argues that when thinking of the typical, ordinary Christian, we should picture a Brazilian woman living in a favela.[10] A similar demographic shift is occurring among the heirs of John Wesley. New maps are being drawn.

Methodist historian and theologian Justo González surveys the landscape and observes that "now there is no real center. When it comes to financial resources, the center is still in the North Atlantic. The same is true when it comes to other parallel resources, such as libraries, educational

---

6. John Wesley, "The 'Large' *Minutes*, A and B (1753, 1763): Minutes of Several Conversations between the Reverend Mr. John and Charles Wesley, and Others," Q.4, *Works* 10:845.

7. See "The Mission and Ministry of the Church," in *The Book of Discipline of The United Methodist Church, 2016* (Nashville, TN: United Methodist Publishing House, 2016), ¶121, 93–94.

8. Pew Research Center, "About Three-in-Ten U.S. Adults Are Now Religiously Unaffiliated" (Dec. 14, 2021), https://www.pewforum.org/2021/12/14/about-three-in-ten-u-s-adults-are-now-religiously-unaffiliated/.

9. Lovett H. Weems, Jr., "The Coming Death Tsunami," *Ministry Matters* (October 5, 2011), https://www.ministrymatters.com/all/entry/1868/the-coming-death-tsunami. See also Weems, *Focus: The Real Challenges That Face The United Methodist Church* (Nashville, TN: Abingdon, 2012).

10. Philip Jenkins, *The Next Christendom: The Coming of Global Christianity*, 3rd ed. (New York: Oxford University Press, 2011), 1–2.

institutions, publishing houses, and the like. But when it comes to growth and vitality, as well as to theological creativity, there are new centers."[11] The centers of Methodism have moved from London, New York, and Nashville to Seoul, Abidjan, and Rio de Janeiro. United Methodism in the United States and Methodists around the world are called to face a sobering and exciting reality: "We are a center that must be nourished by other centers, that must be in dialogue with other centers."[12] These centers of renewal are potentially everywhere the Spirit of God is present; that said, Methodists have found this presence particularly powerful at the margins of society. Peter Storey's experience in Apartheid South Africa convinced him of the gospel truth that "if Jesus had a home address in this world, it was among the poor."[13] Among the people of District 6, this Methodist minister encountered the Jewish carpenter in thickly sacramental ways.

Is there a future for Methodism? Yes, but the future of Methodism is not mainline. It is not even Methodist. When read from the end, the story of Methodism is appreciated for what it is: pages in the divine story of the one, holy, catholic, apostolic church. The plot of the story of Methodism, like that of John Wesley's life, is real Christianity.[14] Its future depends on rediscovering its vocation. At heart, Methodism is not a church but a renewal movement for the sake of the church catholic.[15] Where the flames of this movement have cooled in the North, I go South to learn how Christians in general and Methodists in particular witness to Jesus as they are moved by fresh outpourings of the streaming deity. There are resources among Hispanic and Latin American Christians and Methodists that can renew Methodist doctrine, worship, and mission for the sake of the one

11. Justo L. González, "Beyond Christendom: New Maps," *Toronto Journal of Theology* 27.2 (2011): 189–202, 191.

12. Justo L. González, "Wesley's Heritage and the Global Church," *Methodist History* 43:2 (January 2005): 115–30, 129.

13. Peter Storey, *Protest at Midnight: Ministry to a Nation Torn Apart* (Eugene, OR: Cascade, 2022), 26.

14. See Kenneth J. Collins, *A Real Christian: The Life of John Wesley* (Nashville, TN: Abingdon, 1999), 37.

15. E.g., see Albert C. Outler, "Do Methodists Have a Doctrine of the Church," in *The Doctrine of the Church*, ed. Dow Kirkpatrick (Nashville, TN: Abingdon, 1964), 11–28.

church. Indeed, read from the end, the future of Methodism as real Christianity cannot be fully understood apart from the people called metodista.

Before I proceed, I offer a few caveats. First, I want to avoid pathologizing mainline Methodism in the United States. Sources of renewal spring forth from many places, and I have been blessed with the gift of serving white rural Methodist churches and multicultural urban ones in North Carolina. Moreover, aging mainline Methodism has much to contribute to Christianity's renewal precisely through the wisdom its elders have to share with younger generations. I also want to avoid romanticizing Christians from the Global South and the people called metodista. My sisters and brothers from these communities also struggle with fidelity to the Spirit of God rather than the spirit of the age. If I fall into these errors in the following pages, I welcome correction. Nevertheless, I do not apologize for my focus on the people called metodista. Their voice is seldom heard in conversations about the church, and these valuable voices have much to contribute both to church renewal and to the purpose for which God raised the people called Methodists. In brief, I believe metodistas can help all Methodists feel young and emboldened for mission again, confident the unending hymn sung by the entire company of heaven and earth includes Hispanic and Latin American stanzas.[16]

The People Called Metodista

The people called metodista are the heirs of the Wesleyan movement's spread to Latin America and among Hispanic and Latinx populations in the United States. Texts on church history abound, and excellent accounts of Methodism's historical origins can be found in books like Richard Heit-

---

16. As Raquel Mora Martínez exclaims, "What a vision for the Church and for the world in our days! In the midst of confusion and conflict, of discord and diversity, the Christian community affirms its hope in the harmony of all the voices in praising the Lord of all the nations. As we offer our stanza in the universal hymn, we will be learning the stanzas that other peoples sing to the Lord, and they will be learning ours until there is one flock with one Shepherd!" Raquel M. Martínez, "The Hispanic Stanza," in *Fiesta cristiana: Recursos para la adoración (Resources for Worship)*, ed. Raquel M. Martínez (Nashville, TN: Abingdon, 2003), 293.

zenrater's authoritative *Wesley and the People Called Methodists*.[17] Yet the story of Methodism remains unfinished. A fuller story of the people called Methodists needs to be told that testifies to the work of God, for example, in gathering young and old African Americans at Mother Bethel in Philadelphia at the beginning of the nineteenth century and the rise of Methodism in El Salvador at the end of the twentieth century.

The people called metodista rose in Latin America as the result of missionary expansion, particularly, though not exclusively, from Methodist churches in the United States. Argentinian Methodist theologian José Míguez Bonino speaks of the introduction of Wesley to Latin America in three distinct missionary waves: mainline, Holiness, and charismatic.[18] These waves correspond to what he elsewhere calls the faces of Latin American Protestantism: the liberal face, the evangelical face, and the Pentecostal face.[19]

Although by far the smallest, the mainline wave made a lasting impact through its building of institutions and promotion of social advocacy. This first wave arrived in the early 1900s with immigrants from England and the United States who were allowed to practice their Protestant faith in English within their communities. These immigrants were later followed by missionaries from the Methodist Episcopal Church (MEC) and the Methodist Episcopal Church, South (MECS). These missionaries had two chief goals: evangelizing the poor and educating the wealthy. Míguez Bonino describes the situation: "The Methodist churches pioneered in the educational task, creating both large, modern schools catering to the children of liberal elites and more modest parish schools serving the poor children of the *barrios*."[20] The social outreach to the working classes

---

17. See Richard P. Heitzenrater, *Wesley and the People Called Methodists*, 2nd ed. (Nashville, TN: Abingdon, 2013).

18. José Míguez Bonino, "Wesley in Latin America: A Theological and Historical Reflection," *Rethinking Wesley's Theology for Contemporary Methodism*, ed. Randy L. Maddox (Nashville, TN: Abingdon, 1998): 169–82.

19. José Míguez Bonino, *Faces of Latin American Protestantism* (Grand Rapids, MI: Eerdmans, 1995).

20. Míguez Bonino, "Wesley in Latin America," 170.

resulted in economic uplift, and the Methodist churches in Latin America became increasingly identified with an emerging middle class.

Early critics of the mainline wave of Protestantism decried it as a tool of US colonial expansion and a Western civilizational project. In 1928, the Peruvian writer José Carlos Mariátegui observed, "Protestantism is not able to penetrate Latin America by virtue of its spiritual and religious power but by its social services (YMCA, Methodist missions in the mountains, etc.). These and other signs indicate that their possibilities of normal expansion are exhausted."[21] Of course, Mariátegui's critique could be equally leveled at Roman Catholic expansion in Latin America during the time of the conquest.[22] However, he accurately identifies the channels through which this first Protestant wave flowed to Latin America. Its missionary endeavors were wedded to the project of democracy as the key to human development. Although embraced by small enclaves within Methodist churches and elite progressive sectors of society, the project's supporters later shed its religious garment for more secular versions. Míguez Bonino sums up the tragic outcome: the liberal face of Protestantism presented by this first wave of Methodism "ended up defeated or absorbed by the dependent capitalist model."[23]

The second wave grew from the Holiness movement in the United States and the resultant missionary efforts of its offshoots like the Free Methodist Church, the Church of the Nazarene, and the Salvation Army. This second wave has proven more enduring than the first. Testaments to its endurance include the Church of the Nazarene's widespread presence, with nearly half a million members throughout Mesoamerica.[24] Yet the Holiness wave also poses challenges stemming from the influence of

---

21. José Carlos Mariátegui, cited in Míguez Bonino, *Faces of Latin American Protestantism*, 53.

22. For more on the European colonial-imperial conquest of the lands and peoples now often called Latin America, see Walter D. Mignolo, *The Idea of Latin America* (Malden, MA: Blackwell, 2005).

23. José Míguez Bonino, *Faces of Latin American Protestantism*, 17.

24. See the Church of the Nazarene's Mesoamerica region website: http://www.meso americaregion.org/en/about-us/. Mesoamerica includes Mexico, Central America, the Caribbean, and South America (including the Guayanas).

fundamentalist theology on evangelical and Holiness churches. These challenges include an individualist and legalistic account of holiness, an inerrantist scriptural hermeneutic that prioritizes the Bible over Christ, a premillennial eschatology that turns the church into a waiting room for heaven, and a reflexively anti-Catholic posture. Indeed, in some evangelical churches, the cross (not the crucifix, but the cross) is not displayed in buildings or sanctuaries because it is considered too Catholic. In spite of these challenges, Míguez Bonino holds out hope that Christian life in evangelical churches is not confined to the often-limited perspectives promoted by pastors and congregational leaders. Indeed, "Jesus Christ is larger than our images of him, and the Spirit is more powerful than our paltry expectations and works *in spite* of our theological distortions."[25] In this optimistic spirit, he suggests, "the future of Latin American Protestantism will be evangelical or it will not be."[26]

The Pentecostal wave of Methodism—the third and presently ongoing wave—was first felt in Valparaíso, Chile. There, the Methodist missionary Willis Hoover led a congregation that experienced charismatic manifestations of the Holy Spirit in 1909. As Míguez Bonino explains, "Two years later a baffled and 'orderly' Methodist Church expelled the 'rebellious' missionary and congregation on charges of being unbiblical, irrational, and decidedly un-Methodist."[27] The expelled group became the Iglesia Metodista Pentecostal (Methodist Pentecostal Church). Scholars disagree on how to account for the tidal wave of Pentecostalism in Latin America, but they generally trace its origins to the seismic upheaval caused by the transition "from a traditional society to a modern one, or more specifically, from a largely agrarian society to a partially industrialized one, from a rural to an urban society."[28] In this reading, the attraction of Pentecostalism resides in its ability to recreate a traditional, pre-modern community in an urban, postmodern landscape. Míguez Bonino does not dismiss the

---

25. Míguez Bonino, *Faces of Latin American Protestantism*, 47.

26. Míguez Bonino, *Faces of Latin American Protestantism*, 46.

27. Míguez Bonino, "Wesley in Latin America," 171.

28. Míguez Bonino, *Faces of Latin American Protestantism*, 58.

explanatory power of these sociological approaches but cautions against an overly reductive reading.

Whatever the historical factors contributing to the growth of Pentecostalism in Latin America may be, the impact of this wave on Methodism is undeniable. To the extent churches in the Wesleyan tradition from the first and second wave are growing numerically, it is because they have undergone charismatic revival, as seen in Brazil, Costa Rica, and Cuba. In Cuba, Methodism started in 1883 as a small missionary effort of the MECS, with 190 members, and it remained tied to mainline US Methodist efforts—interrupted by challenges like the Spanish-American War—until the Cuban Revolution, with The Cuban Methodist Church declaring its autonomy in 1968. Then, as Linda Bloom puts it, "what was once a carbon copy of the US order of worship...transformed into music-filled calls to prayer with a Pentecostal vibe." By 2017, the Cuban Methodist Church had grown to forty thousand members.[29] Admittedly, from a Wesleyan theological perspective, the impact of the charismatic wave has been ambiguous. The theological postures of anti-Catholicism, dispensationalism, and biblical inerrancy dominate the Pentecostal face of Methodism. Even so, Míguez Bonino's judgment regarding the importance of the evangelical wave may be extended: the future of the Methodist church in Latin America will be Pentecostal or it will not be.

The story of the people called metodista in the United States shares common elements with the broader Latin American story.[30] It is a story of missions and national expansionism. The annexation of Texas in 1845 and the Treaty of Guadalupe Hidalgo in 1848—ending the Mexican-American War—brought half the territory of Mexico into the United States, opening the way for new Protestant missionary outreach in the

---

29. Linda Bloom, "Cuban Methodists Are Packing the Pews," United Methodist News (Jan. 31, 2017), https://www.umnews.org/en/news/cuban-methodists-are-packing-the-pews. See also the "Cuba, Methodist Church" entry in "World Methodist Council Member Denominations in South America" directory on the World Methodist Council website: https://worldmethodistcouncil.org/south-america/name/cuba-methodist-church/. The World Methodist Council website lists the denomination's membership at 33,000, whereas Bloom's article suggests the denomination considers its membership to be 43,000 in 2017.

30. Justo L. González, ed., *Each in Our Own Tongue: A History of Hispanic United Methodism* (Nashville, TN: Abingdon, 1991).

Southwest.[31] The annexation of Puerto Rico following the war of 1898 brought Methodist missionaries to the Caribbean island and final holdout of Spanish colonialism. The three waves of Latin American Methodism have been felt by Latinx people too. The mainline face of Methodism typically shows itself in congregations led by pastors trained in US seminaries and theological schools, whereas the evangelical and Pentecostal faces appear more often among Holiness congregations led by immigrant pastors.

Despite Methodism's relatively recent date of birth in Latin America, metodistas are not newcomers. As Uruguayan Methodist theologian Mortimer Arias avers, "We did not invent or reinvent the church, we are incorporated into it. We join a caravan of a people with a history, a people called by God into existence and with a mission to the entire world."[32] The metodista caravan is diverse. It includes a multiplicity of nationalities, ethnicities, races, and languages who share a common ecclesial identity. The identity of the people called Methodists and metodistas are not intelligible apart from each other or from the story of God's work in and through the church. In this sense, to encounter Wesley's story is to encounter the church's story.[33] The Methodist missionaries that rode the waves to Latin America brought with them their own way of being church. In other words, the people called Methodists travelled to Latin America with a Methodist House.

The Methodist House

To speak of a Methodist House is to speak of a Methodist way of being Christian. To understand the Methodist House, we must consider its fundamental design, its core doctrines, its integration of doctrine with

31.   Benigno Cárdenas, a former Catholic priest, preached a sermon in Spanish in a Methodist church in Santa Fe, New Mexico, in 1853. In 1874, Alejo Hernández was the first person of Mexican descent ordained in the Methodist church. See Noel J. Martínez, "The South Central Jurisdiction," in *Each in Our Tongue*, 39–64. See also Juan Francisco Martínez, *The Story of Latino Protestants in the United States* (Grand Rapids, MI: Eerdmans, 2018), 3–47.

32.   Mortimer Arias, "Por qué y para qué estudios wesleyanos," in *Teologia e prática na tradiçao wesleyana*, ed. Claudio de Oliveiro, Helmut Renders, José Carlos de Souza, and Rui de Souza Josgrilberg (San Bernardo do Campo: Editeo, 2005), 18.

33.   Arias, "Por qué y para qué estudios wesleyanos," 18.

worship and mission, and, finally, what happened to the House when it moved from Aldersgate to the Americas.

Fundamental Design

On one occasion, Wesley describes his understanding of the essentials of Methodist doctrine using the metaphor of a house. Wesley's metaphor captures a sense of movement, a Methodist way of doing theology, and a discrete structure based on specific doctrines. He writes:

> Our main doctrines, which include all the rest, are three, that of repentance, of faith, and of holiness. The first of these we account, as it were, the porch of religion; the next, the door; the third is religion itself.[34]

A few features of the house merit attention. First, notice the ecclesial location of the house. The Methodist House sits at the crossroads of the Appian Way, Geneva Avenue, Canterbury Road, and Aldersgate. In other words, Methodist doctrine and practice builds on the foundations of and in dialogue with the traditions of Roman Catholicism, Calvinism, the Church of England, and the Moravians.

Second, notice the size of the house. Unlike majestic gothic cathedrals and soaring medieval *summae* of grand proportions, the Methodist House is designed to be simpler, plainer, and more practical.[35] Its scale is more human, offering "plain truth for plain people."[36] It is a school of practical divinity, designed to form a people of holy love who share in God's mission to the

---

34. John Wesley, "Principles of a Methodist Farther Explained," VI.4, *Works* 9:227.

35. What John Wesley said of his sermons could be said of Methodist doctrine in general: "Nothing here appears in an elaborate, elegant, or oratorical dress. If it had been my desire or design to write thus, my leisure would not permit. But in truth I at present designed nothing less, for I now write (as I generally speak) *ad populum*—to the bulk of mankind—to those who neither relish nor understand the art of speaking, but who notwithstanding are competent judges of those truths which are necessary to present and future happiness." John Wesley, Preface to "Sermons on Several Occasions," §2, *Works* 1:103–104. See also Edgardo Colón-Emeric, *Wesley, Aquinas, and Christian Perfection: An Ecumenical Dialogue* (Waco, TX: Baylor University Press, 2009), 5–6.

36. Wesley, Preface to "Sermons on Several Occasions," §3, *Works* 1:104.

world. Its doctrines are communicated through worship, through structures and practices and witnesses like sermons, general rules, holy lives, and hymns.

Third, the house rests upon a triune foundation. To quote Wesley, "The knowledge of the Three-One God is interwoven with all true Christian faith, with all vital religion."[37] By vital religion, Wesley means a living, breathing faith, "a heart right toward God and man."[38] Although anti-trinitarianism was rampant among Wesley's peers, with Christian leaders rejecting the doctrine as needlessly complicated,[39] Wesley could "not see how it is possible for any to have vital religion who denies that these Three are one."[40] Although Wesley wrote only one sermon on the Trinity, his sermons are deeply trinitarian because his goal is not simply to inform the Methodist people about the doctrine of the Trinity but to form trinitarian faith—vital religion.[41]

The design of the Methodist House connects doctrine with worship and mission. One manifestation of this design appears in the role of hymnody. The Wesley brothers sang the doctrine of the Trinity because they understood the importance of hymns for forming faith.[42] As a result,

---

37.   John Wesley, Sermon 55, "On the Trinity," §17, *Works* 2:385.

38.   John Wesley, Sermon 7, "The Way to the Kingdom," I:10, *Works* 1:223.

39.   As evidenced by such writings like John Toland's *Christianity not Mysterious* (1696), Matthew Tindal's *Christianity as Old as Creation* (1730), and Joseph Priestly's *Appeal to Serious and Candid Professors of Christianity* (1770).

40.   Wesley, "On the Trinity," §18, *Works* 2:386.

41.   Wesley, "On the Trinity," §17, *Works* 2:384. When discussing Wesley's pneumatology, Albert Outler highlights Wesley's "persistent concern for a *trinitarian* doctrine of the Holy Spirit—a concern that appealed to Scripture tradition and to rational argument for his vivid experience of the radical difference between nominal orthodoxy and fruitful Christian spirituality" (emphasis original). In brief, Wesley sees an essential link between *trinitarian* pneumatology and practical divinity. Albert C. Outler, "A Focus on the Holy Spirit: Spirit and Spirituality in John Wesley," *Quarterly Review* 8.2 (Summer 1988): 3–18, 7–8.

42.   See Barry E. Bryant, "Trinity and Hymnody: The Doctrine of the Trinity in the Hymns of Charles Wesley," in *Wesleyan Theological Journal* 25.2 (Fall 1990): 64–73. Bryant notes that "although John published at least two sermons on the same subject, both Wesleys thought perhaps the best way to combat the Unitarian heresy was through the hymnal, not through declarations from the pulpit. The pulpit was used to convert. The hymnal was used to instruct in Christian doctrine in order to influence the lives of the Methodists" (66). For more on the Wesleys' use of hymns for formation and instruction, see Randy L. Maddox, *Responsible Grace: John Wesley's Practical Theology* (Nashville, TN: Abingdon/Kingswood, 1994), 208, and Joanna Cruickshank, *Pain, Passion and Faith: Revisiting the Place of Charles Wesley in Early Methodism* (Lanham, MD: Scarecrow, 2009), 21.

Charles Wesley's 1767 collection of hymns of the Trinity included 188 hymns enjoining singers to a vitally trinitarian faith.[43]

This way of being church and doing theology—called "practical divinity"—unites doctrine, worship, and mission by emphasizing the Spirit-empowered human response in praise to God's saving action in Christ.[44] As one enters Wesley's doctrinally framed House, one cannot help but encounter doctrine's inherent interconnections with worship and mission. Wesley's insistence on the connection between trinitarian doctrine, hymnody, and faith raises a question for his heirs. How trinitarian is our praise? A recent study of contemporary church music (Vineyard) showed that most songs are either addressed to the Son (32%) or to an unspecified "You Lord" (51%). Only a small percentage are addressed to the Father (6%), the Spirit (1.4%), or all three (1.4%).[45] Can we expect a robustly trinitarian faith without trinitarian songs?[46]

Having established the original Methodist House's ecumenical location, maneuverable size, and trinitarian foundation for a living faith, we can now tour its interior. As we move from the porch, through the door, and into this home, we move through the essential doctrines, the formative worship they inspire, and their missional orientation.

---

43. E.g., see Charles Wesley, Hymn 19, *Hymns on the Trinity* (Bristol, UK: Pine, 1767). Reflecting on John and Charles Wesley's contribution to theological renewal, Jason Vickers writes, "To be sure, Wesley did not write a major work in systematic theology or a technical treatise on the Trinity. This does not mean, however, that he did not help to restore the vital link between the doctrine of God and the doctrine of salvation in English Protestant theology. Indeed, it may be that the restoration of this link was at least partly responsible for the revival with which he is customarily associated." Jason Vickers, "'And We the Life of God shall Know': Incarnation and the Trinity in Charles Wesley Hymns," *Anglican Theological Review* 90.2 (2008): 329–44, 344.

44. Chapter 1 further considers this topic.

45. Robin Parry, *Worshipping Trinity: Coming Back to the Heart of Worship* (Eugene, OR: Cascade, 2012), 115.

46. Chapter 6 returns to such burning questions about Methodist hymnody.

Integrating Doctrine, Worship, and Mission

The Methodist House's design integrates doctrine, worship, and mission with God's mission of holy and transformative love as its foundational *raison d'être*. The purpose of this house is clear: salvation by grace, sanctification, holiness. Wesley describes the design of this house not for the speculative purpose of defining Methodist ideas but for the practical purpose of moving Methodists on the way to full salvation and communion with the God who is communion.

The Methodist House exists by grace. The way onto its porch is made possible by God's prevenient grace. Through the life, death, resurrection, and ascension of Christ, God has made available a universal degree of regeneration, empowering humans to awake and repent. Once on the porch, convincing grace enables true contrition for sin and the beginning of the Christian journey. This leads to the door of forgiveness, opened by justifying and sanctifying grace. God forgives us our past sins for the sake of Jesus Christ. The journey into the house's interior is sanctification—the process of restoring the image of God in human beings. As Christians abide in the house, they grow in grace and go on to perfection, meaning freedom from sin and freedom for love.

The Methodist House is furnished with the means of grace. Christians attain communion with the triune God not by the sheer exercise of heroic virtue but by participating in Christ's body. The church is the primary community for the way of salvation. It is the privileged place where God mediates grace to humanity in an orderly and dependable way through the means of grace, such as prayer, fasting, reading Scripture, and the sacraments. The Methodist House may not be a cathedral, but neither is it a pop-up tent. It is spacious enough to welcome a vast variety of people at various stages of their spiritual pilgrimage. Indeed, one of the attractions of the Methodist House for metodistas is its fundamental reliance on grace rather than laws.

The integration of doctrine, worship, and mission in the Methodist House appears in Wesley's accounts of Methodism's origins. In his sermon "The General Spread of the Gospel," Wesley recalls how "between fifty and sixty years ago, God raised up a few young men, in the University of Oxford, to *testify those grand truths*, which were then little attended to." To which grand truths did they testify? Wesley answers by offering a brief biblical compendium of Methodist doctrine, in which Methodists affirm

That without holiness no man shall see the Lord;
That this holiness is the work of God, who worketh in us both to will and
to do;
That he doth it of his own good pleasure, merely for the merits of Christ;
That this holiness is the mind that was in Christ, enabling us to walk as
Christ also walked;
That no man can be thus sanctified till he is justified; and
That we are justified by faith alone.[47]

In his "Short History of Methodism," Wesley again narrates the origins of Methodism by starting with those four young men, but this time he focuses less on their doctrines and more on their distinctively "Methodist" way of life: reading from the Bible and the Apostolic and Church Fathers in the original languages, praying, fasting, and visiting prisoners and the sick. Describing the emergence of Methodism as "three rises," Wesley writes that

the first rise of Methodism (so-called) was in November 1729, when four
of us met together at Oxford: the second was at Savannah, in April 1736,
when twenty or thirty persons met at my house: the last, was at London, on
this day, when forty or fifty of us agreed to meet together every Wednesday
evening, in order to a free conversation, begun and ended with singing and
prayer.[48]

Wesley relates each rise of Methodism to a gathering of people united by a common purpose and set of practices—ways of life that seamlessly in-

---

47. John Wesley, Sermon 63, "The General Spread of the Gospel," §13, *Works* 2:490–91.
48. John Wesley, "Short History of the People Called Methodists," ¶¶8–9, *Works* 9:430.

tegrate theological study, worship, and mission. Each rise is accompanied by a ripple effect. Each successive gathering grows larger.

The story of the origins of Methodism is the story of a people building a house where doctrine, worship, and mission are integrated into a saving way of life, a way of being real Christians. The Methodist House was so distinctive in the eighteenth-century English landscape that Wesley referred to its very existence as a sign of God's coming reign.

> At this day the gospel leaven—faith working by love, inward and outward holiness, or (to use the terms of St. Paul) "righteousness, and peace, and joy in the Holy Ghost"—hath so spread in various parts of Europe, particularly in England, Scotland, Ireland, in the islands, in the north and south, from Georgia to New England and Newfoundland, that sinners have been truly converted to God, thoroughly changed both in heart and in life; not by tens, or by hundreds only, but by thousands, yea, by myriads![49]

The Methodist House formed a people with purpose, and at the heart of that purpose was praise.

The Methodist House on American Soils

A strange thing happened when the blueprint of this house was handed down to the people called Methodists, especially as it crossed the Atlantic and grew to massive proportions in the US during the nineteenth century. Some pieces of furniture acquired dust through disuse. First, North American Methodism lost sight of the sacramental dimension of holiness. Second, the eagerness of Methodist preachers to bring people through the door of religion often led to the virtual neglect of doctrine. For many today, the influence of American evangelical zeal dominates—that is, the urgent message is not *be perfect* but *repent*. Third, when Methodists did heed the doctrine of holiness, it became the focus of almost obsessive attention, and not in a holistic way

---

49.   John Wesley, Sermon 66, "The Signs of the Times," II.4, *Works* 2:527.

that places perfection on the grace-filled path of sanctification via the means of grace and our concretely expressed participation in God's love.[50]

The Brazilian theologian and Bishop Ayres Mattos argues that "Wesley's soteriology was deeply changed by the early controversy over slavery immediately after the Christmas conference."[51] When the Methodist House traversed the Atlantic, the soteriological significance of the poor for Wesleyan ecclesiology was largely lost. Indeed, "church growth, understood as increasing membership numbers, was not a priority in the very beginning of the Methodist church—holiness was."[52] John Wesley's emphasis on holiness over unity was reversed when it came to slaveholding, with Francis Asbury's shifting emphases reflecting this change. The Conference gatherings became business meetings more than revivals; preaching was more concerned with free will than free grace; sanctification was individualized, and so on. The church itself was eclipsed as a means of grace.[53]

Emblematic of the changes that the Methodist House experienced, US Methodism revised Methodism's mission statement. In England, Wesley designed Methodism "to reform the nation, and in particular the

50. The seeds of the shift in emphasis from holiness to repentance were planted early in the US, as seen in Methodist "camp meeting" revivalism in the opening decades of the nineteenth century, fueled by the fervor of the Second Great Awakening. See John Butler, Grant Wacker, and Randall Balmer, *Religion in American Life: A Short History* (New York: Oxford University Press, 2003), 184–85. Methodist Sunday Schools of that era likewise carried a concern for conversion, where growth in character had less to do with forming a holy heart and more to do with learning formal doctrines. Alongside holiness-as-conversion-through-education, Wesleyan notions of "holiness" further shifted in meaning within the Holiness movement associated with Phoebe Palmer. During the nineteenth century, the role of the camp meeting in Methodism evolved and contributed to these diverging doctrinal emphases, including both the emphasis on education, on the one hand, and, on the other, the Holiness movement's belief in a "second blessing" of the Spirit (which differs from the typically gradual growth of sanctification as Wesley understood it). See Russel E. Richey, Kenneth E. Rowe, and Jean Miller Schmidt, *The Methodist Experience in America: A History*, vol. 1 (Nashville, TN: Abingdon, 2010), 120–23; 247–48.

51. Paulo Ayres Mattos, "'The World Is My Parish'—Is It? Wesleyan Ecclesio-Missiological Considerations from a Contemporary Latin American Perspective," *Our Calling to Fulfill: Wesleyan Views of the Church in Mission*, ed. M. Douglas Meeks (Nashville, TN: Abingdon/Kingswood, 2009), 125–42, 132.

52. Ayres Mattos, "'The World Is My Parish'—Is It?" 133–34.

53. See the chapter on evangelism for more on this eclipse.

Church, to spread scriptural holiness over the land."[54] On American soil, the MEC redesigned it "to reform the Continent, and to spread scriptural Holiness over these Lands."[55] When it crossed the Atlantic, the Methodist House lost its clear ecclesial referent (no mention of the church) and its commitment to national reform (no mention of the nation). It gained an emphasis on territorial expansion (the continent, with lands in the plural), which replicates the colonizing ideology of empty lands waiting to be filled. Ayres Mattos states, "The understanding of the continent as *terra nulla* led North American Methodism to reinforce and deepen its theological and practical schizophrenia already implied in its compromises with slavery interests and in the alterations that broke continuity with Wesley's social religion as means of grace."[56]

The transitions did not end in North America. The three waves that carried Methodism to Latin American shores transplanted the Methodist House yet again. The Wesley who arrived in Latin America was mediated through North American (and to a lesser extent, English) Methodism. Methodist missionaries unreflectively transmitted and translated the theological reflexes of the Second Great Awakening into the Spanish language, the Portuguese language, and Latin American cultural contexts. These missionaries painted Wesley as a warm-hearted evangelist and downplayed the place of entire sanctification and the Eucharist in the Methodist House. His theological output was limited to the fifty standard sermons and some hagiographical anecdotes of his life and famous sayings (including apocryphal ones). The bifurcation of evangelism from ministries of mercy and justice common in North America was carried over to Latin America. As Míguez Bonino explains, "Many churches were helping the poor at a local level, and some created and supported schools

---

54. John Wesley, "The 'Large' *Minutes*, A and B (1753, 1763)," Q.4, *Works* 10:845.

55. MEC General Conference (1784), *Minutes of Several Conversations between the Rev. Thomas Coke, LL. D., the Rev. Francis Asbury and others, at a Conference, Begun in Baltimore, in the State of Maryland, on Monday, the 27th of December, in the Year 1784* (Philadelphia: Charles Cist, 1785), 3–4. This became part of the MEC's Book of Discipline. For discussion, see Jean Miller Schmidt, Kenneth E. Rowe, and Russell E. Richey, "Preface," *The Methodist Experience in the Americas, Volume 1: A History* (Nashville, TN: Abingdon, 2010), xvi.

56. Ayres Mattos, "'The World Is My Parish'—Is it?" 138.

and orphanages. But this service was not integrated into their evangelistic and theological self-understanding."[57] Latin American Methodists inherited a constricted version of the Wesleyan theological vision, which failed to properly distinguish the Christian faith from Deism, Christomonism, moralism, individualism, and sentimentalism. On the whole, Míguez Bonino believes "the life of Protestant Christians is much richer than this picture—their love, service, evangelistic passion, and compassion, far exceed the limitations of their theology."[58] Nevertheless, the people called metodista experience significant challenges as they seek to live in the Methodist House they inherited. Ayres Mattos acknowledges that, despite decades of dedicated work in difficult social circumstances, "many of our Methodist churches in today's Latin America live through serious instabilities and deficiencies in their praxis as God's people."[59]

Repairing the Methodist House

We can renew and enrich the Methodist House by intentionally engaging the theological vision of John Wesley from the margins. In this engagement, we must avoid two pitfalls. First, there is the danger of denominational nostalgia. As Míguez Bonino suggests, we should not try "to repristinate some real or imagined Wesleyan heritage, lay claim to some private confessional distinctive, or carve out a space in the annals of Latin American Christianity for Wesleyanism."[60] Second, there is the danger of neocolonialism and "proposing to shape the agenda for Latin American theology by appeal to an eighteenth-century movement, however significant it may have been."[61] With these caveats in mind, our engagements of Wesley's theology bear fruit when we root them in the realities of Latin American and Hispanic Christian experience and con-

---

57. Míguez Bonino, "Wesley in Latin America," 173.

58. Míguez Bonino, "Wesley in Latin America," 174.

59. Ayres Mattos, "'The World Is My Parish'—Is It?" 130.

60. Míguez Bonino, "Wesley in Latin America," 175.

61. Míguez Bonino, "Wesley in Latin America," 175.

nect them to ecumenical developments in theology—a recurring theme in this book's chapters. As Míguez Bonino suggests, Latin American Methodists might "overcome" the limitations of the "mediated forms of Wesleyanism" by "turning to Wesley's theology and ministry." Ayres Mattos commends a reappropriation of Wesley that allows for rereading Wesley's theological vision (as expressed in such lapidary phrases like "I look upon all the world as my parish,"[62] "you have nothing to do but save souls,"[63] and "to reform the nation, and in particular the Church, to spread scriptural holiness over the land"[64]) as pointing to a soteriological account of the church.[65]

The crisis of identity and inferiority complexes afflicting Methodists will be solved not by simply going back to Wesley (ressourcement) or bringing Wesley up to date (aggiornamento) but by attentive listening to the Spirit who makes all things new. The theologians called metodistas studied in this book exemplify how the Methodist House can be rebuilt on Latin American soil and in Hispanic contexts for the revival of Methodism as a whole. Indeed, the church universal stands to benefit from a heightened, ecumenically driven engagement between Latin American ecclesial contexts and the original flames of Wesleyanism.[66]

Renewal of the Methodist House is for the sake of the church catholic. Not only Wesleyans but all Christians gain from a practical form of trinitarian faith that empowers and inspires action to anticipate God's eschatological intentions. The church desperately needs a trinitarian reading of Wesley in conversation with ecumenical trends in theology and Latin American struggles to affirm the dignity of human rights, protect and uplift the poor, and care for the environment. Following

---

62. John Wesley, [Letter to the Revd. John Clayton?], ([Mar 28, 1739?]), in *Letters I, Works* 25:616.

63. Wesley, "The 'Large' *Minutes*, A and B (1753, 1763)," Q.37.11, *Works* 10:854.

64. Wesley, "The 'Large' *Minutes*, A and B (1753, 1763)," Q.4, *Works* 10:845.

65. Ayres Mattos, "'The World Is My Parish'—Is It?" 129.

66. Míguez Bonino, "Wesley in Latin America," 175.

Justo González, I refer to this reading strategy as "reading in Spanish."[67] Read in Spanish, Wesley can help correct the tendency of some Latin American theologies to equate the new birth with a newfound social awareness and to equate an encounter with Jesus with solidarity with the poor, thereby freeing each to find their place in a holistic life of faith. And from the people called metodista comes forth a bold call to action for parts of the church universal whose spiritual and social complacency severs the vital lifelines between doctrine, worship, mission, and the marginalized.

Renewing Doctrine, Worship, and Mission from the Margins

The connection of doctrine, worship, and mission represented by the Methodist House is not new. According to legend, the origin of the Apostles' Creed goes back to the first Pentecost. At the end of a long day of mighty signs, powerful preaching, and surprising conversions, the apostles rested in the Upper Room and planned their next steps. They knew Pentecost marked a turning point in world history and in their own biographies. This realization prompted a question: How do you have a consistent message when witnesses of the risen Lord are scattering across the world? The answer came from the Holy Spirit, who moved Peter to proclaim, "I believe in God, the Father Almighty." He was followed by Andrew—who added "maker of heaven and earth"— and then James, and John, and so on as they extemporaneously authored the Creed.[68]

Although a legend, this story names an important truth: doctrine, worship, and witness belong together. The creed of the apostles is woven

---

67. Justo L. González, "Can Wesley Be Read in Spanish?" *Rethinking Wesley's Theology for Contemporary Methodism*, ed. Randy L. Maddox (Nashville, TN: Abingdon, 1998), 161–68; Justo L. González, *Santa Biblia: The Bible through Hispanic Eyes* (Nashville, TN: Abingdon, 1996), 28–29.

68. E.g., see a brief account of this origins myth in "Apostles' Creed, The," in *International Standard Bible Encyclopedia*, ed. Geoffrey Bromiley et al. (Grand Rapids, MI: Eerdmans, 1979–1988), 1:204.

from the deeds of the apostles for the sake of mission. It connects to the history of Christian worshipping communities in Rome and the initiation of pagans into the church through baptism. In that context, the Apostles' Creed was a kind of baptismal gift, a summary of the highlights of God's story in the world. The creed confesses faith in a missionary God, a God who is both sender and sent, a God who is the Lord of history because God in Christ emptied himself and took the form of a servant in a given time and place.

Renewing the church requires returning to worship as the common source for all theological disciplines.[69] Historically, the liturgical act of baptism propelled the development of the Apostles' Creed.[70] Theologically, the church's *lex credendi* (rule of faith) and *lex orandi* (rule of prayer) are born together, and the rebirth of one is not possible without the revival of the other.[71] As Eastern Orthodox theologian Alexander Schmemann says, "Theology must rediscover as its own 'rule of faith' the Church's *lex orandi*, and the liturgy reveal itself again as the *lex credendi*."[72] To the rediscovery of this duo, we must add *lex vivindi*—the rule of life, how we live and move in love toward the world. In this renewal, I look to the margins

---

69. This correlates with the interconnections of what theologians sometimes refer to as "first order" and "second order" theology, in which the more practical activities of the Christian community—like worship, pastoral care, and the desire to form disciples—inspires the intellectual activities of formulating and articulating doctrine. Doctrinal belief and commitment also inform and inspire practical activities; their relationship is more dialogical and codependent than unidirectional. See Maddox, *Responsible Grace*, 16–17.

70. See Arthur Wainwright, *The Trinity in the New Testament* (Eugene, OR: Wipf & Stock, 2001), 6–7: "The creed acknowledges the character of a worship already being practiced.... The nature of Christian worship influenced the development of Christian thought, and, conversely, the development of thought influenced the nature of worship." See also Luke Timothy Johnson, *The Creed* (New York: Doubleday, 2003), 10: "This profession was rooted in deep religious experience. Indeed, in the early baptismal rites we see the close connection between the confession and the first Christians' experience."

71. The origins of the concept of *lex credendi, lex orandi* are commonly traced to Prosper of Aquitaine (c. 435–442). He famously refuted the heresy of semi-Pelagianism by arguing for the primacy of grace over works on the basis that we believe as we pray and we pray as we believe. See Geoffrey Wainwright, *Doxology: The Praise of God in Worship, Doctrine, and Life* (New York: Oxford University Press, 1980), 225–45.

72. Alexander Schmemann, *Church, World, Mission: Reflections on Orthodoxy in the West* (Yonkers, NY: St. Vladimir's Seminary Press, 1979), 146.

as places of encounter with the wounded Christ and the Holy Spirit who groans with Christ's bruised body, the church.[73]

This book is divided into three sections: doctrine, worship, and mission. By approaching each in turn, I invite readers to recognize threads of renewal from converging angles as they knit together, revealing a future for Methodism and its emblematic flames. The ongoing story of Methodism animates these chapters, beckoning us to participate in the unfolding drama of a church renewal movement. Renewal requires serious engagement with and from the margins of society, and studying the intersection of Wesleyan theology and Latin American and Hispanic Christian life is a step along the way.

A few notes on language may be helpful to the reader. First, I wish to clarify how I use terms like Hispanic, Latino/a, and Latinx. These terms seek to describe people of Latin American ancestry who were born in or moved to the territory currently comprising the United States. Each term has its history and nuances. Hispanic has the benefit of not being a gendered term. Some prefer Latino because the term is not seen as an imposed US Census designation and can include those of Brazilian origin who do not identify as Hispanic due to the latter's association with Spanish colonial culture and language. The term Latino, unlike Hispanic, is gendered and requires the addition of feminine endings to be inclusive of both men and women.[74] Different conventions have developed over the years to signal this inclusion, from Latino/a to Latin@ and, more recently, Latinx.

---

73. The language of the margins is related to the language of the preferential option for the poor, which arose in Latin American liberation theology to express the church's commitment to solidarity with the poor and to transforming unjust structures. In recent years, these terms have been contested as insufficiently capacious to express the range of forms of injustice, exclusion, and violence suffered by vast numbers of Latin Americans. See Joerg Rieger, *Opting for the Margins: Postmodernity and Liberation in Christian Theology* (New York: Oxford University Press, 2003). Pope Francis speaks of the margins and peripheries as social locations and of the marginalized and vulnerable as signs of the times calling for the church to act in mercy. See Michel Simo Temgo SCJ, *Jon Sobrino and Pope Francis: A New Springtime for the Preferential Option for the Poor/Vulnerable?* (London: Xlibris UK, 2019), Kindle Edition.

74. For more on the complexities of this nomenclature, see Fernando F. Segovia, "Aliens in the Promised Land: The Manifest Destiny of U.S. Hispanic American Theology," *Hispanic/Latino Theology: Challenge and Promise,* ed. Ada María Isasi-Díaz and Fernando Segovia (Minneapolis, MN: Fortress, 1996), 31–42.

The latter term has gained traction in the academy as a non-gendered and even nonbinary descriptor. However, a 2020 Pew Research Study found only 25 percent of Hispanics have heard the term and only 3 percent use it.[75] In this book, I use the term Hispanic on most occasions because it is the term most commonly used by the Latin American diaspora populations I engage, but I also use Latino, Latina, and Latinx interchangeably.

Second, I wish to clarify my usage of non-English terms. In this book, I draw on primary sources in a variety of languages. Unless otherwise stated, all translations are my own; however, in some cases, I choose not to translate terms but instead to transplant them. I do so to suggest that genuine dialogue among mainline Methodists and Hispanic, Latino, Latina, Latinx, and Latin American Methodists cannot happen in English alone. The accents of the voices I engage matter, and one way of gesturing to the importance of these particularities is to present these without translation or italics.[76] Hence, I use the term metodistas—a term that is identically written in Spanish and Portuguese—to name the people who are continuing God's mission of spreading scriptural holiness in the lands of Latin America and the barrios of the United States.

Doctrine

What does it mean to renew the theological task—the task of doctrine—from the margins? The three chapters in part 1 afford distinct yet complementary perspectives, ranging from the benefits of reimagining key doctrines from a metodista perspective to how metodistas might gain a greater self-understanding through an intentional focus on doctrine.

Chapter 1 explores how the Wesleyan concept of practical divinity enacts Christian theology from the margins. In conversation with Jon Sobrino and Elsa Tamez, the chapter reviews how John Wesley's practical divinity

75. Luis Noe-Bustamante, Lauren Mora, and Mark Hugo Lopez, "About One-in-Four U.S. Hispanics Have Heard of Latinx, but Just 3% Use It," Pew Research Center (Aug. 11, 2020), https://www.pewresearch.org/hispanic/2020/08/11/about-one-in-four-u-s-hispanics-have-heard-of-latinx-but-just-3-use-it/.

76. For more on the fluid use of Spanish terms in theological writing, see Carmen Nanko-Fernández, *Theologizing en Espanglish: Context, Community, and Ministry* (Maryknoll, NY: Orbis, 2010), xv–xvi.

resonates with the metodistas, the important role of place or location for theological practice, and how practicing divinity deliberately from social margins renews the theological task. From the margins, we recognize the goal of new creation as beginning in history through the humanization of the person—what we might call mercy in search of understanding. The chapter concludes with practical signposts for renewal, as the people called metodista invite all Christians to renew the doctrinal task by locating theology in its rightful place—in Christ reaching out in mercy to a wounded and lost world.

Chapter 2 formulates a distinctively Latinx Wesleyan Christology, which complements Western Christology precisely where it needs such complement. To do so, it places John Wesley's Christology alongside images of Christ from Latin American and Hispanic/Latinx perspectives. The overlapping of these lenses yields a Latinx Wesleyan Christology that affirms Christ as the liberator, prophet, priest, and king, and shows Christ present today in a mestizo body. In the process, Latinx Wesleyan Christology summons Christians to embrace Christ's present power to transfigure the world.

Chapter 3 examines the 1968 conference of Latin American Catholic Bishops that met in Medellín, Colombia. This event has often been referred to as the Pentecost of the Latin American church. Drawing on the reflections of Argentinian Methodist theologian José Míguez Bonino, who was a Protestant observer at Vatican II and Medellín, I study Medellín's ecumenical currents and its focus on liberation of the poor. I further consider how, in the mirror of Medellín, metodistas see more clearly the Latin American, catholic, and Wesleyan aspects of their theological identity and vocation.

Worship

What happens when we consider worship from marginalized Latinx and Latin American ecclesial contexts? Chapters 5, 6, and 7, each in its own way, address opportunities for worship-related renewal within metodista communities and beyond.

Chapter 4 returns to chapter 1's theme of theology's location but digs deeper into the dynamics of culture, creed, and worship as the fiesta cristiana. Akin to John Wesley himself, the metodistas value tradition and translation, appreciating how Christianity is always culturally embodied. Thus, metodistas profess the faith multiculturally in symbols old and new, from the Apostles' Creed to the Hispanic Creed, embracing solidarity with particular cultural heritages and marginalized communities. Using the Hispanic Creed as a guide, the chapter unpacks the scandalous claim at the heart of worship: the God of the people called metodista, the host of the day of the great fiesta, is a minoritized God who works for the liberation, reconciliation, and sanctification of all peoples and cultures.

Chapter 5 steps into controversial territory of Guadalupanismo, or the reverence of the Virgin of Guadalupe associated with Mexican Catholicism. Guadalupanismo exposes painful fault lines among Latinx and Latin American Christians, including racism, Catholic-Protestant tensions, international animosities, and historic wounds from the imperial-colonial conquest; but it also carries the potential for an ecumenically vibrant renewal of worship. In this chapter, I mine Methodist theology to point the way for a Methodist reception of Guadalupe—a Wesleyan Guadalupanismo—which inspires our hope for holiness and our worship of a God who performs miracles.

Chapter 6 examines how Charles Wesley's hymns have never played a significant role in Methodist worship among Spanish speakers. This is, in part, because Methodists have not adequately pursued translations attuned to both Indigenous expression and the spiritual gifts of Wesleyan hymnody. To kindle the flames of renewal, Wesleyans in the Americas would benefit from knowing and singing more of Charles's hymns—which, in turn, frees us to sing new songs in a Wesleyan spirit.

Mission

Renewal of the church's doctrine and worship cannot be considered apart from the mission of the church to the world. The remaining chapters address these topics by bringing the Wesleyan tradition into ecumenical engagement with Roman Catholic figures.

Chapter 7 brings the Wesley brothers into conversation with Bartolomé de las Casas, a Spanish conquistador turned defender of the Indigenous. From this conversation, we learn how the only legitimate way to bring people into communion with God is by persuading the intellect and alluring the will with an evangelistic life characterized by nonviolence, poverty, and holiness.

Chapter 8 frames mission as ambassadorship of God's message of reconciliation. Methodists can renew their voice in the public square by attending to the witness of El Salvador's Archbishop Óscar Romero, martyred in 1980 for opposing grave social injustices. Romero's practice of the ministry of reconciliation resonates with John Wesley's theology and models how the church might better engage the public square.

The volume concludes with reflections on rediscovering the heart of Methodism. By applying the hermeneutic of "reading in Spanish" to the three landmark moments in the rise of Methodism in Oxford, Savannah, and London (in particular Aldersgate), I present a vision of Methodist renewal that goes South and learns from Pope Francis how to dream in Spanish.

Dreams of Future Renewal

Different theological accounts have been advanced to explain the weakness of the church in its mission to the world.[77] At a time when many Methodists and Christians are wondering if the Spirit of the living God can fall afresh on the church, we urgently need dreamers and visionaries. Dreams of renewal are born from below. Visions are common among the

---

77. Ephraim Radner diagnoses the current state of the church in the West since the time of the Reformation as one of pneumatological deprivation. As in the case of Israel during the monarchy, disunity makes itself felt in the church by an "increase in sin," to which God responds by divine hardening and withdrawing the Holy Spirit (see Ps 106:33; Is 6:10). Ephraim Radner, *The End of the Church: A Pneumatology of Christian Division in the West* (Grand Rapids, MI: Eerdmans, 1998), 26–47. R. R. Reno advances a similar thesis with different imagery: the church is in ruins. Reno borrows this metaphor from Scripture's description of the besieged Jerusalem and from John Nelson Darby, who clearly perceived that a church whose witness to holiness and unity lacks empirical corroboration has failed. An invisible church is a ruined church. See R. R. Reno, *In the Ruins of the Church: Sustaining Faith in an Age of Diminished Christianity* (Grand Rapids, MI: Brazos, 2002), 13–28; R. R. Reno, "Theology in the Ruins of the Church," *Pro Ecclesia* 12.1 (2003): 15–36.

powerless.[78] Renewal from the margins connects us with neglected peoples and forgotten stories, which remind us that divisions within the church do not go all the way down. We are radically united.[79] By situating the witness of the people called metodista within the broader story of God and tracing its rise in Latin America, hope in the Spirit's power to renew today's church is invigorated. This hope is grounded in everyday life, in *lo cotidiano*, and it gives meaning and energy to marginalized people's daily struggles to survive.[80]

Renewal begins with a dream. Edith Molina Valerio, a presbyter in the Methodist Church of Mexico, says it well: "As in the reform of Josiah, Nehemiah, Wesley, Martin Luther King, Gandhi, and Dietrich Bonhoeffer, the church needs to turn to the signs of the times, to, as Jesus would say, be reformed and not be conformed."[81] After naming this great company of dreamers, she declares, "Yes, sisters and brothers, everything begins with a dream, with something that we can build together."[82] Carmen Nanko-Fernández, a hurban@ (Hispanic and urban)[83] Catholic theologian, speaks of Hispanic theologies as "theologies dreamed in Spanish, articulated in English, and lived in Spanglish."[84] Renewal begins with a dream, and dreams are related to hope and prophecy. Thomas Aquinas writes of how the gift of prophecy, unlike the virtue of hope, is not a habit; rather, it is a

---

78. "Utopias have to do with the hopes and expectations of the poor and all the marginalized as they face the everyday reality of oppression." Ada María Isasi-Díaz, *"Burlando al Opresor*: Mocking/Tricking the Oppressor: Dreams and Hopes of Hispanas/Latinas and *Mujeristas," Theological Studies* 65 (2004): 349.

79. I expand on this in Edgardo Colón-Emeric, "A Radical Unity," *Circuit Rider* (May 2019).

80. "Hope itself is impossible to maintain—dissolving into confusion, futility, anguish, and frustration: despair—if it does not have at least the tiniest of footholds in the world of the tangible." Ada María Isasi-Díaz, *"Burlando al Opresor,"* 353.

81. Edith Molina Valerio, "La reforma de la iglesia del siglo XXI," *Memorias del congreso de renovación y reforma de la iglesia metodista de México*, AR-CAM (México: Comisión un llamado al corazón, 2004), 130–33, 130.

82. Molina Valerio, "La reforma de la iglesia del siglo XXI," 133.

83. Carmen Nanko-Fernández, "¡Bienvenido Pope Francisco to Améric@ Latin@!" *HuffPost* (Sept. 22, 2015), https://www.huffpost.com/entry/bienvenido-pope -francisco_b_8170442.

84. Carmen Nanko-Fernández, *Theologizing en Espanglish*, xv.

passion that leaves an impression on the soul. He explains how "after the actual enlightenment has ceased, there remains an aptitude (*habilitas*) to be enlightened anew."[85] When persons open themselves to the Holy Spirit, dreams and visions may come and go, but a certain aptitude or ability to dream again remains. I believe the aptitude to dream remains present in the church and among the people called Methodists. I write this book in the hope that learning from and with the people called metodista might kindle dreams of renewal and a new Pentecost.

---

85. Thomas Aquinas, *Summa Theologiae* 2-2.171.2.ad2.

Chapter One

Practical Divinity as Christian Theology from the Margins

In 2009, I visited the Methodist University in Brazil. I was particularly excited to meet their theological faculty. The FaTeo (short for Faculdade de Teologia), as they are known, is home to many of the most significant Methodist scholars in Latin America. They write prolifically, and their teaching impacts not only the Methodist church in Brazil but Methodists in Portuguese-speaking countries in Africa and, indeed, Methodism as a whole. As it happened, the day I arrived coincided with the final faculty meeting of the academic year, and I was invited to attend. The meeting resembled a Methodist class meeting at prayer. Sitting in a circle, the attendees took turns naming personal and professional triumphs and trials. After each testimony, a member of the faculty led the group in singing a refrain of gratitude and supplication to God. The overall experience was distinctively Methodist.

The people called metodista approach theological reflection in close conversation with the life of Christian discipleship. One of the faculty members present at the meeting I attended, Rui de Souza Josgrilberg, writes, "Doctrines cannot be considered, in a Wesleyan and Biblical sense,

31

apart from a committed spirituality and the practices that these entail."[1] In an eighteenth-century English context that normalized the contrary, Wesley promoted a sound balance of doctrine and life, of personal and social holiness, of the evangelical and the sacramental. The Methodist tradition embodied this dynamic equilibrium in the way it approached the theological task as practical divinity.

In this chapter, I explore how practical divinity is characteristic of Methodist theological reflection as Christian theology from the margins. First, I examine John Wesley's understanding of practical divinity and how the metodistas receive it. Second, I consider the place of theology, the location from which it is practiced. In particular, I put Wesley in conversation with Jon Sobrino, who advocates for a practical divinity that is oriented by mercy and located in the margins. Third, this formal study of the nature and location of practical divinity clears the way for a concrete example: Elsa Tamez's understanding of the Wesleyan *via salutis* (the way of salvation) from a Latin American perspective. Finally, I consider how practicing divinity from the margins renews the Methodist theological task. What I witnessed at the faculty meeting in the FaTeo was not simply a faculty body in prayer but theologians fully devoting themselves to their academic work as mercy in search of understanding.

Practical Divinity

Theology was not a common term in Wesley's day.[2] Christians in eighteenth-century England often used the term *divinity* to name a diverse set of theological investigations and practices. First, *speculative divinity* is the form of theology one associates with systematics and the works of medieval theologians and classic reformers. Wesley believed speculative divinity plays a vital role in preaching and teaching Christian doctrine. In his "Address to the Clergy," he asks, "Do I understand metaphysics; if not the depths

---

1.   Rui de Souza Josgrilberg, "Espiritualidade comprometida," *Teologia em perspectiva wesleyana*, ed. Duncan Alexander Reily, José Carlos de Souza, and Rui de Souza Josgrilberg (São Bernardo do Campo: Editeo, 2005), 53–60, 53.

2.   Frank Baker, "Practical Divinity: John Wesley's Doctrinal Agenda for Methodism," *Wesleyan Theological Journal* 22.1 (1987): 7–15, 7.

of the Schoolmen, the subtleties of Scotus or Aquinas, yet the first rudiments, the general principles, of that useful science?"[3] Speculative divinity is a "useful science." Its linguistic precisions and distinctions are valuable, and Wesley drew on these when he preached on the distinctions between time and eternity.[4] However, even though Wesley considered speculative divinity an important step in the mind's journey to God, it is only "the threshold of perfection," and Wesley encouraged his followers to press on to "know all that love of God which passeth all (speculative) knowledge."[5]

Wesley recognized the necessity of a second type of divinity: *controversial divinity*, or what we might call apologetic theology. As he led the Methodist people in a time of religious foment, Wesley countered the teaching of those who denied the Fall of humanity in his treatise *The Doctrine of Original Sin: According to Scripture, Reason, and Experience* (1757). Against the Calvinists, he wrote *Predestination Calmly Considered* (1752). In both cases, Wesley sought to follow the biblical injunction, "Always be ready to make your defense to anyone who demands from you an accounting for the hope that is in you" (1 Pet 3:15).

In addition to speculative and controversial divinity, Wesley spoke of *mystical divinity*, or what we might call spiritual theology. In Wesley's own personal journey, mystical divinity both attracted and repelled him. He was drawn to the works of mystics like Gregorio López, the Mexican hermit whose works Wesley read in Spanish and published in English in the Arminian magazine.[6] At the same time, Wesley counseled care. By

3.   John Wesley, "Address to the Clergy," in *The Works of John Wesley, Volume 10: Letters, Essays, Dialogs and Addresses*, ed. Thomas Jackson, 14 vols. (Grand Rapids, MI: Zondervan, 1958–1959), 492; hereafter *Works* (Jackson).

4.   John Wesley, Sermon 54, "On Eternity," *Works* 2:358–72.

5.   John Wesley, Letter to Miss March (June 9, 1775), *The Letters of John Wesley*, ed. John Telford (London: Epworth, 1931), 6:153–54.

6.   John Wesley included his abridgement of Francisco de Losa's Spanish-language *The Life of Gregory Lopez* in Wesley's *A Christian Library* (e.g., in volume 27 of the London, 1836 edition). López's biography was among Wesley's most frequently republished; see Isobel Rivers, "John Wesley and Religious Biography," the tercentenary conference on John Wesley at the University of Manchester, June 2003, cited in David Hempton, *Methodism: Empire of the Spirit* (New Haven, CT: Yale University Press, 2005), 235. See also Jean Orcibal, "The Theological Originality of John Wesley and Continental Spirituality," in *A History of the Methodist Church in Great Britain, Volume One*, ed. Gordon Rupp and Rupert E. Davies (Eugene, OR: Wipf & Stock, 2017), 93.

his own account, mystical divinity was the rock on which his faith nearly shipwrecked, and he concludes mystical divinity overvalues experiences of darkness on the way of salvation and obscures the gospel. Similarly, he suggests, "They seek mysteries in the plainest truths, and make them such by their explications. Whereas the Christian religion, according to the scriptural account, is the plainest, clearest thing in the world."[7]

In contrast to mystical divinity, distinct from controversial divinity, and completing speculative divinity, Wesley commends and exemplifies *practical divinity*. Practical divinity, according to Frank Baker, attempts to "understand the hazards and the way-stations traversed by a pilgrim along the path of salvation."[8] Wesley never offers a precise definition of practical divinity, and, when discussing it, he shows equal concern for what it is *not*. Practical divinity is "all agreeable to the oracles of God"; it is "all practical, unmixed with controversy of any kind, and all intelligible to plain men"; it is "not superficial, but going down to the depth, and describing the height, of Christianity; and yet not mystical, not obscure to any of those who are experienced in the ways of God."[9] Instead of straining to define practical divinity, Wesley exemplifies it. If speculative divinity is represented by works like Malebranche's *Search after Truth* and Clarke's *Demonstration of the Being and Attributes of God* (both on Wesley's recommended reading list for clergy), practical divinity is represented by works like Wesley's *A Christian Library* and *A Collection of Hymns for the People Called Methodist*. The first of these contained "Extracts from and Abridgements of the Choicest Pieces of Practical Divinity"[10]; the latter was "a little body of experimental and practical divinity."[11]

Significantly, Wesley considers the Methodist hymnbook a kind of primer to practical divinity. Methodism is inconceivable without music

---

7. John Wesley, Preface to *A Christian Library: Consisting of Extracts from, and Abridgements of, the choicest pieces of Practical Divinity which have been published in the English Tongue*, §7, in *Works* (Jackson) 14:221–22.

8. Baker, "Practical Divinity," 9.

9. John Wesley, Preface to *A Christian Library*, §9, *Works* (Jackson) 14:222.

10. As phrased in *A Christian Library*'s subtitle.

11. John Wesley, Preface to *A Collection of Hymns for the People Called Methodists*, ¶4, *Works* 7:74.

and song. From the beginning of the Wesleyan movement, Methodists have expressed their theology in hymnic form. As Thomas Langford explains, "It is a theology with which one can praise; it is a theology with which one can pray, a theology with which one can teach; it is a theology which one can use to initiate, to guide, and to envision the final hope of Christian experience."[12] Practical divinity emphasizes the Spirit-empowered human response to God's saving action in Christ. It is a doxological theology where proclamation through word and service prepares and anticipates the new creation. In Langford's words, "For the Methodist tradition, theology is never an end in itself; it is always a means to the transformation of life. As such, theology is developed to underwrite proclamation and the renewal of personal and corporate life. It possesses no independent existence. One does not do theology then apply it; the doing of theology is itself transformative."[13]

Doing Christian theology as practical divinity resonates among the metodistas. According to Rui de Souza Josgrilberg, what distinguishes Wesley's theology from that of other Protestant theologians like Luther or Calvin is not what Randy Maddox calls "responsible grace," which Josgrilberg believes also appears in the great reformers in their own fashion. "The difference is that Wesley begins 'from below' with practical divinity. The grace of God is understood as stages of the way and the walk."[14] The starting point for theology is "the human condition, our practices, personal and social needs which end being taken up by divine grace."[15] José

---

12. Thomas Langford, "Charles Wesley as Theologian," in *Charles Wesley: Poet and Theologian*, ed. S. T. Kimbrough, Jr. (Nashville, TN: Abingdon, 1992), 97–105, 97.

13. Langford, "Charles Wesley as Theologian," 105.

14. Rui de Souza Josgrilberg, "A motivação originária da teologia wesleyana: o caminho da salvação," *Prática e teología na tradição wesleyana: John Wesley 300 anos* (São Bernardo do Campo, Brazil: Editeo, 2008), 93–112, 111. Randy Maddox speaks of "responsible grace" as Wesley's "orienting concern"—that is to say, as the integrating theme of Wesley's theology. Josgrilberg appreciates the centrality of this theme in Wesley's theology but finds the theme of "the way of salvation"—or, even better, "the way of social salvation"—to be a more accurate reading of Wesley and a more meaningful message for the Latin American context. See also Randy Maddox, *Responsible Grace: John Wesley's Practical Theology* (Nashville, TN: Abingdon/Kingswood, 1994).

15. Josgrilberg, "A motivação originária da teologia wesleyana," 93.

Carlos de Souza considers Wesley's theology to be chiefly concerned with the economy of salvation, in that Wesley's "fundamental search does not consist in unveiling who God is in himself but rather what God means for the human being."[16]

In this practical search for what God means for us, metodistas turn first to Scripture and then to tradition, reason, experience, and creation. This last one is of particular importance for Brazilian Methodists, who have expanded the Wesleyan quadrilateral into a pentalateral. When Wesley speaks of the Scripture way of salvation, or the way to heaven, these expressions contain social and historical density. His soteriology has an expansive, inclusive scope that embraces all created reality. As Josgrilberg puts it, "The new creation synthesizes the salvific horizon for Wesley."[17] Practical divinity has an eschatological orientation because, in the journey, the destination comes first. At the same time, the journey's contextually specific starting point matters, demanding theology likewise begin with the concrete. For this reason, we now turn to consider the question of the place from which theologians perform practical divinity.

Theology from the Way

Theologians live and work in particular places. The theologian's location powerfully shapes the kind of theology she produces. In John MacKay's rich metaphor, theologians do theology either from the balcony (teología del balcón) or from the way (teología del camino).[18] The contrast echoes the experience of religious processions in Latin America. Some people view the unfolding drama from the balconies of their residence, while others experience it from the midst of the procession. Theology from the balcony is theology from above. On the balcony, theologians

16. José Carlos de Souza, "Fazendo teologia numa perspectiva wesleyana," *Prática e teología na tradição wesleyana: John Wesley 300 anos* (São Bernardo do Campo, Brazil: Editeo, 2008), 113–30, 127.

17. Josgrilberg, "A motivação originária da teologia wesleyana," 109.

18. John MacKay, *Prefacio a la teología cristiana* (México, D.F.: Casa Unida de Publicaciones, 1957).

are comfortable spectators with an excellent view of all that happens below; they observe and describe but are uninvolved with what transpires.
Theology from the way is different. It developed on street level, dynamic
and always in motion. Theologians on the balcony are safe from the vicis-
situdes of the crowd. Theologians of the way are pilgrims swept up by the
people's movement; intimately connected to the people, they run the same
risks as the multitude.

We must interrogate the place from which Christians do theology. In
the words of Jon Sobrino, "The problem of determining where theologians stand—that is, the reality in and from which they will develop and
expand and interpret their data (revelation, Scripture, tradition, the mag-
isterium, other theologies)—is a fundamental problem whose solution
will determine all the subsequent concrete reflections that the theologians
will be making."[19] More specifically, we must determine the relationship
between theology's location and suffering, because "the development of
every Christian theology has been determined, explicitly or implicitly, by
the way it has responded to suffering, for in one way or another, all theology claims to be a form of soteriology."[20] When theology takes place in
the margins, the soteriological nature of theology grows in missional urgency. From this location, theologians better understand the confession of
faith that the Word became flesh for us and for our salvation. As Sobrino
explains, "when this salvific 'pro' is understood mainly as 'pro me' or 'pro
nobis'—no matter how real, necessary, or convincing this understanding
may be—it is utterly different from an understanding that sees the salvific
'pro' as primarily 'pro aliis,' 'pro pauperibus'"—for others, for the poor.[21]
Decentering the self and church for others and for the poor allows us to
live the gospel as a joyous proclamation of salvation, as good news to the
poor.

---

19. Jon Sobrino, *Principle of Mercy: Taking the Crucified People from the Cross* (Maryknoll,
NY: Orbis, 1994), 36.

20. Sobrino, *Principle of Mercy*, 29.

21. Sobrino, *Principle of Mercy*, 34.

The place from which Christians do theology entails a choice. Some historical and social circumstances resonate more closely with the scriptural witness and the life of the early church than others. Theologians should choose places that facilitate seeing suffering "from the partiality of those who suffer and not from the (apparently) universal perspective of the metaphysical suffering characterizing all finite being."[22] Theologians know reality best when engaging it in its density. "Reality," Sobrino says, "gives rise to thought insofar as it stirs admiration, promises something radically new, or displays suffering that cries for liberation."[23] In the technical language of Ignacio Ellacuría, this engagement entails understanding, taking responsibility, taking charge of reality. "In biblical terms, one knows God when one does justice (Jeremías, Ósea); one knows by loving (1 John); one realizes what it means to be human when one serves those in need (although such knowledge may not be explicit) (Matt. 25)."[24]

In a world of injustice, theologians are called to feel the suffering of the poor enough to share their weakness and strive for their liberation. Sobrino (following Henri de Lubac) argues, "All theology can be, and must be, in the final analysis 'apologetic'—a rational defense of something that has been given, not discovered as a human achievement."[25] The apologetic character of theology manifests in a compassionate praxis of liberation that seeks to end the suffering of the crucified peoples. Sobrino refers to this apologetic character as *the principle of mercy*. In a church guided by the principle of mercy, Christians believe in and worship the God who identifies with the victims lying wounded beside the road. The theology that serves a church guided by the principle of mercy does not remain indifferent to the plight of the crucified peoples; its intellectual energies must aim to bring the suffering ones down from the cross. In brief, theology must assume the form of *intellectus misericordiae*.[26]

---

22. Sobrino, *Principle of Mercy*, 33.

23. Sobrino, *Principle of Mercy*, 43.

24. Sobrino, *Principle of Mercy*, 38.

25. Sobrino, *Principle of Mercy*, 40.

26. Sobrino, *Principle of Mercy*, 25.

Intellectus misericordiae is the form of theology from the place of suffering. Western theologians have traditionally adopted the Anselmian motto that posits theology as *intellectus fidei*—as faith in search of understanding. God enables this search by way of God's self-revelation, as transmitted through the church's tradition. From revelation, Christians can name the true God and turn away from idols. However, by itself, *intellectus fidei* does yield complete understanding. Following the Pauline path of the trio of theological virtues, Sobrino also calls attention to *intellectus spei* and *intellectus amoris* or "hope in search of understanding" and "love in search of understanding." He argues, "the *intellectus fidei*, in order to be true *intellectus* or understanding and not just doctrine, needs help from the *intellectus spei* and the *intellectus amoris*."[27] Theology is a second act that follows the mystagogical encounter with God. It is an act of mercy in search of understanding God's mercy. Hope helps preserve the mystery of faith, and love helps make faith concrete in the world of the poor.

Sobrino's reflections on the place and person of the theologian are valuable but not without ambiguity. Some of his statements understate the gratuitousness and surprise of God's initiative. For instance, Sobrino declares that "the end purpose of theology is to clarify and facilitate how humanity is to respond and correspond to God within history."[28] This assertion and others like it would benefit from a stronger language of grace and participation.[29] The *intellectus misericordiae* is only possible through graced participation in God who is *dives in misericordia* (rich in mercy).[30] Jesus Christ is the liberator, and, by the power of the Holy Spirit, humans can join in the Father's work of establishing the kingdom from the margins.

---

27.   Sobrino, *Principle of Mercy*, 43.

28.   Sobrino, *Principle of Mercy*, 39.

29.   Sobrino states, "When theology understands itself as *intellectus amoris*, it seeks to operate within reality in order to save it, incarnating itself within humanity as it is, responding from an original compassion." Sobrino, *Principle of Mercy*, 42.

30.   See Ephesians 2:4 and John Paul II's 1980 encyclical *Dives in misericordia* on the topic of mercy.

Tamez and the Way of Salvation from the Margins

The people called metodista represent a spiritual and theological renewal mission. One of the most significant Latin American exponents of this movement is Elsa Tamez. In true Wesleyan fashion, she brings together Scripture and theology in conversation with the Methodist tradition and from a Latin American context. In her work, we find an example of practical divinity done from a place of solidarity with the margins.[31]

Latin American Methodists need John Wesley. The cultural distance of Wesley might seem to suggest otherwise. What does an eighteenth-century priest of the Church of England have to say to a pastor serving in Mexico City or the highlands of Guatemala? Tamez engages Wesley and his theology in these contexts and offers three hermeneutical keys for a missionally faithful reading.[32]

First, "it is extremely important to consider *who* reads the Methodist tradition, *from what concrete situation* they read it, and *for whom* they read it."[33] Tamez proposes a "correspondence of relationships" that connects Wesley with his context, Latin American Methodists with theirs, and both to one another. The point of contact in this analogy is human life. "Both then and now there is a theological conviction that life is a gift of God; we are created in his image, and it is his will that we have life."[34]

---

31. As a young Methodist woman in Mexico in 1969, Tamez moved to Costa Rica to pursue theological studies—at the time, Mexican seminaries did not admit women. Despite such obstacles, she earned four degrees, including her Doctor of Theology from the University of Lausanne in Switzerland. She has published widely in biblical studies, including notable books like *Bible of the Oppressed* and *Through Her Eyes: Women's Theology from Latin America*. She helped develop the Ecumenical Association of Third World Theologians (EATWOT) and, with other women from the Global South, sparked the EATWOT Women's Commission. In 1995, she was the first woman president of the Universidad Bíblica Latinoamericana, and she has taught around the world. For a sample of the Women's Commission's work, see "Feminist Theology Reaching New Borders: Búsquedas de la Teología Feminista (Multilingual Issue)," *Voices* 39.1 (2016).

32. Elsa Tamez, "Wesley as Read by the Poor," *The Future of the Methodist Theological Traditions*, ed. M. Douglas Meeks (Nashville, TN: Abingdon, 1985), 67–84.

33. Tamez, "Wesley as Read by the Poor," 68.

34. Tamez, "Wesley as Read by the Poor," 72.

Second, Latin American Methodist readings of Wesley bear great fruit because of Methodism's historic affinity for the marginalized. The early Methodists were not known simply for preaching *at* the poor but for preaching *as* the poor.[35] For practical divinity, exemplars offer concreteness to theological arguments. The "Wesley of the poor" and his witnesses—if better known—could resonate in hopeful ways in the Latin American context. Tamez thus highlights the ministry of Joseph Chapman, a Methodist union member in England whose labor-organizing efforts were guided by the eschatological vision of a "grand union" in which "prince and peer and peasant shall combine and cooperate for the good of one and all."[36] She also lifts up the name of H. J. Crabtree, a North Carolina preacher who announced, "God's a poor man's God."[37]

Third, the inclusion in the Methodist tradition of a social creed alongside the Apostles' Creed frames a Methodist identity that reaches to the origins of Christianity and to the margins of society. At its best, the social creed offers one concrete instantiation of the form of life embraced by the apostles.

Doing practical divinity from Latin America highlights the social dimensions of Wesley's understanding of the *via salutis*. The journey along the way of salvation from sinner to saint is one of grace, a grace that gives the people called metodista meaning and hope as they advance toward the new creation. In the words of a Bolivian Methodist declaration, "To the extent that [human beings] become similar to God and give themselves to him to be transformed, they become truly human."[38] The way of salvation entails a journey of true humanization. In her writings, Tamez brings into conversation the Wesleyan *via salutis*—

---

35. Richard P. Heitzenrater, ed., *The Poor and the People Called Methodists* (Nashville, TN: Abingdon/Kingswood, 2002), 15–38. Heitzenrater states, "Wesley did not have to search out the poor; they sat right there in front of him on the benches of his preaching houses. He did not have go to another part of town to find some poor people to assist—he could have put signs on the Methodist preaching houses that read, 'The Poor R Us'" (28).

36. Tamez, "Wesley as Read by the Poor," 75.

37. Tamez, "Wesley as Read by the Poor," 76.

38. Tamez, "Wesley as Read by the Poor," 80.

including its inherently social and humanizing dimensions—with Paul's teaching on justification by faith.[39]

The itinerary of the way of salvation begins with the human predicament as experienced in Latin American society. The human condition under the condition of sin is one in which people are "being governed by a system that insists on a logic of death."[40] Given this reality, Tamez asks, "How can one affirm the relevance of an interpretation of justification by faith as the forgiveness of the ungodly in a situation where the most obvious sin is structural?"[41] Received doctrines, including the doctrine of justification, must answer the burning questions people are asking. After all, "What does justification say to the poor Indigenous person of Peru, Guatemala, Bolivia, or Mexico, who suffer both hunger and permanent discrimination?"[42]

The doctrine of justification transplanted to Latin America was individualistic and abstract. Too often, it promoted social impunity, washing away the guilt of those who still benefited from oppressive structures. Moreover, it sometimes condoned passivity by commending trust in divine sovereignty as the sole remedy for injustice, and it reinforced prejudice by labeling as sinners those already demonized by society. By contrast, a concrete doctrine of justification by faith begins with a clear affirmation of the life of the poor; the lives of people on the margins are worth living and saving. Teaching justification by faith commits the theologian to naming and resisting that which negates or forecloses the possibilities of human life. "By being justified by faith in the one who raises the dead and brings to life that which does not exist, the excluded person is incorporated with power into a new logic. That new logic is the logic of faith whose criterion is the life that Jesus Christ brought, a life both dignified and free, that is granted to others."[43]

---

39. Elsa Tamez, *The Amnesty of Grace: Justification by Faith from a Latin American Perspective* (Eugene, OR: Wipf & Stock, 2002).

40. Tamez, "Wesley as Read by the Poor," 76.

41. Tamez, *The Amnesty of Grace*, 20.

42. Tamez, *The Amnesty of Grace*, 21.

43. Tamez, *The Amnesty of Grace*, 166.

From a Latin American Methodist perspective, being born again by God's grace awakens deadened senses from their slumber. "We can identify those who produce death, the principalities and powers that govern the earth, the anti-Christs. We become aware of the meaning of real life and realistic possibilities of achieving it. We see God as the source of life and justice who gives his life for our life."[44] With this new awareness of God's love for all God's creatures, especially the more vulnerable ones, the process of sanctification begins. Integral to this process is the commission to "accept the challenge and risk the struggle for the fullness of life, to make visible the kingdom of God: the kingdom of love and justice."[45] By committing to these struggles, the wayfarers along the *via salutis* grow in holiness and go on to Christian perfection in ways that challenge the perfectionism many aspire to in contemporary society. "For people today, perfection is linked to success, competition, excelling at the expense of others."[46] For Wesley, by contrast, Christian perfection is the result of a radical interior transformation that unites the Christian with God and with God's poor, outcast children.

The way of salvation is a journey of humanization where embodied creatures grow in the likeness of God. Indeed, the recovery of the image of God is, according to Wesley, the goal of the *via*; it is the one thing needful.[47] This image has been wounded and defaced in all human beings, rich and poor, victim and victimizer. However, as Tamez avers, "God chooses a meeting place so that God's image might be reproduced in every living being. God makes this choice not in order to exclude some people, but precisely in order to negate exclusion by including all people, beginning among those presently excluded."[48] To restore God's image to its full splendor, God begins with those who have been discarded in the garbage dumps of history.

---

44. Tamez, "Wesley as Read by the Poor," 80.

45. Tamez, "Wesley as Read by the Poor," 81.

46. Elsa Tamez, *The Scandalous Message of James: Faith without Works Is Dead* (New York: Crossroad, 2002), 71.

47. John Wesley, Sermon 146, "The One Thing Needful," *Works* 4:351–59.

48. Tamez, *The Amnesty of Grace*, 132.

This restoration is the occasion for fiesta. When a person who has been relegated to the role of an extra in the story of a society learns they are protagonists in the story of the triune God's love for the world, life becomes a gift that calls for public celebration.[49] The life of the poor, against all odds, calls for fiesta and song. In translation, one such song declares:

> Come! … Let us make a giant loaf of bread
> And prepare much wine as in the wedding of Cana.[50]

Practical Divinity as Mercy in Search of Understanding

Practical divinity charts the way of salvation, to guide human beings from alienation to communion with God. In this chapter, I have reflected on how practical divinity as practiced by the people called metodista is located deliberately along the margins of society and how the theologian's option for this placement grants her the perspective to recognize the goal of new creation as beginning in history through the humanization of the person. One way of interpreting this approach to theology is to speak of practical divinity as mercy in search of understanding. Here, I harvest some of the insights from the previous sections and present a sketch of practical divinity from the people called metodista with the intent of offering signposts for Christian doctrinal renewal.

First, practical divinity is a work of mercy. When John Wesley preaches on the way of salvation, he speaks of works as conditionally necessary for participating in God's grace. First, Wesley highlights *works of piety*, "such as public prayer, family prayer, and praying in our closet; receiving the Supper of the Lord; searching the Scriptures by hearing, reading, meditating; and using such a measure of fasting or abstinence as our bodily health allows."[51] Practical divinity embodies the patristic tradition of theology as

---

49. Tamez, *The Amnesty of Grace*, 138. Translated by the author.

50. Elsa Tamez, "Vengan celebremos la cena," in *Un cántico nuevo*, ed. Jorge Maldonado (Quito, Ecuador: Eirene, 1989), 145.

51. John Wesley, Sermon 43, "The Scripture Way of Salvation," III.9, *Works* 2:166.

eusebeia, a concept expressed with admirable succinctness by Evagrius of Pontus: "If you are a theologian, you will pray truly, and if you pray truly, you will be a theologian."[52] The works of piety are, for the Wesleyan tradition, constitutive of the theological task. John Wesley's way of salvation does not only call for works of piety; it also calls for *works of mercy* as a proper response to God's grace. Works of mercy address the neighbor as a whole person, in both body and soul, which means "feeding the hungry, clothing the naked," entertaining strangers, and visiting the sick and imprisoned; and it also means feeding souls by teaching, encouraging, and inspiring, to "contribute to the saving of souls from death."[53] Teaching and visiting the poor are both works of mercy; they are means of grace that help theologians become what Hans Urs von Balthasar calls "complete theologians."[54]

Second, practical divinity as a work of mercy calls on theologians to choose the peripheries over the centers of power. It is an option, as Harold Recinos insists, for the barrio. "The rejected people of the barrio call…for a radical discipleship that opts for the poor, builds a church that does not separate God from the poor, and promotes activity directed to the restructuring of the social order and dominant culture in the direction of the reign announced by the Crucified Jesus."[55] This mode of theology modeled by John Wesley has strong christological and missiological orientations. The Wesley brothers, each in their own way, patterned their lives after the medieval, and indeed biblical, vision of Jesus as the poor one. As Ted Campbell puts it,

---

52. Evagrius Ponticus, "De oratione," in *The Praktikos and Chapters on Prayer,* trans. John Eudes Bamberger, OSCO (Kalamazoo: Cistercian, 1972), 52–80, 60. Khaled Anatolios speaks of *eusebeia* as follows: "Divine self-disclosure is available through its inspired witness in the Scriptures, as interpreted by acts of ecclesial communion (synodal councils) and as appropriated and performed in worship and discipleship. The combination of these three elements constitutes what fourth-century theologians referred to as *eusebeia.*" Khaled Anatolios, *Retrieving Nicaea: The Development and Meaning of Trinitarian Doctrine* (Grand Rapids, MI: Baker, 2011), 282. *Eusebeia* as a principle of trinitarian theology assumes hermeneutical significance.

53. Wesley, Sermon 43, "The Scripture Way of Salvation," III.10, *Works* 2:166.

54. Hans Urs von Balthasar, "Theology and Sanctity," in *Word and Redemption: Essays in Theology, Volume One* (New York: Herder & Herder, 1965), 57.

55. Harold Recinos, "Barrio Christianity and American Methodism," in *Methodist and Radical: Rejuvenating a Tradition,* ed. Joerg Rieger and John Vincent (Nashville, TN: Abingdon/Kingswood, 2003), 77–93, 93.

for the Wesleys, "the poor are connected intimately with Christ. If unconnected to the central *religious* meaning of Christian faith—unconnected to Christ—the poor become a problem, an obligation, an exception, and in any case, they become peripheral."[56] Indeed, as Emilio Castro explains, contextual and global theologies "are basically missiologies. They are not explanations of God's being but represent a passionate search for new options for the mission of the churches."[57] They are missiologies with ecclesiological and christological principles. As Castro notes, "We are the church of the powerless Christ who made his own the fate of the poor and the least."[58]

Third, practical divinity practiced from the peripheries properly takes the form of *intellectus misericordiae,* **mercy in search of understanding.** To do so, one must unite doctrine and life. Wesley valued orthodoxy and orthopraxis, but for these to achieve their goal, one also needs what Methodist and Catholic theologians call *orthopathy.* Orthopathy refers to the right passions (in the sense of feelings and affections) someone who has been born of God experiences through participation in Jesus's filial relation.[59] Theology as *intellectus misericordiae* entails an affec-

---

56. Ted A. Campbell, "The Image of Christ in the Poor," in *The Poor and the People Called Methodists,* ed. Richard P. Heitzenrater (Nashville, TN: Abingdon/Kingswood, 2002), 39–57, 57. Campbell notes the theme of Christ's material poverty was understated in most Protestant piety. The Wesley brothers are an exception. Of the Wesley brothers, Charles reflected on the medieval vision of poverty most. Charles's hymns include themes of voluntary poverty, which are absent in John's sermons. Campbell acknowledges the difference may not be one of personal temperament or of theological convictions but of theological genre. Charles wrote in verse and John in prose, "and poetry sometimes carries echoes of notions that have long since perished in prose. For example, although the church lost sight of the doctrine of the poverty of Christ, devotion to Christ's material poverty persisted in the dramatic paradoxes of religious verse" (56). John, for his part, has been compared to the founders of medieval orders and practiced and commended an almost mendicant lifestyle for the Methodist preachers.

57. Emilio Castro, *Sent Free: Mission and Unity in the Perspective of the Kingdom* (Geneva: World Council of Churches, 1985), 16.

58. Castro, *Sent Free,* 3.

59. For Ted Runyon, orthopathy denotes "the new sensitivity to and participation in spiritual reality that mark genuine faith." Theodore Runyon, *The New Creation: John Wesley's Theology Today* (Nashville, TN: Abingdon, 1998), 146–67, 149. It is "experience that is rooted in the activity of the Spirit, experience that is consistent with past Christian experience reflected in Scripture and tradition" (167). Sobrino likewise finds the term useful in describing the "correct way of letting ourselves be affected by the reality of Christ." Jon Sobrino, *Christ the Liberator: A View from the Victims* (Maryknoll, NY: Orbis, 2001), 210.

tive disposition, an openness to being moved by the truth of God and the reality of suffering in the world. Reflecting on the significance of mercy for Christian life, Todd Walatka observes, "Callousness or inattention toward the cruel lot of the poor and oppressed indicates a fundamental lack of attunement to God's love for the world and a failure to cooperate with God's de-privatizing grace."[60] By contrast, like the Good Samaritan, the merciful refuse to avert their gaze from those struggling in the ditches. At the same time, mercy is more than a feeling; it is a habitual disposition and power to act in concrete, socially effective ways.

Fourth, practical divinity practiced from the margins is guided by a trinitarian vision of the end and the way. In the words of Tamez, "The glory of the Father is in seeing God's sons and daughters mature in freedom and justice to the stature of God's Son, by faith—a capacity that is granted by the gift of justification."[61] Theology along the *via salutis* is more than pious feelings or personal opinions. As José Carlos de Souza puts it, "It is not enough to be pious" if we wish "to promote a theological understanding that responds both to the needs of the gospel and to the needs of the current realities."[62] Practical divinity discerns the spirits by the power of the Spirit, who aids the complex navigation of revelation, tradition, and location, resulting in a sound balance. The equilibrium of Wesley's theology is not static but dynamic; it reflects his concern that theology be born from the life of the believer and the church in movement toward the

---

60. Todd Walatka, *Von Balthasar and the Option for the Poor: Theodramatics in the Light of Liberation Theology* (Washington, DC: Catholic University of America Press, 2017), 160. Walatka argues Balthasar's theodramatic theology, despite its complex relation to liberation theology, locates mercy at the core of all genuine Christian vocations and missions in their rich diversity (160). In a very Wesleyan move, Balthasar frames his understanding of Christian mission in terms of the love of God and neighbor "in which one's whole being is placed at the disposal of God for the sake of the salvation of the world" (152). Balthasar's anthropological missiology draws on the *Suscipe* of the Ignatian Spiritual Exercises. Wesley's draws on Richard Alleine's Covenant Prayer. Both are ways of embodying the same mind that was found in Jesus, who, being God, emptied himself for us and for the salvation of the world.

61. Tamez, *The Amnesty of Grace*, 145.

62. De Souza, "Fazendo teologia numa perspectiva wesleyana," 121.

world. Theology "seeks to serve the mission and cause of the gospel, while, at the same time, being expressed as the daily life of the people."[63]

Christian theology as practical divinity is not a Methodist patrimony. Rather, it is a missional movement that converses with the ecumenical tradition and reflects on cultural contexts, integrating these with a trinitarian spirituality lived out in solidarity with the people of God. Doing theology as practical divinity is not the only valid option. For example, kerygmatic theology and scholastic theology likewise have merit. What de Souza says regarding practical divinity could be applied more broadly: "Wesley did not intend to disqualify the task of theological understanding, but rather, he endeavors to locate it in its rightful place, as an instrument in service to Christian faith and life and not as its substitute."[64] The people called metodista invite all Christians to renew the doctrinal task by locating theology in its rightful place—in Christ reaching out in mercy to a wounded and lost world.

Postlude

The theologians I met at the FaTeo were deeply engaged in their churches. In some cases, this was an economic necessity, to supplement the low salaries their institution could afford to pay. In every case, their communal involvement reflected an option for the church in its mission to the world as the place for doing theology as practical divinity. Wesley's doctrinal articulations of the way of salvation are secondary in importance to the actual walking of the way. "Wesley proposes a practical Christianity in the sense that it is a lived Christianity."[65]

After the faculty meeting, several of the faculty in attendance took me on a tour of Methodist churches and ministries in Sao Paolo. One of these was a shelter for homeless persons supported by the Methodist church.

---

63. José Carlos de Souza, "Um modo equilibrado, dinâmico e vital de fazer teologia," *Teologia em perspectiva wesleyana*, ed. Duncan Alexander Reily, José Carlos de Souza, and Rui de Souza Josgrilberg (São Bernardo de Campo: Editeo, 2005), 13–23, 22.

64. De Souza, "Um modo equilibrado, dinâmico e vital de fazer teología,"15.

65. Josgrilberg, "A motivação originária da teologia wesleyana," 103.

The facility and the people were like those I have seen in many other places, except for one person I met. He was a former police officer who had been convicted of murdering a homeless person. While in prison for this crime, Methodist pastors evangelized him, and after being released, he heard Christ calling him to follow him by serving the very homeless people whom he had once victimized. Now, this former police officer dedicated his life to running the shelter. He was not an academic theologian, though he called several of them friends. He embodied practical divinity as mercy in search of understanding.

The shelter is not the only proper place for doing theology. The academy also has a role, provided it adopts the proper posture before the wounded wayfarers on the *via salutis*. Pope Francis addresses the question of place and posture with his usual frankness: "Let us not forget that the only legitimate way to look at a person from the top down is when you stretch out a hand to help them get up."[66] To put it differently, the world urgently needs the theological academy, provided the academy serves not as an ivory tower but as a watchtower. In a world corrupted by pervasive personal and structural sin, the true theologian is not only one who prays truly. The true theologian is one who stoops down to lift others up.

---

66.   Pope Francis, Angelus address, Saint Peter's Square (Sunday, February 7, 2021), https://www.vatican.va/content/francesco/en/angelus/2021/documents/papa-francesco_angelus_20210207.html.

Chapter Two

Jesus Was Born in Guatemala: Towards a Latinx Wesleyan Christology

In the spring of 2019, the Central American Methodist Course of Study where I regularly teach hosted a concert in Ahuachapán with the Salvadoran composer Guillermo Cuéllar. The students sang along as he played music from the Salvadoran Popular Mass, but the song that elicited the most vigorous response was one by the Nicaraguan composer Carlos Mejía Godoy, which proclaims "Cristo ya nació en Palacagüina" (Christ Was Born in Palacgüina).[1]

The final decades of the twentieth century were a fruitful time in Latin American Christianity. New theologies like the theologies of liberation were written from contexts where previous generations had only yielded translations and adaptations of European works. New expressions of Christian life like the Base Ecclesial Communities sprang up across the landscape. New songs, like the Christ of Palacagüina, set to music these new theologies and forms of life. Christology is always embedded in a web of cultural practices. The Christ of Palacagüina is not simply a Latin American christological song; it is Nicaraguan. The language and imagery

---

1. The Spanish text of the song is found in Josep Ignasi Saranyana and Carmen José Alejos Grau, eds., *Teología en América Latina, Volumen III: El siglo de las teologías latinoamericanistas (1899–2001)* (Madrid: Vervuert, 2002), 358. The translation into English is my own.

of its refrain and verses is situated in a land groaning under the dictatorship of Anastasio Somoza Debayle. For Mejía Godoy, the christological titles commonly sung of Jesus in church were honey-flavored poison pills handed out by those in power.[2] This is a Christology born in a context of civil unrest, church protest, and the struggle for dignity. The Christ of Palacagüina dreams of growing up to be not a carpenter like his father but a guerrilla fighter.

Why did my Central American Methodist friends resonate strongly with a Nicaraguan Catholic's protest song? The answer, I suggest, is that it affirms faith in a Christ incarnate in their own history. In this essay, I trace the contours of a Latinx Wesleyan Christology.[3] To accomplish this goal, I begin by reviewing Wesley's Christology with the help of John Deschner's magisterial work on this topic. Next, I consider images and faces of Christ from Latin American and Hispanic perspectives. The overlapping of these two lenses yields a Latinx Wesleyan Christology that finds confirmation in a Methodist pastor's witness that Jesus was born in Guatemala.

Wesley's Christology

John Deschner's work on Wesley's Christology is the most significant exploration of Wesley's understanding of Christ written to date.[4] His book draws on Wesley's standard sermons and *Notes on the New Testament* and

---

2.   Regarding this abuse of Christology, see Paul in Romans 16:18: "For such people do not serve our Lord Christ, but their own appetites, and by smooth talk (*chréstologia*) and flattery (*eulogia*) they deceive the hearts of the simple-minded?" When Cyril of Jerusalem reads Paul's letter, he interprets the apostle to mean "the heretics do this by coating over their poison pills of godless doctrines with the honey of the name of Christ." In Catechetical Lectures 4.2, *Ancient Christian Commentary on Romans* (Downers Grove, IL: InterVarsity, 1998), 377. The usage of the term *Christology* to name the church's teaching of Christ is relatively recent: see Rafael Ramis-Barcelo, "En torno al surgimiento de la noción moderna de 'cristologia,'" *Gregorianum* 100.1 (2019): 27–47.

3.   For discussion on the use of terms like Latinx, Hispanic, and Latin American, see 24–25.

4.   John Deschner, *Wesley's Christology: An Interpretation* (Dallas, TX: Southern Methodist University Press, 1985).

displays the results in the categories of Barthian theology. Deschner identifies two distinctive aspects of Wesley's Christology.

First, there is in John Wesley's theology a valorization of the "whole Christ." This means, says Deschner, "Christ in all his offices, not only atoning for our sins, but also guiding and empowering our recovery of the image of God."[5] Wesley believed that Jesus of Nazareth was "a Prophet, revealing to us the whole will of God; that He was a Priest, who gave Himself a sacrifice for sin, and still makes intercession for transgressors; that He is a King, who has all power in heaven and in earth, and will reign till He has subdued all things to Himself."[6] As the hymns for Ascension Sunday make clear, the return of Jesus to his Father entails the exaltation of the true Elijah, the consecration of the true Aaron, and coronation of the true David.[7] Jesus super-fulfills the roles of prophet, priest, and king because he is truly God. He is the holy one of God; "His divine righteousness belongs to his divine nature, as he is ὁ ὤν, 'He that existeth, over all, God, blessed for ever': the supreme, the eternal, 'equal with the Father as touching his godhead, though inferior to the Father as touching his manhood.'"[8] Christ teaches us who God is, enables us to participate in the divine nature, and guides us into the communion of the Father, the Son, and the Holy Spirit.

The centrality of the "whole Christ" is consistent with Wesley's holistic soteriology. Christ is both the justifier and the sanctifier; he forgives and heals; he is for us and in us. Wesley warns, "We are not ourselves clear before God unless we proclaim him in all his offices."[9] The whole Christ must be preached and sung. Thus, on the anniversary of his conversion, Charles Wesley sings,

---

5.   Deschner, *Wesley's Christology*, xvi.

6.   John Wesley, "A Letter to a Roman Catholic," §7, *Works* (Jackson) 10:81.

7.   See Charles Wesley, *Resurrection Hymns* (1746), hymn 16, and *Ascension Hymns* (1746), particularly hymns 2 and 4, https://divinity.duke.edu/initiatives/cswt/charles-published-verse.

8.   John Wesley, Sermon 20, "The Lord Our Righteousness," I.1, *Works* 1:452.

9.   John Wesley, Sermon 36, "The Law Established through Faith II," I.6, *Works* 2:37.

> O for a thousand tongues to sing
> My great redeemer's praise,
> The glories of my God and King,
> The triumphs of his grace.[10]

Second, Wesley teaches his fellow Methodists to focus their attention on the "present Christ." Wesley does not neglect the cosmic Christ or the coming Christ. However, Deschner notes that Wesley emphasizes "the Christ whose cross is the present ground of a divine forgiveness which underlies everything, whom one encounters 'now' in the means of grace, and whose 'mind' takes form today in the renewed 'affections' of the believer's heart."[11] Methodists take Paul's words to heart: "See, now is the acceptable time; see, now is the day of salvation!" (2 Cor 6:2). In the present Christ, we "anticipate our heaven below."[12] In Christ, we see what it means to be truly human—holiness of heart and life, internally and externally righteous—and receive the power to become like him.

Christ is holy of heart:

> His internal righteousness is the image of God stamped on every power and faculty of his soul. It is a copy of his divine righteousness, as far as it can be imparted to a human spirit. It is a transcript of the divine purity, the divine justice, mercy, and truth. It includes love, reverence, resignation to his Father; humility, meekness, gentleness; love to lost mankind, and every other holy and heavenly temper: and all these in the highest degree, without any defect, or mixture of unholiness.[13]

And Christ is holy in life: "It was the least part of his external righteousness that he did nothing amiss; that he knew no outward sin of any kind, 'neither was guile found in his mouth'; that he never spoke one improper word, nor did one improper action."[14] Moreover, "'He did all

---

10. *The United Methodist Hymnal* (Nashville, TN: United Methodist Publishing House, 1989), Hymn 57.

11. Deschner, *Wesley's Christology*, xvi.

12. *The United Methodist Hymnal*, Hymn 57.

13. John Wesley, Sermon 20, "The Lord Our Righteousness," I.2, *Works* I:452–53.

14. Wesley, "The Lord Our Righteousness," I.3, *Works* I:453.

things well.' In every word of his tongue, in every work of his hands, he did precisely the 'will of him that sent him.' In the whole course of his life he did the will of God on earth as the angels do it in heaven. All he acted and spoke was exactly right in every circumstance. The whole and every part of his obedience was complete. 'He fulfilled all righteousness.'"[15]

There is a clear correspondence between the human righteousness of Christ and the Methodist General Rules: avoid evil, do good, and attend to all the ordinances of God. The correspondence is not accidental, for everything in Wesley's Methodism was oriented toward the renewal of the image of God in the human being. By participating in the means of grace, humans are empowered to avoid evil, do good, and thus grow into the stature of Christ. The transformation of the sinner into a saint depends on Christ's graceful presence today. Faith will fail "unless we be endued with power from on high; and that continually, from hour to hour, or rather from moment to moment."[16] The "now" is all important because our justification and sanctification depend on a continual indwelling of the whole Christ.

Deschner's interpretation of Wesley's Christology is respectful and appreciative. At the same time, Deschner worries that the clarity of Wesley's christological vision is impaired by an inadequate account of the humanity of Christ. Deschner offers two pieces of evidence to substantiate his suspicion. First, Wesley's translation of 1 John 4:2 relegates the Christ's human nature to a subordinate clause. Second, Wesley omits the phrase "of her substance" from the edited version of the Articles of Religion that he sent to the Methodist Episcopal Church. For Deschner, Wesley's "lack of precision with respect to Mary as mother of Christ in both natures, taken together with the reserve about the human nature" raises the specter of Nestorianism in Wesley's Christology.[17]

The anti-Chalcedonian specter raised by Deschner haunts the agenda of interpreters of Wesley's Christology. For example, Edward Oakes writes,

---

15. Wesley, "The Lord Our Righteousness," I.3, *Works* I:453.

16. John Wesley, Letter 408 to Mrs. Elizabeth Bennis (September 10, 1773), *Works* (Jackson) 12:397.

17. Deschner, *Wesley's Christology*, 30.

"Wesley's account of the sufferings of Christ in the passion carries a whiff of Apollinarian Logos-Sarx Christology."[18] Clearly, these interpreters agree there is a problem with Wesley's Christology, but they do not agree with the exact nature of the problem. Does Wesley's Christology lean towards Apollinarianism or Nestorianism? Geoffrey Wainwright offers a helpful alternative to Deschner's reading. What we find in Wesley is not Apollinarianism, Nestorianism, or monophysitism, but "a healthily Alexandrian view of Christ's person."[19] Deschner's interpretation of Wesley's Christology is not simply retrospective but also prospective. He looks ahead to how this Christology could benefit from entering the theological conversation with ecumenical and liberation theologians. It is important for Wesleyan theology to engage ecumenical theology precisely on the point of Christology. Deschner states, "We have learned with Outler's help how limiting it can be to understand Wesley simply as a Protestant, and how insistent he himself was upon the ecumenical tradition as the foundation and interpretive context for the Methodist message of salvation."[20]

Deschner believes that engaging ecumenical theology deepens the Chalcedonian moorings of Wesley's Christology. He also believes that engaging liberation theology would strengthen the practical dimension of Wesley's theology. According to Deschner, Wesley's theology can be read at different levels: the "articulated" theology of his sermons and treatises, the "presupposed" theology of these writings, and the "enacted" theology of his ministry. "That enacted theology asks for much more reflection from students of Wesley's theology than it has yet received, and it may be that a liberation theology schooled in praxis-reflection methodologies will have the insight and will to undertake it."[21] It is to the Latin American and Latinx versions of these theologies that we next turn.

---

18. Edward Oakes, *Infinity Dwindled to Infancy: A Catholic and Evangelical Christology* (Grand Rapids, MI: Eerdmans, 2011), 288.

19. Geoffrey Wainwright, "Wesley's Christology: An Interpretation," Book Review, *Perkins Journal*, 39.2 (1986): 55–56, 55.

20. Deschner, *Wesley's Christology*, ix.

21. Deschner, *Wesley's Christology*, xiii.

Latin American and Latinx Christology

Two of the most important collections of essays on Christology from Latin American and Latinx perspectives were directed by Methodists. In 1977, José Míguez Bonino published the book *Jesus, ni vencido ni monarca celestial.* It was published in English in 1984 as *The Faces of Jesus in Latin America.*[22] In 2009, Harold Recinos and Hugo Magallanes published *Jesus in the Hispanic Community.*[23] Both books are ecumenical in scope, making ample room for Protestant and Catholic voices. In this sense, they embody well the Wesleyan Catholic spirit. John Deschner was familiar with Míguez Bonino's theology. Indeed, it is quite possible that the faces of Christ represented in this work are precisely those that Deschner thought needed to be considered carefully by Wesleyan theologians.[24] At the same time, the Wesleyan heritage is not particularly evident in these works. Indeed, the terms Wesley and Methodism do not appear in either book. Despite these lacunae, the books are extremely helpful guides to the images of Christ at work in shaping the Christian imagination of Latin American and Latinx people. The purpose of identifying these images is to point out their cultural captivity in order to be freed of them for more biblical, life-giving images of Jesus Christ as liberator and mestizo.

Jesus the Liberator

Embedded in Latin American Christologies is a distinction between the "historical Jesus" and the "Christ of faith." The former is the source; the latter is the interpretation. The history of interpretation has

---

22.   José Míguez Bonino, ed., *Jesus: Ni vencido ni monarca celestial* (Buenos Aires: Editorial Tierra Nueva, 1977); Míguez Bonino, *Faces of Jesus: Latin American Christologies* (Maryknoll, NY: Orbis, 1984).

23.   Harold J. Recinos and Hugo Magallanes, eds., *Jesus in the Hispanic Community: Images of Christ from Theology to Popular Religion* (Louisville, KY: Westminster John Knox, 2009).

24.   For Deschner's engagement with Míguez Bonino, see "More Than Inclusiveness: The New Christian Majority and the Shift in the Ecumenical Conversation about Church Unity," *The Ecumenical Review* 43.1 (1991): 57–67, and "The Changing Shape of the Church Unity Question," *Mid-Stream* 29.1 (1990): 23–32, 26.

bequeathed images of Christ that have normalized oppression in Latin America. The title of Míguez Bonino's book accurately names two dominant images: *vencido* (beaten victim) and *monarca celestial* (heavenly monarch). In churches throughout Latin America, images of Christ's crucified, bleeding, tortured, nearly naked body can be found near images of Christ clothed in a splendid, gold-and-silver-embroidered gown while wearing a jeweled crown and looking imperiously detached from the troubles of the world. The colonial Jesus was a Janus-like figure who looked like a dying Atahualpa or like the apotheosis of King Ferdinand I.[25] By starting with the historical Jesus, Latin American theologians seek to unmask the Spanish Christ that came to the Americas, hoping to discover a new, more hopeful face.

The path followed by Wesley's Alexandrian, Johannine Christology yields precedence to an Antiochene, synoptic Christology from below. Jesus is fully human. Latin American theologians call attention to Jesus's prayer life, his radical openness and surrender to God, and his solidarity with the marginalized. In *Jesus the Liberator,* Jesuit theologian Jon Sobrino speaks of Jesus as one who "belongs, then, to the current of those who hope in history, in the midst of oppression, who again and again formulate a utopia, who believe justice is possible. And in this way we can say that Jesus's humanity is true humanity."[26] Jesus's life and ministry reveal true humanity as oriented toward the kingdom of God. The kingdom is a utopia that fulfills the dreams of a people caught up in suffering; it is a liberating reality that comes in the midst of the oppression and resistance of the anti-kingdom.[27] The anti-kingdom is in force wherever true humanity is being denied, even in the visible church, for example, in its oppressive Christologies. In this christological vision, salvation is the integral liberation of the oppressed, and sanctification can only be attained in joining the struggle with the poor for the sake of the poor.

---

25. See George Casalis, "Jesus, Neither Abject Lord nor Heavenly Monarch," in *Faces of Jesus: Latin American Christologies,* 72–76.

26. Jon Sobrino, *Jesus the Liberator* (Maryknoll, NY: Orbis, 1993), 75.

27. Sobrino, *Jesus the Liberator,* 72.

Jesus is the liberator. This is the chief title for Jesus in the Latin American Christologies of the 1970s and 1980s. It is also a theme present in Latin American Methodist hymnody. The translation of "O for a thousand tongues to sing my great redeemer's praise" reads "Mil voces para celebrar a mi libertador" ("A thousand voices to celebrate my liberator"). The theme of liberation is developed more fully in another Methodist hymn, "Tenemos esperanza" ("We have hope").[28]

Porque El entró en el mundo y en la historia;
porque El quebró el silencio y la agonía;
porque llenó la tierra de su gloria;
porque fue luz en nuestra noche fría.

> Because he entered the world and history,
> because he broke the silence and the anguish,
> because he filled the earth with his glory,
> because he was light in our cold night.

Porque nació en un pesebre oscuro;
porque vivió sembrando amor y vida;
porque partió los corazones duros
y levantó las almas abatidas.

> Because he was born in a dark manger,
> because he lived sowing love and life,
> because he broke the hard hearts
> and raised the crushed souls.

Por eso es que hoy tenemos esperanza;
por eso es que hoy luchamos con porfía;
por eso es que hoy miramos con confianza,
el porvenir en esta tierra mía.
Por eso es que hoy tenemos esperanza;
por eso es que hoy luchamos con porfía;

---

28. *Mil voces para celebrar* (Nashville, TN: United Methodist Publishing House, 1996), Hymn 129. The translation into English is my own.

por eso es que hoy miramos con confianza,
el porvenir.

> This is why today we have hope,
> this is why today we fight with boldness,
> this is why today we look with confidence
> to the future in this land of ours.
> This is why today we have hope,
> this is why today we fight with boldness,
> this is why today we look with confidence
> to the future.

"Porque El entró en el mundo y en la historia . . . hoy miramos con confianza el porvenir en esta tierra mía": because he entered the world and history, today we look with confidence to the future of this land of ours.

In this hymn, Bishop Federico Pagura looks at the national crisis and widespread human rights violations during Argentina's dirty war and anchors his hope on a Christ who sides with the oppressed against the oppressor. Two Wesleyan notes stand out in this hymn. First, the hymn emphasizes today. The hope that Christ makes possible is not just for life in glory but for life in history. We hope for today, and it is hope for today that gives us confidence to look to the future. Second, the hymn emphasizes human participation. Hope in Christ encourages Christians to join the struggle to make this hope real today. The vision of life revealed by Christ becomes a commission for the Christian.

Jesus the Mestizo

Despite the many connections between them, the Latinx context differs from the Latin American one in significant ways. Hispanics are marginalized in distinctive ways. The experience of hyphenation and hybridity renders them too Latin for Americans and too American for Latins. The faces of Jesus in the Hispanic communities envisioned by Recinos and Magallanes are more fluid than those in Latin America because, in the United States, Jesus is a *sato*—a mongrel, a mutt. In the words of Loida Martell-Otero, to call Jesus a *sato* "underscores the experience of being relegated to the bottom rung of society precisely as one who is perceived to be nonhuman, impure, and of no intrinsic value—*sobraja* [leftovers]."[29]

The Latinx christological vision of cultural hybridity has been strongly influenced by the work of the Mexican American theologian Virgilio Elizondo.[30] Latin American history is marked by mestizaje, a term used to denote the mixing of Spanish and Indigenous cultures that followed the conquest. The ambiguities and tensions that accompany mestizaje have characterized Latin American and Hispanic identity. Elizondo owes his renown as the father of Latinx theology to being the first to bring this experience into a theological register. According to Elizondo, "The human scandal of God's way does not begin with the cross, but with the historic-cultural incarnation of his Son in Galilee."[31] Jesus of Nazareth in Galilee is a mestizo. As Elizondo understands it, "Galilee was the home of the simple people—that is, of the people of the land, a hardworking people, marginated and oppressed regardless of who was in power or what system of power was in effect. They were the ones who were left out and exploited by everyone else. They shared the fate of other peoples living on the margins of 'better' civilizations."[32] The borderland status of Galilee justified Nathanael's question to Jesus: "Can anything good come out of Nazareth?" (Jn 1:45). Elizondo explains, "Nobody looks for leadership from or has high expectations of those who live in the sticks, the *barrios,* the *ranchitos,* or inner-city slums."[33] There is a Galilean principle at work in God's salvation history. "It is in the unsuspected places and situations of the world and through 'unlikely' persons that God continues to work today."[34] God chooses the borderlands as the setting for his drama of redemption and border-crossers as his privileged audience. Elizondo's

29.   Loida Martell-Otero, "Encuentro con el Jesús Sato: An Evangélica Soter-ology," in *Jesus in the Hispanic Community*, 74–91, 77.

30.   Virgilio Elizondo, *Galilean Journey: The Mexican-American Promise* (Maryknoll, NY: Orbis, 1997).

31.   Elizondo, *Galilean Journey*, 53.

32.   Elizondo, *Galilean Journey*, 52.

33.   Elizondo, *Galilean Journey*, 52.

34.   Elizondo, *Galilean Journey*, 92.

Galilean principle coincides with the theological vision of a hymn by the Cuban American Methodist theologian, Justo González.[35]

> From all four of earth's faraway corners,
> flows together the blood of all races
> in this people who sing of their trials,
> in this people who cry of their faith;
> hardy blood that was brought by the Spanish,
> noble blood of the suffering Indian,
> blood of slaves who stood heavy oppression,
> all the blood that was bought on the cross.

González sees in the history of the Americas the tortuous path of God's ministry of reconciliation. From the diversity of ethnicities in these lands, God is creating a new people, a mestizo people who point to a tomorrow without borders where all dwell together in peace and love. Through the blood of the cross of Christ, God is dismantling the walls of separation and reconciling all peoples, Jews and Gentiles, Africans, Indians, Europeans, and Asians. Jesus makes possible a new humanity, a new way of being ethnic. He is, in the words of González's Hispanic Creed, "God made flesh in a person for all humanity, God made flesh in an age for all the ages, God made flesh in one culture for all cultures."[36] Chapter 4 offers a in-depth study of the Hispanic Creed; for now, it suffices to note how González's harmonization of Antiochene and Alexandrian approaches, of a historical Jesus and a cosmic Christ, is an example of the direction for Wesleyan Christology proposed by Deschner.

Towards a Latinx Wesleyan Christology

In his book on Wesley's Christology, John Deschner hoped engagement with the methodologies of theologies from the Global South would

---

35. *Mil voces para celebrar*, Hymn 378.
36. González, "Hispanic Creed," *Mil voces para celebrar*, 70.

bring to the fore the practical theological orientation of Wesley's ministry. In effect, Deschner longed for a Christology that is classically Chalcedonian and contextually concrete. In this final section, I overlap the focal points of Wesleyan, Latin American, and Hispanic Christology with a view towards a Latinx Wesleyan Christology. The resulting image can be expressed in two axioms: the whole Christ liberates and the present Christ is mestizo today.

The Whole Christ Liberates

Wesley rightly insists that Christ must be preached in all his offices, but his heirs have not always been faithful in discharging this responsibility. The emphasis has been on Christ as priest and mediator of forgiveness. The Latin American and Hispanic voices considered here would encourage the Wesleyan to preach Christ as prophet and king also. At the same time, looking at the whole Christ through the overlapping of Wesleyan and Latin American lenses brings two other significant features to the fore.

First, the whole Christ is human and divine. The Alexandrian and Antiochene approaches need to be held together. Followers of the Antiochene way must be ever mindful of the inherent ambiguity in all the "historical" works of Jesus. Indeed, his disciples frequently misunderstood his signs and sayings. Followers of the Alexandrian way can never forget the limitations inherent in all knowledge of God. Both paths converge on the second person of the Trinity, the Son of God. The Latinx Wesleyan Christology that I envision here would resist a hard distinction between the Jesus of history and the Christ of faith. Failure to keep these united results in the christological dead ends described by Míguez Bonino. "We seem to have both a Christ who is the Second Person of the Trinity but historically inoperative, and localized 'Christs' from whom actions (magical, perhaps) are looked for in the natural, human world."[37] It is through the witness of the church in the power of the Holy Spirit that we know Jesus Christ today. The whole Christ includes Christ as head and his body.

---

37. Míguez Bonino, *Faces of Jesus: Latin American Christologies*, 6.

Second, the whole Christ is the liberator. There is no need to play off the roles of Christ against each other, as if being a prophet was connected to the struggles for liberation and being a priest to the maintenance of the status quo. The threefold office of Christ as a whole is oriented to the liberation of humanity and creation from bondage to sin and to leading it on to perfection in the kingdom of God. The development of a Latinx Wesleyan Christology calls for a rereading of the *munus triplex* of the whole Christ from the periphery. Elsa Tamez explains, "What is novel for us is the consideration of justification and liberation from a historical perspective of oppression, poverty, and struggle."[38] The significance of a historical perspective leads us to the second christological feature.

The Present Christ Is Mestizo Today

The presence of Jesus, Emmanuel, is central to a Latinx Wesleyan Christology. At the end of his life's journey, John Wesley's deathbed declaration says it well, "The best of all is, God is with us."[39] Jesus is "God incarnate, and dwells by his Spirit in the hearts of his people."[40] Pablo Andiñach is being a good Wesleyan biblical scholar in titling his theology of the Old Testament *El Dios que está* ("The God who is present"). He writes, "The God who is present is no mere spectator in the drama of creation. The Scriptures highlight a God who is committed to human life and who, far from being isolated, inserts himself into the ways of humanity and follows closely the destiny of human beings."[41]

A Latinx Wesleyan emphasis on the present Christ calls for a double concretion of that present. First, the present becomes concrete in every-

38. Elsa Tamez, *The Amnesty of Grace: Justification by Faith from a Latin American Perspective* (Portland, OR: Wipf & Stock, 2002), 36.

39. John Whitehead, *The Life of the Rev. John Wesley* (Auburn, NY: J.E. Beardsley, 1793), 542.

40. John Wesley's note on Mt 1:23 in *Explanatory Notes Upon the New Testament,* 3rd ed., 2 vols. (Bristol, UK: Graham & Pine, 1760–61), 15; hereafter *NT Notes.*

41. Pablo Andiñach, *El Dios que está* (Pamplona, España: Editorial Verbo Divino, 2014), 25.

day life. Jesus inserted himself into ordinary life. Echoing the thought of Irenaeus of Lyons, Wesley writes, "So our Lord passed through and sanctified every stage of human life."[42] Jesus hallows infancy, childhood, youth, and adulthood. Since these stages are not lived in the abstract but in the concrete, Jesus's sanctification of the stages of human life has implications for the conditions of human life. Elsa Tamez writes, "The first sign of life is the recovery of the image of God in humanity choked by sin, where death lies in ambush, in hunger and insignificance. It is a matter of feeling the pulse of God 'in the depths of Hell,' and of experiencing grace on the garbage dump."[43]

God in Christ is most immanent in the places of exclusion. Elsa Tamez states it accurately, "Though all human beings manifest a broken image of God (the victimizers as well as the victims), God chooses a meeting place so that God's image might be reproduced in every living being. God makes this choice not in order to exclude some people, but precisely in order to negate exclusion by including all people, beginning among those presently excluded."[44]

Second, the present becomes concrete in history. Thus, discerning the present Christ calls for reading the signs of the times. For Wesley, the signs

---

42.   John Wesley, *NT Notes*, Lk 2:43, 1:220. Wesley did not follow Irenaeus in the latter's positive assessment of old age. Wesley adds, "Old age only did not become him." By contrast, Irenaeus writes of Christ, "He was an old man for old men, that He might be a perfect Master for all, not merely as respects the setting forth of the truth, but also as regards age, sanctifying at the same time the aged also, and becoming an example to them likewise. Then, at last, He came on to death itself, that He might be 'the first-born from the dead, that in all things He might have the pre-eminence, [Col 1:18] the Prince of life [Acts 3:15], existing before all, and going before all" (Irenaeus, AH 2.22.4). Wesley's judgment on this point follows a strand of Christian tradition picked up by Hans Urs von Balthasar, who writes, "Jesus appears before the world at thirty, at the age of full maturity, beyond which no essential development could humanly be expected." Balthasar, *Man in History* (London, UK: Sheed & Ward, 1968), 268. More positively, and perhaps by way of a synthesis, Balthasar also observes, "There are no 'old' saints. All of them are youthful even in advanced age." Balthasar, "Young until death," *Explorations in Theology, V: Man Is Created* (San Francisco, CA: Ignatius, 2014), 223.

43.   Tamez, *The Amnesty of Grace*, 132.

44.   Tamez, *The Amnesty of Grace*, 132.

of the times are christologically centered and soteriologically oriented.[45] A Latinx Wesleyan reading of the signs of the times would look for tokens of Christ's advent within the violent, mestizo-making history of Latin America and the United States because Christ entered into our history. The present Christ is mestizo because the body of Christ in history is mestizo. Jesus ended the hostility between Jews and Gentiles and made them into a new humanity through his crucified flesh (Eph 2:13-16). This Ephesian Moment, as missiologist Andrew Walls terms it, is relived throughout the church's long history of mestizo-bearing encounters, yielding Latin American and Hispanic Christs.[46]

A Latinx Wesleyan Christology starts from the mystery of the conception and birth of Jesus but does not stop there. A Christology centered on the mystery of the incarnation to the exclusion of the transfiguration underappreciates the possibility of the status quo being swept up by the Holy Spirit into the history of salvation. All cultures, historical ages, and peoples bear the marks of sin. We can profess faith with González in the "God made flesh in one culture for all cultures" only if we read the "for" missiologically. Latinx Wesleyan theologians would benefit from engaging the theological vision of Saint Óscar Romero, whose christological thought centers on the transfigured Christ who transfigures the people of God and the land of El Salvador.[47] God is "for all cultures" in that God promises the healing and transfiguration of all nations. Commenting on the mountain to which Jesus led his disciples in Matthew 28:18, Wesley says "this was probably Mount Tabor, where (it is commonly supposed) he had been before transfigured. It seems to have been here also, that He

---

45.   John Wesley, Sermon 66, "The Signs of the Times," I.1, *Works* 2:523: "What times were those concerning which our Lord is here speaking? It is easy to answer: the times of the Messiah, the times ordained before the foundation of the world wherein it pleased God to give his only-begotten Son to take our nature upon him, to be 'found in fashion as a man,' to live a life of sorrow and pain, and at length to be 'obedient unto death, even the death of the cross'; to the end 'that whosoever believeth on him should not perish, but have everlasting life.'"

46.   See Andrew Walls, *The Cross-Cultural Process in Christian History* (Maryknoll, NY: Orbis, 2002), 72–84.

47.   See Edgardo Colón-Emeric, *Óscar Romero's Theological Vision: Liberation and the Transfiguration of the Poor* (Notre Dame, IN: University of Notre Dame Press, 2018): 115–68.

appeared to above five hundred Brethren at once."[48] Tabor is the starting point for the Great Commission and its goal. Christ sends his church to make disciples for the transfiguration of the world.

Conclusion

What keeps Christology from becoming an exercise in biblical eisegesis and cultural affirmation? Do Nicaraguans sing of a Christ born in Palacagüina simply because they are Nicaraguans? Míguez Bonino warns us of the risk of this kind of Feuerbachian approach to Christ. "In that case Christology would be either nothing but a manner of speaking, or a form of the projection of such conditions and ideologies. . . . Christology could serve only to justify an already existing historical praxis."[49] Míguez Bonino's solution to this conundrum is hermeneutical, namely "a hermeneutics that respects not only the original historicity of the text but also the singularity of the reader's locus."[50] This is wise counsel, to which Charles Wesley would recommend adding a doxological coda.

> Furnished with intellectual light,
> In vain I speak of thee aright,
> While unrevealed thou art:
> That only can suffice for me,
> The whole mysterious Trinity
> Inhabiting my heart.[51]

A few years ago, I was teaching theology at Duke's Pastoral Program in Guatemala. Because the native language of a number of my students was K'iche', one of the Mayan tongues, I required the assistance of a translator; and because it was an oral culture, I dispensed with written examinations.

---

48. Wesley, *NT Notes*, Mt 28:18, 1:142.

49. Bonino, *Faces of Jesus: Latin American Christologies*, 3.

50. Bonino, *Faces of Jesus: Latin American Christologies*, 4.

51. Charles Wesley, *Hymns on the Trinity* (1767), Hymn 19, https://divinity.duke.edu /initiatives/cswt/charles-published-verse.

Instead, I tested my students by asking a series of true or false questions like, "Marcion loved the Old Testament, true or false?" My students had never taken this kind of test before, so I offered a sample question: "Jesus was born in Guatemala, true or false?" Most students caught on quickly until it was Juan's turn. He paused, and then said, "True." I assumed that Juan had misunderstood me, so I asked again. "Jesus of Nazareth, not Jesús your cousin, was born in Guatemala. True or false?" Again, he paused, thought hard, and answered, "True." I admit that I became a little flustered. If he was having trouble with this question, what would happen when we turned to questions about Irenaeus? So I asked him, "Why do you say that Jesus was born in Guatemala, the Bible says that he was born in Bethlehem?" "Yes," he said, "but he was born in my heart." Marvin, my translator, tried to help, but Juan remained resolute. Jesus was born in Guatemala. Later, as I reflected on this experience, I remembered reading that Atticus of Constantinople, the predecessor of Nestorius instructed the empress and her sisters that "if they imitated the virginity and chastity of Mary, they would give birth to God mystically in their souls."[52] Juan was a good Wesleyan theologian; he was no Nestorian. By the power of the Holy Spirit, the whole Christ had become present in his life. Yes. Jesús was born in Guatemala.

52. Maxwell Johnson, "*Sub Tuum Praesidium*: The *Theotokos* in Christian Life and Worship before Ephesus," *Pro Ecclesia* 17.1 (2008): 52–75, 69.

Chapter Three
Medellín through Methodist Eyes

The ecumenical movement appears to be past its prime. As early as 1989, Robert Runcie, then Archbishop of Canterbury, spoke of "the winter of ecumenism."[1] When the Norwegian pastor Olav Fykse Tveit, the General Secretary of the World Council of Churches (WCC), visited Pope Benedict, he gave the pontiff a thick pair of woolen gloves.[2] The theological academy has clearly lost interest in ecumenism. Whereas the giants of the European and North American theological schools were conspicuously present at the conferences of the WCC in the mid-twentieth century, this was no longer true by the end of the century. Mark Heim credited this parting of ways to a number of factors, including "the divergence of academic theology from churchly concerns as well as the growing urgency of issues of liberation and

---

1. According to Jelle Creemers, *Theological Dialogue with Classical Pentecostals: Challenges and Opportunities* (New York: T&T Clark, 2015), 1 fn.1.

2. According to Bruce Myers, Tveit explained to Benedict XVI that, for Norwegians, winter is not something to be dreaded: "We know that winter can be beautiful, and we know that winter is only one of four seasons. In winter, we have time for reflection, time to think about what we have experienced in the past and what we expect from the future, and, of course, how we can prepare for the future." Myers, "Keeping Warm: Reception in the Ecumenical Winter," *The Ecumenical Review* 65.3 (October 2013): 376. See also Minna Hietamäki, "Finding Warmth in the Ecumenical Winter: A Nordic Viewpoint," *The Ecumenical Review* 65.3 (October 2013): 368–75.

religious pluralism."[3] The church, too, lost interest. For some, the ecumenical movement achieved such great success that it no longer seemed as urgent. For others, questions around human sexuality and women's ordination heated up and introduced new divisions. Ricardo Assolari has pointed to the collapse of the Iron Curtain in 1989 as a contributor to the ecumenical winter.[4]

From the beginning of the ecumenical movement, there were questions regarding the theology and the politics of the WCC. In Latin America, in particular, the preferential option for the poor made by the theologies of liberation became a catalyst for the ecumenical movement. The theme of the fifth assembly of the WCC in Nairobi, "Jesus Christ liberates and unites," resonated strongly among many Latin American theologians.[5] Emilio Castro—a Uruguayan Methodist and former General Secretary of the WCC—suggested that his Northern friends may be misreading the signs because "In Northern imagery, winter is the time when not many things happen. In my part of the world, winter is the contrary."[6]

Whatever the ecumenical temperature may be, a turn to the Southern hemisphere may be helpful in bringing some global perspective to the weather forecasts. In particular, I want to take us back to Medellín. It has been fifty years since the Council of Latin American Catholic Bishops (CELAM) held a conference in Medellín, Colombia. The event has been rightly regarded as a watershed moment in Latin American church history. It has been celebrated or condemned as a fountainhead of liberation theology. As might be expected, it has generated a vast amount of scholarly reflection over the decades, but its legacy is now be-

---

3. S. Mark Heim, "Montreal to Compostela: Pilgrimage in Ecumenical Winter," *The Christian Century* 109.11 (April 1, 1992): 334.

4. Ricardo Assolari, "As estações ecumênicas: implicações do conceito de tradição para os desafios do inverno ecumênico," *Protestantismo em Revista* 42 (2016): 49–51.

5. See Julio de Santa Ana, *Ecumenismo y liberación* (Sao Paulo: Ediciones Paulinas, 1987).

6. Emilio Castro, "Ecumenical Winter," *Mid-Stream* 32.2 (1993): 12.

ing read through the optic of Francis's pontificate.[7] His call for "a church which goes forth" to the peripheries of society universalizes the lessons of Medellín.[8]

In this essay, I read Medellín through Methodist eyes, in particular through the writings of José Míguez Bonino (1924–2012). In so doing, I hope to show the impact of the conference on the Latin American ecumenical scene and to answer the Argentine Methodist's question: "How do we understand ourselves as Methodists in light of Medellín?"[9] The dominant role that I accord Míguez Bonino in posing and addressing this question is warranted by his widespread recognition as the dean of Latin American Protestant theology.[10] When Methodists gathered in 1983 to explore the prospects for a Latin American Methodist theology, four of the ten essays dedicated to reinterpretation of the Methodist heritage for the Latin American context were written by Míguez Bonino.[11]

In order to address the question of the significance of Medellín for Methodists, I will structure the essay as follows. First, I will give a brief overview of the background and content of the conference of Medellín. Then, I will examine Míguez Bonino's reading of the documents from the conference before considering the impact of this Catholic gathering on the Latin American Protestant ecumenical and evangelical movements. Finally, I will conclude with some tentative answers to the framing question: How do Methodists understand themselves in light of Medellín?

---

7.   See Juan Miguel Espinosa Portocarrero, "Memoria, gratitud y profecía: De Medellín a Francisco," *Páginas* 43.249 (2018): 36–43.

8.   See *Evangelii gaudium*, nos. 20–24.

9.   José Míguez Bonino, "¿Conservar el metodismo?—En busca de un genuino ecumenismo," in *La tradición protestante en la teología latinoamericana Primer intento: Lectura de la tradición metodista*, ed. José Duque (San José, Costa Rica: Departamento Ecuménico de Investigaciones, 1983), 329.

10.   See Orlando Costas, *Theology of the Crossroads in Contemporary Latin America: Missiology in Mainline Protestantism: 1969–1974* (Amsterdam: Editions Rodopi, 1976), 91.

11.   Orlando Costas, *Theology of the Crossroads in Contemporary Latin America*, 91. Not only did Míguez Bonino author numerous essays in this collection, many of the other presentations and the final documents from that congress referenced his reading of Wesley as basically normative for all Latin American engagement.

Medellín—A Catholic Pentecost

Recalling his experience at the 1968 Conference, Bishop Marcos Mc-Grath said, "We left Medellín inspired as by a new Pentecost."[12] The meeting of Latin American Catholic bishops in Medellín marked the first time a pope had visited Latin America. In his opening speech to the assembly at Medellín, Paul VI stated, "The first personal visit of a Pope to his brothers and children in Latin America is not just a simple, singular news event. It is, in our opinion, a historic event that inserts itself into the long, complex, toilsome, evangelical work of these immense territories."[13] In that long history, the Catholic Church in Latin America had convened many councils, which were meant to serve as instruments for disseminating the teachings of the councils taking place in Europe. A brief overview of this history is important in order to understand the significance and surprise of Medellín.

Historical Context

The toilsome history of Latin America to which Paul VI alluded in his discourse closely overlapped the Protestant Reformation. The Council of Trent (1545–63) was convened for the purpose of offering a Catholic version of ecclesial reform that would distinguish it from that of the Protestant Reformers. A few Latin American prelates were present at Trent. Also present were Spanish theologians such as Melchor Cano, who made important contributions to the deliberations of Trent. Overall, it was a council of and for Europeans. Even so, Trent's teachings were binding for all Catholics, and they made their way to Latin America through the Council of Lima (1582–83) and the Council of Mexico City (1585).[14]

---

12. Cited by Carlos Schickendantz, "Un enfoque empírico-teológico. En el método, el secreto de Medellín," *Teología y Vida* 58.4 (2017): 423.

13. Medellín (hereafter, M), "Discurso Inaugural." The source used herein is Catholic Council of Latin American Bishops, *Las Cinco Conferencias Generales del Episcopado Latino-americano* (Bogotá, Columbia: CELAM, 2014) for Medellín, Puebla, and Rio documents.

14. See Brian Larkin, "Tridentine Catholicism in the New World," in *Cambridge History of Religions in Latin America*, ed. Virginia Garrard-Burnett, Paul Freston, and Stephen C. Dove (New York: Cambridge University Press, 2016), 107–32.

The Tridentine Catholicism transplanted from Europe by these councils found fertile soil in the Latin American lands.

The First Vatican Council (1869–70) was convened by Pius IX in order to address the European crises arising from the European Enlightenment. Fifty-three Spanish-speaking bishops and seven Portuguese-speaking bishops attended from Latin America (twenty-three did not attend). By way of comparison, forty-six bishops attended from the United States, even though they had just gone through a civil war. The nearly yearlong stay in Rome of many Latin American bishops contributed to the Romanization of the Latin American churches and to the "modernization" of ecclesial life from contact with the currents of renewal circulating in Europe.[15] Following Vatican I, a Latin American Plenary Council was held in Rome in 1899 under the auspices of Leo XIII. His chief purpose for this council was to consolidate the Latin American churches that had experienced fragmentation following the independence movements of the nineteenth century. The Latin American Council was, in general, successful in accomplishing this goal. The Catechism of Trent was frequently cited in the proceedings of the council, and Vatican I's teachings on faith and revelation were ratified. Nearly half of the Latin American bishops participated in this council, and the experience yielded fruits in a greater sense of shared life and mission in Latin America. Among these fruits, two are worth mentioning. First, a series of eucharistic congresses were held throughout Latin America;[16] second, CELAM was founded with the approval of Pius XII and met in Rio de Janeiro in 1955.

When the second conference of Latin American bishops met in Medellín in 1968, there was a strong expectation that the conference would

15. Josep Ignasi Saranyana, ed., *Teología en América Latina, Vol II,2* (Vervuert: Iberoamericana, 2001), 78.

16. For instance, an international gathering was celebrated in Buenos Aires in 1934, the thirty-second such congress, but the first of its kind in Latin America. A number of themes in this congress are worth pointing out, as they become significant for future regional congresses. A hymn was composed that expressed devotion to the Sacred Heart of Jesus, a christocentric form of piety much promoted by Pius XI. The hymn also voiced strongly patriotic notes, praising "the geographic and agricultural particularities proper to Argentina, like the blue color (present in the flag of the republic) as an allusion to the river, the gold of the wheat and sun (also on the flag); the boundary-less expanse of the Pampa, etc." (Saranyana, *Teología in América Latina*, 72).

be focused on the reception of the Second Vatican Council (1962–65). This was, after all, the historic pattern. For almost 500 years, the church in Latin America had been a reflection of the church in Europe. Latin American councils were convened for the purpose of translating, adapting, and disseminating the teaching of councils that were regarded as "catholic" or "ecumenical" but were also undeniably "European." The light of Vatican II certainly shone on Medellín, but what this light revealed was not a dim reflection of the Church of Rome but a nascent Latin American church that would become a source for the Catholic Church as a whole.

The Latin American Pentecost of Medellín occurred in a historically dense moment.[17] Latin American independence was an incomplete project, which led to political autonomy from Spain but economic dependence on Great Britain. With World War II and the rise of the United States as a world power, the economic reins of Latin America switched from the eastern shores of the North Atlantic to the western ones. During the 1950s, Latin America sought an equivalent of a Marshall Plan to promote the kind of economic development in the southern hemisphere that would protect it from the Soviet threat. No such plan was made. The year 1959 proved to be a watershed moment, as the Cuban revolution showed the possibility of a Latin America free from economic and political dependence on the United States.

The Kennedy administration responded to this event by propping up Puerto Rico as a model of liberal democracy and capitalist investment, a model that would be offered to all Latin America by means of the Alliance for Progress. The work of the Alliance for Progress, with its emphasis on development through technical and economic assistance, was well received by both Christian and social democrats in Latin America. It was hoped that the assistance of the United States would help stabilize the economic and political situation in Latin America and thus prevent the conditions that led to leftist revolutions. However, the lack of adequate funding and internal inefficiencies doomed this work to failure. The 1960s saw a rise in hyperinflation in many Latin American countries, which contributed to

---

17. See Norman Rubén Amestoy, "De la crisis del modelo liberal a la irrupción del movimiento Iglesia y Sociedad en América Latina (ISAL)," *Teología y Cultura* 8.13 (2011): 7–11.

social unrest and political instability. The "Doctrine of National Security" the United States had developed at the outset of the Cold War became the basis for an alliance between Latin American economic elites and various US administrations, resulting in right-wing coups all over Latin America. When the bishops gathered at Medellín, all the signs of the time pointed to an intolerably sinful situation.

The Conference of Medellín

At Medellín, the bishops expressed their commitment to being ecclesially engaged in the social transformation already occurring throughout the continent. Toward that end, the report from the council is organized around three areas: first, the raising of the Latin American peoples toward the human values of justice, peace, education, and the family; second, the evangelization of the populace and the social elites through catechesis and the liturgy; third, the adaptation of the structures of the church to the new social realities in the continent. In addressing this new situation, the bishops adopted the "see, judge, act" methodology of the Young Catholic Worker (JOC) movement. Two examples will help to clarify how the method was employed.

Medellín addresses the topic of justice by seeing the pertinent facts in the continent: "There are in existence many studies of the Latin American people. The misery that besets large masses of human beings in all of our countries is described in all of these studies. That misery, as a collective fact, expresses itself as an injustice which cries to the heavens." After noting these sociological and historical facts, it judges them on a doctrinal basis: "The Latin American Church has a message for all men on this continent who 'hunger and thirst after justice' . . . for our authentic liberation, all of us need a profound conversion so that 'the kingdom of justice, love and peace,' might come to us" (M 1, 1). From this vision and theological judgment, a concrete pastoral action follows: "The Latin American Church encourages the formation of national communities that reflect a global organization, where all of the peoples but more especially the lower classes have, by means of territorial and functional structures, an active and receptive, creative and decisive participation in the construction of a new society" (M 1, 7).

Medellín's call for a church of the poor begins by attending to the Latin American scene: "A deafening cry pours from the throats of millions of men, asking their pastors for liberation that reaches them from nowhere else" (M 14, 2). As a result, Medellín concluded that "the Latin American bishops cannot remain indifferent in the face of the tremendous social injustices existent in Latin America, which keep the majority of our peoples in dismal poverty, which in many cases becomes inhuman wretchedness" (M 14, 1). These social injustices are judged by holding them up to a christological account of the Church's poverty: "Christ, our Savior, not only loved the poor, but rather 'being rich He became poor,' He lived in poverty. His mission centered on advising the poor of their liberation and He founded His Church as the sign of that poverty among men" (M 14, 7). This christological judgment helps the bishops distinguish between different kinds of poverty and exhorts Catholics to respond to the sinful poverty of the continent by evangelizing the poor, seeking solidarity with the poor, and becoming poor.[18]

Medellín did promote the reception of the teachings of Vatican II. Its adaptation of *Gaudium et spes* was particularly rich.[19] However, the teachings of Medellín were more than mere translations of Vatican II. Participants felt that something new, reminiscent of Pentecost, was taking place.

18. Medellín distinguishes three kinds of poverty. "Poverty, as a lack of the goods of this world necessary to live worthily as men, is in itself evil. The prophets denounce it as contrary to the will of the Lord and most of the time as the fruit of the injustice and sin of men" (M 14, 4a). "Spiritual poverty is the theme of the poor of Yahweh. Spiritual poverty is the attitude of opening up to God, the ready disposition of one who hopes for everything from the Lord. Although he values the goods of this world, he does not become attached to them and he recognizes the higher value of the riches of the Kingdom" (M 14, 4b). "Poverty as a commitment, through which one assumes voluntarily and lovingly the conditions of the needy of this world in order to bear witness to the evil which it represents and to spiritual liberty in the face of material goods, follows the example of Christ who took to Himself all the consequences of men's sinful condition and Who 'being rich became poor' in order to redeem us" (M 14, 4c).

19. Carlos Schickendantz is one of many who argue that "*Gaudium et spes* has been the conciliar text which 'has had the greatest impact in Latin America,' precisely because of the contribution of its method which invites palpating and discerning the signs of the times in the deep aspirations and desires of humanity" (see Schickendantz, "Un enfoque empírico-teológico," 445).

The Holy Spirit was turning the Latin American church into a source for the universal church. This was the surprise of Medellín.[20] Although it was a regional conference, Medellín was inspired by an ecumenical and catholic spirit. Robert Curnow stated, "The conclusions of Medellín became questions asked of the broader Christian community. What was the Universal Church going to make of them?"[21]

A Protestant at Medellín

The Pentecostal winds that blew open the windows of the Vatican and surprised the bishops at Medellín were ecumenical in spirit. Vatican II invited Protestant observers to attend. Among these were Methodist eminences such as Robert Cushman and Albert Outler—and José Míguez Bonino, the only Latin American Protestant invited.[22] Míguez Bonino admired the courage of John XXIII and the bold vision of the council he convened. The Argentine Methodist wrote, "For the first time in the history of Christianity a Council is convened with the specific purpose of opening lines of communication, rather than building trenches and walls for the protection of the Christian faith."[23] Whatever the historical accuracy of his statement, the

20. Of course, not everyone liked this surprise. The Belgian Jesuit Roger Vekemans and Archbishop Alfonso López Trujillo saw too much of Marx in Medellín. From their privileged vantage points (Vekemans founded a think tank and journal, and Trujillo became Secretary and then president of CELAM), they raised serious caveats to the conclusions of Medellín. Even so, the critique of Medellín as a gathering of Christian socialists is shortsighted. An examination of the vocabulary of Medellín is revealing. Such words as "communism" and "Marxism" are used rarely and only critically. Moreover, the resulting action of the "see, judge, act" method is overwhelmingly ecclesial in character.

21. Rohan M. Curnow, "Which Preferential Option for the Poor? A History of the Doctrine's Bifurcation," *Modern Theology* 31.1 (2015): 27–59.

22. For the reports from these Methodist observers on Vatican II, see the following: Albert Outler, *Methodist Observer at Vatican II* (Westminster, MD: Newman, 1967); Robert Cushman, "Protestant View of Vatican Council II in retrospect," *Divinity School Review* 31.3 (1966): 163–74; José Míguez Bonino, *Concilio abierto: una interpretación protestante del Concilio Vaticano II* (Buenos Aires: Editorial La Aurora, 1967). See also Leopoldo Cervantes-Ortiz, "El 'Concilio Abierto' de J. Míguez Bonino," *Protestante Digital.com*, December 30, 2012, http://protestantedigital.com/magacin/13223/El_Concilio_Abiertorsquo_de_J _Míguez_Bonino.

23. José Míguez Bonino, *Concilio abierto*, 16.

missional turn of the Catholic Church was momentous for the Latin American context. Even before the Council concluded, Míguez Bonino referred to it as "a council for Latin America."[24] In a sense, it was even a council from Latin America. Many of the concerns animating the Council and the movements of reform that found their way into its statements were first aired in the Latin American context. Míguez Bonino understood that the ecumenical spirit blowing through Rome would encounter resistance across the Atlantic. Some Protestants would "fear that rapprochement would weaken the nerve of Protestantism."[25] Some Catholics would "fear that the ecumenical attitude may foster indifferentism and open the door to a still more pronounced 'proselytism' on the part of Protestants."[26] When Paul VI convened the Latin American bishops at Medellín a few years later, Míguez Bonino was again invited to observe.

In essays and public addresses, the Argentine Methodist offered an interpretation of the Catholic conference from a Protestant perspective. Here, I focus chiefly on two essays. The first of these, "Medellín and Ecumenism: A Protestant Reading of the Documents," was written in 1969 soon after the conclusion of the conference.[27] The second, "The Church and Puebla," was written in 1979 when the third conference of Latin American bishops met in Puebla.[28] Three themes stand out from these reflections: the ecumenical question of Medellín, the theological method by which it addresses this question, and its ecclesiological proposal.

The Ecumenical Question of Medellín

Reflecting back on the gathering at Medellín, Míguez Bonino noted the contradiction of the Protestant presence and the near total invisibility

---

24. José Míguez Bonino, "Vatican II and Latin America," *The Christian Century* 81.53 (December 30, 1964): 1616.

25. Míguez Bonino, "Vatican II and Latin America," 1617.

26. Míguez Bonino, "Vatican II and Latin America," 1617.

27. José Míguez Bonino, "Medellín y el ecumenismo: Una lectura protestante de los documentos," *Teología* 15–16 (1969): 228–32.

28. José Míguez Bonino, "La Iglesia en Puebla," in *Puebla y Oaxtepec: Una crítica protestante y católica* (México: Tierra Nueva, 1980).

of ecumenism. A few ecumenical notes can be heard. In its final exhortation addressed to the people of Latin America, the bishops spoke directly to "all the churches and Christian communities who share in our same faith in the Lord Jesus."[29] The Catholic prelates rejoiced that "our brothers from these Christian confessions participated in our tasks and hopes." According to Míguez Bonino, "by the beginning of the second week, a few of us were working with the experts in the redaction of the final documents."[30] The Holy Spirit was leading the Catholic Church to renew its witness to Christ in Latin America. In order to be faithful in this task the Catholic Church as a whole needed to "collaborate with other Christian confessions and all people of goodwill who are dedicated to working for a true peace that is rooted in justice and love."[31] One area of concrete collaboration was education, wherein Catholics are called to work with "non-Catholic churches and institutions dedicated to the task of bringing justice to human relations" (M 1, 22).[32] This work involves stirring among Catholics and Protestants in wealthy nations a greater solidarity with the peoples of Latin America.[33] Catholic families are encouraged to be "generously open" to families belonging to different Christian traditions (M 3, 20). Míguez Bonino understood the Conference of 1968 to be of the utmost ecumenical significance: "We do not find here an invitation to discuss inter-ecclesial relations, but any Christian who reads this document will find an irresistible invitation to face the call and mission of Jesus Christ in this continent today."[34]

Medellín accurately diagnosed the context in which the gospel is to be announced: "The Church has tried to understand the historic moment of the Latin American person in the light of the Word, who is Christ,

---

29. M, "Mensaje a los pueblos de América Latina." In his inaugural discourse at Medellín, Pope Paul VI exhorted his fellow bishops to preach, talk, and write about "the roads that lead to dialogue with the separated brethren."

30. Míguez Bonino, "Medellín y el ecumenismo," 228.

31. M, "Mensaje a los pueblos de América Latina," 23. See also M 2, 26.

32. See M 4, 28.

33. See M 2, 30.

34. Míguez Bonino, "Medellín y el ecumenismo," 229. Translation my own.

in whom the mystery of the human is made manifest" (M, Intro.). The phrase encapsulates succinctly the manner in which Medellín extended and applied the teachings of Vatican II to the Latin American situation. It echoes *Gaudium et spes*, no. 22, which states that "only in the mystery of the incarnate Word does the mystery of man take on light"—but the generic "man" is now "Latin American." The universal has become concrete. The signs of the times constitute a significant *locus theologicus* in the document.[35] The ecumenical call comes not from Rome but from the Latin American peoples "who long for their liberation and their humanization" (M, Intro.). Míguez Bonino encountered in Medellín an ecumenical problem that needed to be addressed.

How do we understand and serve the mission of the church in a continent whose situation is defined by the search for justice and peace? This is the problem posed to us by Medellín. This is *our ecumenical problem*.[36] Whatever disappointment Míguez Bonino experienced from the feeling that the contribution of the ecumenical observers was missing from the final documents from Medellín, the questions posited there dissipated those concerns. How does the church catholic serve the peoples of Latin America? How is ecumenism a liberating movement in the continent? What is Jesus Christ's vocation and mission here and now? For answers to these ecumenical questions, Míguez Bonino examined the method of Medellín.

The Method of Medellín

At the heart of Medellín lie missional questions. In discerning the movement of the Holy Spirit in a world marked by poverty, the Catholic

---

35. The possibility of considering history or Vatican II's interpretation of the signs of the times as *locus theologicus* is a complex task, which has been the subject of much scholarly attention. See Jorge Costadoat, "La historia como 'lugar teológico' en la teología latinoamericana de la liberación," *Perspectiva teológica* 47.132 (2015): 179–200; Andrés Tornos, "Los signos de los tiempos como lugar teológico," *Estudios Eclesiásticos* 53.207 (1978): 517–32; Henrique de Lima Vaz, *Escritos de filosofia IV: Introdução à Ética filosófica* (São Paulo: Loyola, 2008), 190–222; Giuseppe Ruggieri, "La storia come luogo teológico," *Laurentianum* 35.2–3 (1994): 319–37; Carlos Schickendantz, "Una elipse con dos focos: Hacia un nuevo método teológico a partir de *Gaudium et Spes*," *Revista teología* 110 (2013): 85–109.

36. Míguez Bonino, "Medellín y el ecumenismo," 229.

bishops employed a method that would help them look up to God without losing sight of the world. It is curious that Míguez Bonino omitted any mention of the "signs of the times" or of the "see-judge-act" method so obviously integrated into the architecture of the document. Instead, he drew attention to the dynamic tension of two movements in the document, which he identified as synthesis and concentration.

By synthesis, Míguez Bonino meant "the attempt to find a relation of continuity and complementarity between the secular and Christian spheres."[37] This dynamic is at work in several places throughout the document, starting with its introduction, which calls for a new exodus, a passing over "from less human living conditions to more human ones" (M, Intro., 6).[38] Supporting this social transformation, "there is a longing to integrate the whole range of temporal values into a global vision of the Christian faith" (M, Intro., 7).[39] One of the key passages that expresses the synthetic move is found in the bishops' reflections on the longed for catechesis:

> Without falling into confusion or simplistic identifications, we should always manifest the profound unity that there is between God's salvific project fulfilled in Christ and the aspirations of humanity, between salvation history and human history, between the church, the people of God and the temporal communities; between the revelatory action of God and human experience, between supernatural gifts and charisms and human values. (M 8, 4)

By concentration, Míguez Bonino meant "the attempt of understanding secular reality in the light of the gospel."[40] He found the presence of this movement conspicuous throughout the document, but he offered no examples. Instead, he offered terms that serve as evidence of this dynamic at work: "the Word," "salvation history," or "the plan of God." The problem with using these terms as signposts of the dynamic of concentration is

---

37. Míguez Bonino, "Medellín y el ecumenismo," 230.

38. The Medellín document's reflection on this point leans on a passage from *Populorum progressio*, nos. 20–21, which has become a leitmotif in Latin American theological reflection.

39. See M 1, 4; 1, 6; 8, 2.

40. Míguez Bonino, "Medellín y el ecumenismo," 229.

that they are also used in the synthetic move. So, for instance, the Catholic universities are expected to create the conditions for a dialogue between theology and the sciences that "offers the light of the gospel in order to draw all human values together in Christ" (M 4, 6). In any case, what Míguez Bonino seems to have had in mind is that concentration on the Word of God serves as a resistor to the synthetic movement of the Catholic "and" (nature *and* grace, faith *and* works, Scripture *and* tradition). In Europe, this synthesis provoked the Reformation protest slogans of *sola gratia, sola fide, sola scriptura*. In Latin America, the Catholic synthesis led to an integration of church *and* state, cross *and* sword—which Medellín was trying to disrupt.

On this point, Míguez Bonino posed a Protestant question to Medellín: Is the synthesis by the Latin American bishops too harmonious? Yes, Medellín is right in saying that the light of Christ "heals and elevates the dignity of the human person, consolidates the unity of society and gives new sense and deeper meaning to all human activity" (M 1, 5). But, is not Jesus also an agent of division who sets "father against son and son against father, mother against daughter and daughter against mother, mother-in-law against her daughter-in-law and daughter-in-law against mother-in-law" (Luke 12:53)? This is an ecumenical question, not because it is posed by a Protestant to Catholics, but because the question concerns the mission of the church. It is not a matter of finding Protestant or Catholic answers to perennial questions of continuity and crisis in the proclamation of the gospel but of walking together in search of greater clarity. Míguez Bonino wrote, "Insofar as we can accept the invitation of Medellín and feel called to a common undertaking of the mission of Jesus Christ in a continent spurred by the immediate need for transformation, then we will be manifesting a deeply biblical view of unity."[41] Missional questions are best answered ecumenically, and ecumenical questions can only be answered missionally. This is why Míguez Bonino expressed frustration with the "observer" status extended to Protestants, which relegated them largely to the role of visitors instead of contributors. Medellín challenged

---

41. Míguez Bonino, "Medellín y el ecumenismo," 232.

Catholics and Protestants to invite ecumenical *periti* to each other's conferences and gatherings.

The Church according to Medellín

Medellín's engagement with the Latin American reality was not simply diagnostic. If the secret of Medellín was methodological, its most important proposals were ecclesiological. Míguez Bonino's thoughts regarding the ecclesiology of Medellín are clearest in light of his reflections on the conference of CELAM III at Puebla in 1979. It is interesting to note that he made no mention of the method of the Medellín document on that occasion. Instead, he highlighted three significant ecclesiological moves from Medellín. First, there is the identification of the church with the poor. In Latin America, the Catholic Church wants to be "the evangelizer of the poor and in solidarity with them, a witness to the goods of the kingdom and the humbler servant of all the peoples of our countries" (M 14, 8). Obedience to the mission of God for Latin America calls for a poor church. Second, because of its solidarity with the poor, the Latin American church is committed to their liberation. From all over the continent, "A deafening cry is heard from millions of people asking their pastors for liberation that which they find nowhere" (M 14, 2). It is Christ who cries and calls the church to answer with the message of liberation.

Third, Medellín promotes an ecclesiology of communion. All children of God, not just the hierarchy, "share responsibility for the common mission of witnessing to the God who saved them and made them brothers in Christ" (M 15, 6). Medellín gave impetus to the already emerging movement of Base Ecclesial Communities and other parachurch groups committed to the transformation of Latin American society. These groups, at times, entered into conflict with the hierarchy, but Míguez Bonino was quick to correct any reading of Medellín that pits an ecclesiology of communion against a hierarchical church. Instead, he pointed to widely recognized tensions within Catholic ecclesiology. The church is constituted from two principles: a christological principle "from above" and a pneumatological principle "from below."[42] There are two constitutive principles in the church. The first is best represented by the hierarchical structure of the church and was the dominant principle in the Tridentine Latin American church. The second is best represented by the communion of believers and was the ascendant principle at Vatican II and even more so at Medellín.

The contrasts between Medellín and Puebla sharpen the ecclesiological proposal of the former. At Puebla, the bishops had the opportunity to make explicit the doctrinal foundations of the ecclesiology of Medellín. The documents from this gathering adopt a classical approach to the doctrine of the church, beginning with its origin in Christ and Christ's realm, its nature as a people in communion with God, and its mission in the world. Interestingly, Míguez Bonino deliberately bracketed from his discussion Puebla's reflections on Mary as mother and model of the church, but he offered no reasons why. In any case, he noted that the ecclesiological approach of Puebla builds on the christological principle "from above" rather than on the pneumatological "from below."[43] Míquez Bonino wrote:

> The ecclesiology of Medellín comes across as a moment of breaking walls, it was fated to awaken initiative, stimulate participation, and open the way for all in the church to participate in the common mission in Latin America. Puebla, without renouncing this, tries to set the limits, the conditions, the discipline within which that action is to be carried out. For this reason, it needs to develop a more systematic and robust doctrinal focus which highlights the link and internal integrity of dogma so as to correct or avoid deviations and biases.[44]

The divine origin and nature of the church "from above" finds its most important manifestation in the institutional church, which serves as the criterion for evaluating any claims for a "popular church" born of the people.

---

42. Míguez Bonino attributed this terminology to the Dominican theologian Yves Congar in "La Iglesia en Puebla," 10.

43. See Puebla, no. 263; see also Míguez Bonino, "La Iglesia en Puebla," 13.

44. Míguez Bonino, "La Iglesia en Puebla," 11.

One of the most important aspects of Medellín's ecclesiological proposal is its promotion of Base Ecclesial Communities. Again, the contrasting manner in which Medellín and Puebla treat these illuminates their significance. Puebla locates the discussion of base communities within a section that begins on pastoral ministry with families. Medellín locates the same topic within its core ecclesiological section. One must be careful not to read too much about the relative importance of the base communities from their location in the text, but Míguez Bonino asserted that "the options which start from the 'base communities' and those which begin from 'the family' as initial nuclei of communion and participation tend to diverge profoundly in their social implications."[45] More significant than the question of the location of the topic of base communities is the tone in which they are treated. Whereas at Medellín the positive significance of base communities for the renewal of the church and Latin American evangelization is everywhere highlighted, at Puebla the red flags accompanying the growth of these communities stand out. The Base Ecclesial Communities are not solely "the first and fundamental ecclesial nucleus" (M 15, 10). They are communities "in danger of degenerating toward organizational anarchy on the one hand or a hermetic elitism or sectarianism on the other" (Puebla, no. 261).

Míguez Bonino dismissed as "mistaken and perverse" any interpretations that set the ecclesiology of Puebla over against that of Medellín. In many ways, Puebla ratifies and deepens the ecclesiological trajectories of Medellín. He wrote, "But it is clear that it seeks to place all of them in a framework marked by an ecclesiology 'from above' in its double yet united sense of transcendence and hierarchical ordering."[46] The result is a fundamental ambiguity regarding the compatibility between the basic ecclesial option made at Medellín with the ecclesiological doctrine of Puebla. For Míguez Bonino, the solution to this ambiguity is to be found in making the option for the poor the hermeneutical key for the ecclesiology of Medellín and Puebla. He stated that "theological and ecclesial 'orthodoxy' can be read as an exhortation, an invitation to self-discipline and ecclesial

---

45.   Míguez Bonino, "La Iglesia en Puebla," 16.

46.   Míguez Bonino, "La Iglesia en Puebla," 15.

communion, as warning against idiosyncrasy and the cult of personality *within the fundamental option.*"[47]

In sum, Míguez Bonino was deeply moved by the Conference at Medellín. There he heard a call that was already resounding in many Protestant churches (particularly in those engaged in the ecumenical movement). It was a call for Protestants to end their "social strike" and engage the realities of the Latin American context. It was a call that would prove to be divisive.

Medellín among the Evangelicals

Medellín did not trouble the sleep of Methodists in the US. Dow Kirkpatrick probably spoke for many when he stated, "Most of us were unaware of CELAM II when it was happening. The publication in English of Gustavo Gutiérrez's *A Theology of Liberation* (1973) led to the discovery that five years earlier a major watershed in modern church history had occurred."[48] The fact that most North Americans first heard of Medellín from Catholic sources led to the mistaken belief that Latin American Protestants were idle bystanders in the theological landscape. This is far from the truth. Not only were Methodist theologians such as Míguez Bonino actively participating in the Catholic movements, but also the term "liberation theology" appears to have been coined by Brazilian Presbyterian theologian, Rubem Alves.[49] Further, Medellín was not the only significant outburst of Pentecost in the continent. The ecumenical currents experienced by Míguez Bonino at Medellín converged with the "evan-

---

47. Míguez Bonino, "La Iglesia en Puebla," 21, emphasis in original.

48. Dow Kirkpatrick, "What U.S. Protestants Need from CELAM III," *Cross Currents* 28.1 (1978): 90.

49. Rubem Alves's doctoral thesis, which he defended in 1968 at Princeton, had as its title "Towards a Theology of Liberation." Publishers later changed it to "A Theology of Human Hope" because they thought this title would resonate better with the then-popular theologies of hope coming out of Europe from such theologians as Jürgen Moltmann. See Guillermo Kerber, "Teología de la liberación y movimiento ecuménico: breve reflexión desde una práctica," *Horizonte* 11.32 (2013): 1820, and José Míguez Bonino, "Reading Jürgen Moltmann from Latin America," *Asbury Journal* 55.1 (2000): 106.

gelical" streams of theology working their way through Latin American Protestantism at the time.[50] These currents flowed from three streams: the WCC, Latin American liberation theology, and North American evangelical thought. All of these were, in their own way, trying to answer the ecumenical challenge that Míguez Bonino heard at Medellín: "How do we understand and serve the mission of the church in a continent whose situation is defined by the search for justice and peace?"[51]

The ecumenical and liberationist streams flowed and crisscrossed each other in the work of such Latin American Methodist theologians as Míguez Bonino, Julio de Santa Ana, and Emilio Castro. These theological currents gave rise to the first "Latin American Evangelical Conference" (CELA) in 1949.[52] The origins for this meeting go back to the Edinburgh Missionary Conference of 1910 and the absence of Latin Americans from that conversation. CELA I sought to define Protestantism in Latin America as a single "evangelical" movement that embraced all non-Catholic Christian groups. When CELA met in Peru in 1961, seams were already beginning to show in the "evangelical" unity. One sticking point was the evangelical engagement with ecumenism. Emilio Castro noted that, early in his ministry, the word "ecumenism" was considered anathema. It sounded too close to communism and evoked specters of a modernist, liberal Christianity ill-fitted for the realities of Latin America.[53]

---

50.   In Latin America, the term "evangelical" (*evangélica, evangélico*) has a different sense than that which has become commonly used in the US. These churches see themselves as the heirs of the Reformation and emphasize the traditional Protestant slogans: *solus Christus, sola Scriptura, sola fide, sola gratia.* Unlike their northern counterparts, these churches did not experience the schisms resulting from the modernist controversies or the disillusionment of the social gospel movement. At least, they did not experience these convulsions firsthand, even if their reverberations were felt in Latin America. Traditionally, the evangélicos have been anti-Catholic in ways that only a persecuted Protestant minority could be. Moreover, since their energies have been devoted to the spread of the gospel and the making of disciples, they have typically not been interested in scholarship. See Daniel Salinas, *Latin American Evangelical Theology in the 1970's: The Golden Decade* (Boston, MA: Brill, 2009), 7–11.

51.   Míguez Bonino, "Medellín y el ecumenismo," 229.

52.   The convergence of the ecumenical and liberationist streams also gave rise to the Council of Latin American Evangelical Methodist Churches (CIEMAL) in 1969 and to the Latin American Council of Churches (CLAI) in 1989.

53.   Carlos Sintado and Manuel Quintero Pérez, *Pasión y compromiso con el Reino de Dios: el testimonio ecuménico de Emilio Castro* (Buenos Aires: Kairós, 2007), 466.

An even greater cause of stress in the evangelical garment was the formation of "Church and Society in Latin America" (ISAL) with the support of the WCC. ISAL interpreted the Latin American reality with the help of the "Theology of Revolution" of Richard Shaull and the social analysis of Marx. News of these crisscrossing theological currents caused great anxiety among North American observers such as Carl McIntire of the American Council of Christian Churches and members of the Evangelical Foreign Missions Association (EFMA). They tarred CELA III, the meeting in Peru, as procommunist. This resulted in the arrest of some of the conference's key leaders, including Míguez Bonino.[54] By the time CELA met in Buenos Aires a few months after Medellín, the North American opposition was fully mobilized. The Evangelical Committee on Latin America (ECLA) boycotted that gathering by staging the first Congress for Latin American Evangelization (CLADE) in the same year. Thus, 1969 saw two gatherings of Latin American evangelicals: CELA III and CLADE I.

The CELA meeting in Buenos Aires was backed by the WCC and had a strong Latin American presence in its organization and participation. It even included Roman Catholic observers. Fresh from Medellín, Míguez Bonino gave a keynote address on Catholic-Evangelical relations that met with almost universal affirmation among those in attendance.[55] He described the state of the Latin American Catholic Church as one of crisis. Paul VI's description of "centrifugal tendencies" in the church—arising from "the itch for novelty" by "a practically schismatic ferment" of "vivisectionists of the mystical body of Christ"—was an apt one.[56] The ecclesiological crisis pitted the established church against the people's church, the hierarchical church against the community of love, the church of "religion" against the church of the gospel. Medellín did not cause these conflicts, but it disclosed and contributed to the centrifugal tendencies in Catholicism by favoring the latter of these pairs.

---

54. See Salinas, *Latin American Evangelical Theology*, 54ff.

55. The speech was published in English as "Our Debt as Evangelicals to the Roman Catholic Community," *The Ecumenical Review* 21.4 (1969): 310–19.

56. Míguez Bonino, "Our Debt as Evangelicals," 311.

After Medellín, the Catholic Church sought to become more authentically Latin American. Without compromising its fidelity to Rome, it looked for its own way through the rapid changes impacting the continent. It was divesting itself from its cozy relationship with the social elites to enter into solidarity with the poor; it even admitted "its elements of corruption, superficiality and deformation, and [pled] for a pastoral activity that will be centered in the Gospel, grounded in the knowledge of the Scriptures, which will lead men individually, and collectively toward Christ."[57] Faced with a Catholic Church that is being torn apart by centrifugal forces, Protestants have a responsibility. What Protestants owe the Catholics, said Míguez Bonino, is simply the gospel: "We have nothing else of worth. And nothing else is so necessary, whether it be for the Catholic community, our own, or some other community."[58] This means that Protestants are to engage Roman Catholics filled with the love of God poured into our hearts through the Holy Spirit (Rom 5:5), a love that "believes all things, hopes all things, bears all things" (1 Cor 13:7). The "evangelical attitude" that Protestants owe Catholics includes the willingness to offer and receive admonition and correction.

> It is due to that faithfulness to the Gospel that we have felt it our duty to resist the doctrine and the claims of Roman Catholicism. Other motives have become mingled in our polemic and sometimes have displaced our basic concern. But our opposition can only justify itself in the degree that it is subject to this unique and decisive criterion. And it is this very criterion that also obliges us to recognize today the presence of God's Spirit in many movements that are growing within the Catholic community and are imparting to it a new spirit, a new understanding of its task.[59]

The Latin American Pentecost of Medellín called for a reassessment of the Protestant debt to Catholicism. What they owe each other is not polemics or proselytism. They owe each other the gospel for the sake of the peoples of Latin America. "The gospel is greater than our doctrines.

---

57. Míguez Bonino, "Our Debt as Evangelicals," 312.

58. Míguez Bonino, "Our Debt as Evangelicals," 315.

59. Míguez Bonino, "Our Debt as Evangelicals," 318.

The power of the Spirit transcends our ecclesiastical frontiers. The mission of God in a continent eager for justice and for Christ is greater than all our churches."[60] The first Congress for Latin American Evangelization met in Bogotá, Colombia. The agenda was developed with almost no Latin American input, and it excluded many leading evangélicos from participation because of their association with the WCC. Although Míguez Bonino was invited to attend CLADE I—for what many hoped would be an encore of his address at CELA III—he was not given the opportunity to speak because he was seen to be too influenced by European theologians such as Barth, Brunner, and Bultmann.[61]

In his influential book *Latin American Theology: Radical or Evangelical?*, Peter Wagner described the Latin American ecclesial situation as defined by three camps: "the conservative evangelical Protestants, often called 'fundamentalists'; the conservative Catholics of the establishment; and the radical left-wing group made up of both Protestants and Catholics and characterized generally by secular theology and revolutionary politics."[62] These camps were locked in a high-stakes conflict while the mission of the church in Latin America hung in the balance. In this battle, the evangelical Christians were being outflanked by the literary production of theologians of the radical left, including Ricardo Chartier, Justo González, Emilio Castro, and José Míguez Bonino.[63] Wagner faulted Míguez Bonino's apparent dismissal of the conservative-liberal debate as "sterile and misguided,"[64] but the latter refused to be framed by these banal labels and

---

60. Míguez Bonino, "Our Debt as Evangelicals," 319.

61. See Salinas, *Latin American Evangelical Theology*, 71ff.

62. C. Peter Wagner, *Latin American Theology: Radical or Evangelical? The Struggle for the Faith in a Young Church* (Grand Rapids, MI: Eerdmans, 1970), 9.

63. Wagner warned his readers of ten radical theologians, the four Methodists just mentioned and also Gonzálo Castillo Cardenas, Joaquim Beato, Valdo Galland, Rubem Alves, Jorge Lara-Braud, and Richard Shaull. Interestingly, when it came time to find good Latin American "evangelical" alternatives to the radical theologians, Wagner identified four persons (Fernando Vangioni, Washington Padilla, José María Rico, and José Fajardo) whom he acknowledged were not theologians and are not well known in Latin America, but "they have become aware enough of theological currents in Latin America to address themselves at least once to the issues" (Wagner, *Latin American Theology*, 83).

64. Wagner, *Latin American Theology*, 27.

decried both paths as heretical. The conservative or "fundamentalist" path "tends to ignore the fact that Christ reconciled the world to himself" and the liberal path "fails to recognize the call to faith, conversion, and biblical eschatology."[65]

Wagner was convinced that the Argentine Methodist misread the theological landscape: "Míguez would like to dissociate himself from the right and the left and stay with the center. If our thesis that Latin American theology is becoming polarized is borne out, however, he might find himself in a relatively depopulated middle of the road."[66] Wagner credited Míguez Bonino for his refusal to demythologize the gospel, but he faulted the dean of Latin American theology for relying exclusively on the weapons of the radical left (social analysis, economic reform, political revolution) in the battle with the demonic powers threatening human flourishing. He wrote, "Seldom are prayer, the Word of God, the preaching of the Gospel, and the work of the Holy Spirit in individual hearts and lives mentioned as valid and useful resources for the Christian in the world."[67]

At CLADE, in 1969, Wagner distributed free Spanish editions of his book. The reviews were mixed. Among such evangelicals as René Padilla, there was appreciation for certain aspects of Wagner's argument. Padilla acknowledged, "The equation of ideology (Marxism) and faith (Christianity), the erasing of the boundary between the church and the world, the sanctification of the revolution, the rejection of biblical authority—these are the strands with which the theology of ISAL is woven."[68] In alerting them to this dangerous syncretism, Wagner rendered a valuable service to Latin American evangelicals. However, the Methodists whom Wagner singled out for critique, including González and Míguez Bonino, cannot be included in the company of the theologians of the radical left. Besides, Padilla asked, "Is not the radical leftists' theology itself, at least in part, a reaction against the deadly reduction of the Christian mission that has

---

65. Míguez Bonino, as quoted in Wagner, *Latin American Theology*, 28.

66. Wagner, *Latin American Theology*, 28.

67. Wagner, *Latin American Theology*, 30.

68. C. René Padilla, "A Steep Climb Ahead for Theology in Latin America," *Evangelical Missions Quarterly* 7.2 (1971): 100.

characterized Latin American Protestantism?"[69] Whatever the case may be, Padilla charged Wagner and company of their own brand of syncretism—as exemplified by their uncritical adoption and promotion of the ideology of "church growth"—that separates *kerygma* from *diakonia*.

The convergence of Medellín with CELA and CLADE cannot be framed in the simple liberal-conservative categories that Wagner wanted to use. CELA was not uncritical of Medellín, as exemplified in Míguez Bonino's address on the debt that Protestants owe Catholics, nor was CLADE deaf to the social realities of the continent. Evangelicals such as Padilla deeply appreciated the fact that Medellín and CELA were asking the right questions, even if they did not always agree with the answers that they gave.

Medellín, an Ecumenical Question

The uncertain ecumenical notes that Míguez Bonino heard at Medellín were a great improvement on the prior ecclesial situation. The first gathering of CELAM in Rio de Janeiro in 1955 had addressed the topic of relations with Protestants under the heading "Protestantism and anti-Catholic movements: preservation and defense of the faith" and called for spiritual crusades to guard the faithful, especially the children, from Protestant apostasy.[70] It is fitting that CELAM II met in Colombia, a country that Emilio Castro had noted as a stumbling block for Catholic-Protestant encounters in Latin America on account of the legal proscription of Protestant evangelism in the majority of the country.[71] With Medellín, there

---

69.   Padilla, "A Steep Climb Ahead for Theology in Latin America," 101.

70.   Rio, 69–71.

71.   See Emilio Castro, "Situación y problema del ecumenismo en América Latina," *Teología y Vida* 5.2 (1964): 108–18. Castro stated that "the basic ecumenical work of the Catholic Church will not be credible *as long as there is case like that of Colombia in which an official document of the Catholic Church that serves as a charter for its missionary activity undercuts the freedom of conscience of thousands of Protestants*" (p. 116, emphasis original). Carlos Arboleda Mora acknowledged that the pain caused by historic grievances like the Colombian case hurts the movement toward unity. The Catholic Church has not fully reflected on the significance of this problem, even after the Colombian constitution officially recognized religious diversity in the country in 1991. See Carlos Arboleda Mora, "Medio siglo de ecumenismo: Retos del future," *Cuestiones Teológicas* 40.93 (2013): 199–212.

was, in the words of Patricio Merino-Beas, "a new awareness of the Latin American Church and in this context ecumenical dialogue grows increasingly more relevant."[72] According to Medellín, "ecumenical celebrations" are to be promoted in accordance with *Unitatis redintegratio*, no. 8, which states:

> In certain special circumstances, such as the prescribed prayers "for unity," and during ecumenical gatherings, it is allowable, indeed desirable that Catholics should join in prayer with their separated brethren. Such prayers in common are certainly an effective means of obtaining the grace of unity, and they are a true expression of the ties which still bind Catholics to their separated brethren.[73]

Prayer is no longer a weapon to be brandished against Protestants, as at Rio de Janeiro, but food for the journey that sustains Catholics and Protestants "on the way of fraternal conversion that we call ecumenism."[74]

The Methodist encounter at Medellín gave rise to many questions. How do we answer the call of Jesus Christ today in Latin America? What does faithfulness to the gospel require of Latin American Christians in a continent marred by violence and poverty? These are the questions that the bishops gathered at Medellín heard the Spirit pose, and it is an ecumenical question for all Christians in the continent. This is, Míguez Bonino argued, "our" ecumenical problem. In this final section, I will consider some possible engagements with this problem by way of the question that Míguez Bonino asked: "How do we understand ourselves as Methodists in light of Medellín?"[75]

First, in light of Medellín, Methodists are to understand themselves as bound to Latin Americans. The Brazilian philosopher Henrique de Lima Vaz argues that, prior to Medellín, the Latin American church was simply

---

72. Patricio Merino-Beas, "El diálogo ecuménico desde el CELAM," *Theologica Xaveriana* 67.2 (2017): 397. By the time CELAM met in Aparecida in 2007, there was a general awareness, at least among bishops, that "ecumenical dialogue is an integral part of the evangelizing mission of the church" (404).

73. See M 9, 14.

74. Merino-Beas, "El diálogo ecuménico desde el CELAM," 405.

75. Míguez Bonino, "¿Conservar el metodismo?" 329.

a reflection of the European church.[76] Latin American elites, whether in the social sphere or in the ecclesial one, looked to Europe for the orientation of all projects and the answers to all problems. There was a marked tendency to depend on Europe for ecclesial personnel, spiritualities, theologies, and finances. Mimesis rather than creativity was the most apt descriptor for the action of the church throughout the long years of the colonial period. These tendencies were not immediately overcome by independence. Things changed, however, in 1968. With Medellín, a source-church began to emerge among Roman Catholics. Arguably, something similar was happening at CELA III in Argentina among Protestants.

Resistance to these nascent source-churches was evident among Catholics (especially at the fourth conference of CELAM in Santo Domingo in 1992) and Protestants (especially at CLADE I in Bogotá in 1969). This resistance was expressed through disciplinary measures and theological declarations. Some of these (such as the instructions of the Congregation for the Doctrine of the Faith on liberation theology)[77] were perhaps necessary, even if ham-fisted. Others (such as Wagner's book) were premature, prejudiced, and paternalistic. The driving issue seems to be a noticeable lack of trust and patience in the work of the Holy Spirit among the Latin American theologians. Fear of the spread of communism led to shutting off any trickle of fresh Christian thought in the continent. Yet, the Latin American situation called for theological inquiry to develop in a spirit of Christian freedom. Mortimer Arias asked pertinent questions to Christians who, like Wagner, wanted a theology that addressed the issues of the day but who wanted strictly to predetermine the outcome of this inquiry. He wrote:

> Can the fundamentalist mentality of some conservative evangelical circles provide that kind of freedom? When faith has already been defined once for all, what alternative had the evangelical thinker other than the "anti-Catholic" (anti-ecumenical, anti-secular, anti-radical, or any other anti-)

---

76. See Alfonso García Rubio, "Em direção à V Conferência Geral do Episcopado da AL e do Caribe: fidelidade ao legado de Medellín?" *Atualidade Teológica* 11.25 (2007): 9–42.

77. Congregation for the Doctrine of Faith, "Instructions on Certain Aspects of the 'Theology of Liberation,'" 1984.

polemics or restatements of the traditional evangelical corpus of "systematic theology" of which Wagner complains?[78]

The Holy Spirit, as the wind, blows where it wills. It is always the Spirit that Christ sent from God, but it acts in surprising ways, as at Medellín. The ecumenical winds blowing through the continent led Christians to face squarely the realities of the Americas. Paradoxically, by becoming the voice of the voiceless, they found their own voice, and Latin America became a source of theology for the church catholic. Hence, for Latin American Methodists, Medellín became a reference point for the mission of spreading scriptural holiness across the continent, a mission requiring them to embrace their Latin American history and identity with all its riches and ambiguities. For non-Latin American Methodists, Medellín is a summons to become debtors to their southern sisters and brothers and to listen to what the Spirit is saying to and through the emerging source-churches in Latin America.

Second, in light of Medellín, Methodists are to understand themselves as catholic. Wherein is the catholicity manifested at Medellín? José Duque argued that Latin American theology is intrinsically ecumenical and catholic when "it is articulated from the religiosity expressed by the poor, be they Catholic or Protestant."[79] Míguez Bonino grounded catholicity in the full incarnation of the gospel in the particularities of a given context. Thus, a Latin American Christianity that uniformly reflects its European and North American missionary contexts is not yet truly catholic. Míguez Bonino recognized ambiguities in the Latin American theology heralded by Medellín:

> Even as we tried to liberate ourselves from the burden of our Eurocentric inheritance and to root our theology more and more deeply in the native soil of our land and people, our work betrayed—as many critics have amply documented—the constant use of categories, presuppositions, and methods created and developed overseas. After all, for all their originality—which cannot be denied—Medellín is a Latin American interpretation of Vatican

---

78. Mortimer Arias, as quoted in Salinas, *Latin American Evangelical Theology*, 87.

79. Duque, *La tradición protestante en la teología latinoamericana*, xii.

II and ISAL (the Latin American "Church and Society" movement) is a daughter of the WCC (more specifically, the developments of the Life and Work movement).[80]

Catholicity is fundamentally a theological reality, but it has social ramifications. There is one body of Christ, but there is a difference between spiritual and social connection and dependency. There is one Spirit, but there is a difference between witnessing to how the same Spirit has been at work in Nicaea, Aldersgate, and Vatican II and saying that the Spirit does the same thing in Medellín, Buenos Aires, and Topeka. The catholicity of the Methodist church (Latin American or otherwise) comes not from its relations to European thought but from its fidelity to its Spirit-inspired mission. The European bibliographical presence in this missional context is not a definitive sign for or against its catholicity.

Speaking of the catholicity of Methodism requires talking about doctrine. The first Latin American Protestant theologies were the offspring of the Life and Work movement of the WCC. Drawing on classic Protestant categories, Míguez Bonino speaks of mission as the material principle of Latin American theology. It is the ethos that "permeates the speech, worship, and life of the Protestant community, a self-understanding manifested in all attitudes, conflicts, and priorities."[81] Latin American Protestant Christianity—whether it be in its mainline, evangelical, or Pentecostal faces—is essentially a missionary movement. At Medellín,

---

80. Míguez Bonino, "Reading Jürgen Moltmann," 105. One of the ways in which Míguez Bonino characterized the misunderstandings of Northern from Southern theologians is in their approach to synergism. European theologians such as Moltmann accentuate God's transcendence; Latin American theologians want to call attention to the theological significance of human praxis. He found a possible solution in the Latin American Christology of Guillermo Hansen, who offered a fresh christological account of *enhypostasis*. Míguez Bonino commented, "If 'enhypostatic' means 'to find one's identity in the other' the divine initiative gets its historical 'identity' as it becomes incorporated ('incarnate') in human praxis, and human praxis gets its transcendent meaning and reality as it is assumed by the Holy Spirit" (Míguez Bonino, "Reading Jürgen Moltmann," 112).

81. José Míguez Bonino, *Faces of Latin American Protestantism*, trans. Eugene L. Stockwell (Grand Rapids, MI: Eerdmans, 1997), 131.

Míguez Bonino essentially recognized this same principle at work in the Catholic Church. They may have worked with different formal principles, or perhaps it would be more accurate to say that they received and read Scripture through different hermeneutical lenses: Vatican II in one case, the WCC in the other. The formal principle needs a material principle. Míguez Bonino averred, "Faith and Order never took root in Latin American churches."[82] He credited this to a lack of interest in doctrinal unity. No doubt, there is truth in this assessment of the Latin American ecumenical scene,[83] but doctrinal reflection cannot be sidestepped if the church is to be faithful to its mission. Vatican II offered Catholics the "Pastoral Constitution of the Church in the World" (*Gaudium et spes*) and the "Dogmatic Constitution on the Church" (*Lumen gentium*).

The missional vision of Medellín in 1968 was followed by the christological definitions of the Latin American Catholic bishops who met in Puebla in 1979. Without explicit, robust, and vibrant connections to the church's catholic doctrine, the Latin American church, particularly in its Protestant version, became theologically unmoored. The result is the "reductionism" characteristic of much Latin American Protestantism where "theology is practically swallowed up in Christology, and this in soteriology, and even more, in a salvation which is characterized as an individual and subjective experience."[84] If a Spirit-led freedom is necessary for the church to be authentically Latin American, a Spirit-led reception of church doctrine is equally necessary for that mission to be authentically Christian.

Third, in light of Medellín, Methodists are to understand themselves as Wesleyan. The teaching of Medellín is unambiguously Roman Catholic. Its documents reference Scripture (though not as richly as one would

---

82. Míguez Bonino, *Faces of Latin American Protestantism*, 131.

83. Castro concurred. The church is to be salt and light. The key task at the center of ecumenical dialogue is not the comparison of doctrines, but "what does God want to do with our country? And within our country, what does God want to do with us Christians? . . . How are we witnesses to the kingdom that is coming to society?" (in Sintado and Pérez, *Pasión y compromiso*, 461).

84. Míguez Bonino, *Faces of Latin American Protestantism*, 112.

expect), tradition (especially the writings of Vatican II), and ecclesial structures. By comparison, the theology of the Wesleys is conspicuously absent
from Methodist engagement with Medellín and with the Latin American
questions of the day. There are several reasons that explain this Wesleyan
deficit. First, the Methodism brought to Latin America by the North
American missionaries was more influenced by nineteenth-century revivalism than by eighteenth-century Wesleyanism. Second, Latin American
Methodist theologians came of age when neo-orthodoxy was ascendant.
The already mentioned constellation of Barth, Bonhoeffer, and Bultmann
illuminated their reading of Scripture and the signs of the times. Indeed,
the Uruguayan Methodist Emilio Castro was the first Latin American to
study with Barth.[85]

Next to these theological giants, Wesley appeared to Míguez Bonino
and many Methodists as a pastoral theologian, at best. "In vain would we
seek in him the creative genius of theologians of the stature of Augustine,
Luther, or Calvin. Wesley does not belong to the group of these grand
columns of Christian theology. He lacks the depth, the sure focus, and the

---

85. The impact of Barth on Castro was deep. In Barth's theology, Castro found an alternative to the fundamentalist-liberal dialectic that dominated Protestant church life in Latin
America (see Sintado and Pérez, *Pasión y compromiso*, 114). The manner in which Barth
privileged God's "yes" to humanity over humanity's "no" to God revolutionized the way in
which Castro understood his own Uruguayan context. In a context marked by secularism
(Uruguay was and still is the most secularized nation in Latin America), Castro could preach
with confident expectation of a positive response because, at the end of the day, salvation
was not up to him. He stated, "Salvation is not something that belongs to me. Salvation is
the assurance that God will always be with me and that the experience called salvation is the
presence of God which will be experienced anew tomorrow not because I have any kind of
guarantee but because God promises this" (ibid., 121). At the same time, aspects of Barth's
theology, or perhaps more accurately, his prudential judgments did not resonate with Castro. The Uruguayan student pressed his teacher on his harsh critique of Methodism. Barth's
concerns about the Wesleyan heritage stemmed from reading this tradition as the child of
Zinzendorf's pietism and the grandparent of Schleiermacher's theology of experience. However, Castro could reconcile Barth's critique with the reality of Methodist churches in Latin
America (ibid., 115ff.). Castro greatly appreciated the rigor of Barth's theological approach,
but at the same time he saw it as a very European, indeed, very academic, way of doing
theology (ibid., 109).

insight of the great theologians...he is not a theological genius."[86] Even if this judgment of Wesley as theologian is questionable, the quest for a Methodist identity poses risks. Wesleyan theology may be a flight from the challenges and complexities of the present moment to a safe, nostalgic, airbrushed past. Míguez Bonino warned of these dangers in a series of questions:

> Who are we as evangelical Methodist Christians in Latin America? Does this question matter? Is being identified as a "Latin American Christian" not enough? . . . Is a "Methodist identity" a real thing? Is not the attempt to recognize ourselves in the portraits of our ancestors with whom we have in fact little connection an artificial endeavor? Are we not called to identify ourselves fully with the actual reality of our people rather than to trace a historic connection to the England of the George's?[87]

The difficulties entailed in finding a Methodist identity that is Wesleyan are complex. At the same time, this quest is necessary in order to discern how the people called Methodists can contribute to the exigencies of the Latin American missionary moment. Duque spoke for many when he stated the need for a "re-reading of the tradition and of Protestant theology for the purpose of returning to our roots and [to] recover all those elements of protest and liberating force which were present at the beginning of the Protestant movement which can serve as criteria for Christian practice in the contemporary and difficult process of Latin American transformation."[88] For Methodists, this Latin American *ressourcement* begins with re-reading Wesley. "The horizon of the kingdom of God—in other words, the central message of the Bible—shall be our chief criterion. The missionary practice of Wesley, his identification with the poor, his call to conversion shall be our interpretive key. The troubling reality of

---

86. José Míguez Bonino, "Juan Wesley y la teología de la reforma," *Cuadernos Teológicos* 4 (1951): 63, as quoted in Nellie Ritchie, "¿Existe una pastoral metodista?" in *La tradición protestante en la teología latinoamericana*, 95.

87. José Míguez Bonino, "¿Fue el metodismo un movimiento liberador?" in *La tradición protestante en la teología latinoamericana*, 63.

88. Duque, *La tradición protestante en la teología latinoamericana*, xii.

Latin America will be the place of encounter between our tradition and our obedience."[89]

In this *ressourcement*, Wesleyan theology is well poised to join the pairs so long disjoined: evangelism and liberation.[90] Given the position of the Methodist church in the Latin American and global landscape, the Wesleyan contribution to the missional theology of Medellín may be a modest one. It may only add up to, in the words of Míguez Bonino, "a footnote in the religious life of our continent. But, if faithfully fulfilled, it can be a significant footnote."[91] Indeed, if faithfully fulfilled, the impact of the Wesleyan contribution may be as surprising as that of the mustard seed.

Postlude

I began this chapter with the well-worn trope of an ecumenical winter, and I return to it again. Medellín is not something that can warm those chilled by the theological wintry mix of the north like a pair of gloves. It is a testament to the surprising work of the Holy Spirit. After many years and against all expectations, the seeds of the gospel sown in soil bloodied by the swords of conquistadors, the bullets of narcos, and the money of multinationals have yielded fruit. The Spirit that renews the face of the earth is also the Spirit that manifests the body of Christ in the world. Medellín through Methodist eyes reads like a mission statement even for those who are not Latin American. We are called to be one so that the world, particularly the world of the poor and marginalized, may believe that the Father has sent the Son as one who became

---

89. Duque, *La tradición protestante en la teología latinoamericana*, 346.

90. In Sintado and Pérez, *Pasión y compromiso*, 472, Castro acknowledged that, while the WCC has always been concerned about evangelization, in practice it has been marginalized: "We have internalized the hunger for justice, but we talk about justice. We have internalized the importance of dialogue with other religions while still insisting on treating these subjects in order to deepen our understanding. We are resolute in our fight against all kinds of marginalization and we support the causes of the oppressed peoples. All these, just like evangelization, belong to the gospel and we could take all of it for granted but we treat them explicitly. Likewise, we should speak openly of our passion for evangelism."

91. José Míguez Bonino, "Protestantism's Contribution to Latin America," *The Lutheran Quarterly* 22.1 (1971): 97.

poor so as to make many rich. Reading Medellín through Methodist eyes may actually result not just in a "strangely warmed heart" but also in a "corazón ardiente" unheeding of the ecumenical winter because a new Pentecost is coming. The hope for that day is well sung by Charles Wesley:

> Eternal Paraclete, descend
> Thou gift and promise of our Lord,
> To every soul, till time shall end,
> Thy succour, and thyself afford,
> Convince, convert us, and inspire;
> Come, and baptize the world with fire.[92]

---

92.   Charles Wesley, *Hymns for Whitsunday* (1746), Hymn 17.

Chapter Four

The Day of the Great Fiesta: Renewing Worship from the End

When I graduated from Duke Divinity School, my bishop appointed me to start a United Methodist ministry among Hispanic people in Durham, North Carolina. After fits and starts, a small group of families began meeting for weekly Bible studies in their homes. As Holy Week 1998 drew near, one family suggested we have a worship service for Good Friday and offered their place, a duplex on an unpaved street. I accepted. When I arrived, I saw their front porch decorated with balloons and streamers. A packed table presented a feast, with aluminum chafing dishes full of rice and mole and tortillas, and tres leches cake and piñatas promised more to the celebration. Thirty people packed into a small living room for a Tenebrae service followed by fiesta. We sung praises. We read and proclaimed the Scriptures. We confessed the faith. We offered prayers of lament and hope. We celebrated the Lord's Supper. This was Maundy Thursday, Good Friday, and Easter rolled into one, with a birthday thrown in for good measure.

This gathering of metodistas for worship did not deny the scandal of the cross.[1] It enacted a deep wisdom, recognizing the cross is the tree of life. Only those whose lives are marked by crosses understand this special sensitivity to the light of Easter. This gathering affirmed that—at its core—reality is good, life is beautiful, and the gospel is true. It was the dream of a people who long for a better future, a future that is fiesta.

In this chapter, I consider how worship anticipates this future. In particular, I propose the festive character of Latinx and Latin American worship, when brought into critical conversation with Latinx and Latin American creedal affirmations, can revitalize Methodist worship.

I bring creed and fiesta together because doctrine and worship are yoked. In this volume's introduction, I explore the interconnectedness of doctrine, worship, and mission. There, I review the principle of *lex credendi est lex orandi*, which means we believe as we pray and we pray as we believe. Here, I turn to Justo González, who offers a succinct summary:

> The main source of doctrine is not theological speculation, but the life of worship. Scholars have usually referred to this principle as *lex orandi est lex credendi*—the rule of prayer becomes the rule of belief.... We tend to think that doctrines emerge primarily out of theological debate; but in fact most of them are expressions of what the church has long experienced and declared in its worship.[2]

The dynamic goes both ways, with doctrine influencing practices like worship, but the influence of *lex orandi* on *lex credendi* goes underappreciated and therefore warrants considered attention.

---

1. Liturgically minded readers might wonder if accepting the light of Resurrection during Maundy Thursday violates the progression of Holy Week, seeking what Martin Luther called "a theology of glory" at the expense of a "theology of the cross." Yet this would represent a deep misunderstanding of fiesta cristiana—one this chapter aims to correct. For an introduction to Luther's distinction, see Justo L. González, *The Story of Christianity, Volume 2: The Reformation to the Present Day* (New York: HarperCollins, 2010), 50.

2. Justo L. González, *A Concise History of Christian Doctrine* (Nashville, TN: Abingdon, 2005), 5.

Western Christianity has allowed separation between *lex credendi* and the *lex orandi*,[3] in which the church relegates theology to the margins, often leaving it as little more than an abstract game played in ivory towers. Liturgy suffers as unmoored and sentimental, inadequately forming individual Christian lives or the worldviews of Christian communities. In a real sense, all theology should be liturgical, not because it has the liturgy as its object but because the liturgy is its source. We must renew doctrine to rescue worship from the historicism that ossifies it to a dead text, from the rationalism that evacuates it of mystery, and from the emotivism that reduces it to empty doxology.[4] And we must renew doctrine to anchor the fundamentally eschatological basis of worship. More specifically, we must renew a strong creedal practice for the celebration of worship to orient the congregation toward the day of the great fiesta.

Celebrating the Fiesta Cristiana

Worship in Latinx and Latin American communities often resembles a fiesta. The United Methodist worship resource for metodistas is titled *Fiesta cristiana*. The people called metodista "believe the worship of the Living God who is creator, redeemer and sustainer of life should be all about *fiesta*, a rejoicing in the God of life."[5] Worship as fiesta, says Justo González, is "a celebration of the mighty deeds of God. It is a get-together

---

3.   Alexander Schmemann, *Church, World, Mission: Reflections on Orthodoxy in the West* (Crestwood, NY: St. Vladimir's Seminary Press, 1979), 129–46.

4.   In this last connection, I am thinking of Walter Brueggemann and his category of doxology without reason. See Walter Brueggemann, *Israel's Praise: Doxology against Idolatry and Ideology* (Philadelphia, PA: Fortress, 1988), 89–121. Brueggemann applies this category to psalms that offer praise to God without testifying how God has been acting concretely in history and is working to transform the world, beginning with Israel, in accordance with God's purposes for creation. For example, he identifies Psalm 150 as articulating "a god without reason, a community without memory, a faith without concrete transformation.... Of course it is too much to suggest that Psalm 150 is an act of idolatry. My point is that the tendency in that direction is unmistakable. This god does nothing and has done nothing and will do nothing. Of course one can imagine simply that it is a communal act of utter release and ecstasy. But for what?" (108).

5.   *Fiesta cristiana: Recursos para adoración (Resources for Worship)*, ed. Raquel M. Martínez (Nashville, TN: Abingdon, 2003), 20.

of the family of God."[6] It is an exuberant affirmation of life and anticipation of eternal life that exceeds rational calculus. Fiestas call for *bótates* (splurging). The visual richness of images and colors in a Roman Catholic celebration of the feast of Guadalupe in Durham, the fresh scent from the pine needles covering the floor of a Guatemalan Methodist church, and the pulsating sounds of a band playing coritos in a Pentecostal church in the Peruvian Andes display the existential wealth of God's gift of life in ways that overload the senses.[7]

The fiesta cristiana is rich in food, embrace, and music. The title of the United Methodist Hymnal in Spanish echoes this theme: *Mil voces para celebrar* (a thousand voices to celebrate).[8] In the Wesleyan tradition, music can be considered a means of grace. For instance, Alejo Hernández testifies to his first encounter with Methodist worship while ducking into a chapel, where he sought shelter from the rain. "I felt the Spirit of God there even though I did not understand a single word of what was being said."[9] Hernández became a Methodist and was ordained in Texas in 1871. René de León eloquently expresses the importance of singing for the Christian fiesta in his preface to the hymnal of the National Evangelical Primitive Methodist Church of Guatemala, *Cánticos de vida y esperanza* (Canticles of life and hope). He writes, "We sing because we have life; we believe in the God of life; we proclaim that in him is life and that

---

6. Justo L. González, "Hispanic Worship: An Introduction," in ¡*Alabadle! Hispanic Christian Worship*, ed. Justo González (Nashville, TN: Abingdon, 1996), 20.

7. The concept of excess plays a pivotal role in theological discussions of the arts and aesthetics, and that same excess animates fiesta, in which mundane creaturely materiality can, by God's grace, share in God's abundance. See Jeremy Begbie, "Looking to the Future: A Hopeful Subversion," in *For the Beauty of the Church: Casting a Vision for the Arts*, ed. David O. Taylor (Grand Rapids, MI: Baker, 2010); Rowan Williams, *Grace and Necessity: Reflections on Art and Love* (London: Continuum, 2005), 139–56; Richard Viladesau, *Theological Aesthetics: God in Imagination, Beauty, and Art* (New York: Oxford University Press, 1999), 94–121.

8. *Mil voces para celebrar: Himnario metodistas*, ed. Raquel Martinez (Nashville, TN: Abingdon, 1996). The hymnal was composed in response to the desire of metodistas in the US for music and song with Latino accents, rhythms, and melodies.

9. *Mil voces para celebrar*, v.

he wants to offer fullness of life to all. We sing with hope because by faith we glimpse this fullness."[10]

Fiestas reconcile categories often held in opposition. As fiesta, worship involves both planning and improvisation. Planning includes preparing the worship space. Whether or not the community has an established building, the community plans music, sermons, and aesthetic forms like flowers and decor that point to the beauty of holiness. In many communities, the planning also involves transforming a space designed for a different purpose (a classroom, a living room) into a sanctuary. As fiesta, worship also has an unrehearsed character. For example, one often does not know how many worshippers will join the celebration, or when. Hence, communal worship as fiesta calls for adaptability and generous hospitality.

Just as they reconcile preparation and improvisation, fiestas in the Hispanic community blur the distinctions between sacred and secular. A Catholic *via crucis* in San Juan, Puerto Rico, does not remain confined to the sanctuary but spills into the cobbled streets where Jesus carries the cross flanked by Roman soldiers, worshippers, tourists, and piragüeros (push-cart vendors). Even the fiestas with non-sacred origins or a decidedly civic character are open to the sacred. Fiestas affirm the transcendental grounding of life in what is true, good, and beautiful in the concrete quotidian (birthdays, coming-of-age).

In Hispanic/Latino theology, fiesta is an anthropological category. Modernity privileges a different anthropology, in which the autonomous self constructs its own ends; to be human is to be *homo faber*, a making being. This anthropology finds excellent expression in the English language: we work to "make a living," exhort people to "make something of themselves," and celebrate the "self-made" individual. Postmodern anthropologies, by contrast, value play and elevate the *homo ludens*, the playing being. In its earliest stages, Latin American liberation theology adopted the former anthropology, *homo faber*. Roberto Goizueta observes that for many liberation theologians, to be human is "to be engaged in the

---

10.   *Cánticos de vida y esperanza* (Quetzaltenango: IENMPG, 1996), 3.

transformation of society, to become an agent of change."[11] The centrality of *homo faber* to the Latin American theological vision devalued actions that are an end to themselves and conflated *doing* with *making*. Popular religiosity, liturgical celebrations, and the daily struggles for a beautiful life were seen at best as "useless" and at worst as obstacles for social transformation. However, more recent versions of Latin American and Latinx theology have seen the limitations of the *homo faber* and, building on the postmodern *homo ludens*, they have instead grown in appreciation of the *homo festivus*.[12] As Goizueta explains, "the historical struggle for justice— the construction of a world that truly images the God of life, the 'Giver of life'—must be grounded in the prior, more fundamental attitude and act wherein we acknowledge our dependence on a God who *is* life."[13]

Fiestas celebrate life in the subjunctive. Goizueta, drawing on the work of Victor Turner, contrasts the conjugations of culture in the indicative mood with those of the subjunctive mood. Culture in the indicative mood states how things are and is expressed in economic policies, political ideologies, and life as planned. Culture in the subjunctive mood states how things could be and is expressed in drama, dance, song, carnival, and fiesta. Goizueta cites Turner: "It is perhaps significant that, as the *Concise Oxford Dictionary* puts it, 'subjunctive = verbal mood, obsolescent in English.'"[14] For English speakers, learning how and when to use the subjunctive in Spanish often proves difficult. A helpful clue: the subjunctive always follows the word *ojalá*. This word is a token of the influence of the Moorish culture on the Spanish language. The term derives from the Arabic and literally means "Allah willing," or God-willing. The theological point follows the grammatical one: the subjunctive mood is the prophetic mood; it is a way of living from God's promised future.

---

11. Roberto Goizueta, "Fiesta: Life in the Subjunctive," in *From the Heart of Our People: Latino/a Explorations in Catholic Systematic Theology*, ed. Orlando O. Espín and Miguel H. Díaz (Maryknoll, NY: Orbis, 1999), 84–99, 88.

12. Cándido Pozo, "La teología de la fiesta, ¿ocaso de la teología de la liberación?" in *Teología de la liberación*, ed. Teodoro Ignacio Jiménez Urresti (Burgos: Ediciones Aldecoa, 1973), 411–25.

13. Goizueta, "Fiesta: Life in the Subjunctive," 96.

14. Goizueta, "Fiesta: Life in the Subjunctive," 93.

The fiesta is not just a party. It is not simply a break from work or a coping mechanism. Ramón Luzárraga avers, "The Fiesta is not designed to escape from the daily duties, burdens, and milestones of life."[15] Instead, at the heart of the fiesta lies an eschatological mystery.[16] Fiestas declare life as worth living, even amidst forces that seek to rend it short or render it meaningless. It declares a world where diversity is not divisive but united in praise of the God of life. "Fiesta presents an alternative vision where human beings receive life as a gift from God."[17] As González explains: "Fiesta and mystery go together … we are not required to understand everything that goes on. We are not even expected to agree with everything that everyone says. We are simply invited to join the party, to allow ourselves to be carried and defined by it, to make our own contribution, whatever that might be, and above all, to celebrate whatever the fiesta is about."[18] At its best, Latino worship unites a spirit of fiesta to a deep reverence for the Christian mystery. As the pueblo de Dios gathers in celebration of God's wondrous works, it affirms its faith in—and advances the coming of—the day of the great fiesta.

Professing the Fe Metodista

The fiesta cristiana enacts and empowers the fe metodista. The faith of the people called Methodists is guided by creedal declarations. As noted earlier, the *lex orandi* is the source of the *lex credendi*. The celebration of worship as fiesta finds creedal form in the expectation of the day of the great fiesta. At times, creeds are treated as explanations and are used to evacuate mystery from the faith. Some catechetical and liturgical practices may lend credence to this impression. However, when rooted in the *lex orandi*, creeds celebrate the mystery.

---

15. Ramón Luzárraga, "Fiesta," in *Hispanic American Religious Cultures, Vol. 1*, ed. Miguel de la Torre (Santa Barbara, CA: ABC-CLIO, 2009), 261–68, 266.

16. González, "Hispanic Worship," 21.

17. Luzárraga, "Fiesta," 265.

18. González, "Hispanic Worship," 20.

John Wesley valued the liturgical tradition of the Church of England. As he writes in the preface to *The Sunday Service*, the liturgy he bequeathed to the newly independent Methodists in North America, one can find "no liturgy in the world, whether in ancient or modern language, which breathes more of a solid, scriptural, rational Piety, than the Common Prayer of the Church of England."[19] His appreciation notwithstanding, Wesley revised this liturgy by additions, subtractions, and substitutions as long as experience showed these to be advantageous in promoting the goods of worship. As a member of the Church of England, he adhered to the Apostles' Creed, the Nicene Creed, and the Athanasian Creed. Nevertheless, he rejected the anathemas of the Athanasian Creed, and he did not insist on the necessity of any formal creed for salvation.[20] Given these commitments and concerns, it is telling that Wesley called for the use of the Apostles' Creed in worship. It is precisely as liturgical confessions—rather than as doctrinal explanations—that creeds express the living faith of the people of God.

The fe metodista finds words in new creeds and old. In what follows, I consider two examples drawn from Justo González, the most eminent metodista theologian of his generation.[21] The first offers a reading of the Apostles' Creed in Spanish—that is, in solidarity with Latin American refugees. The second, the Hispanic Creed, affirms the fe viva, voicing the cultural accents of how Wesley's Spanish-speaking heirs live the faith.

---

19. John Wesley, Preface to *The Sunday Service of the Methodists in North America; With Other Occasional Services* (London: J. Kershaw, 1825), 2.

20. John Wesley, Sermon 55, "On the Trinity," §3, *Works* 2:376–77.

21. Justo González (b. 1939, Havana, Cuba) amassed six degrees by the age of twenty-three, becoming the youngest ever to earn Yale's PhD in historical theology. He has taught in several theological institutions, including Evangelical Seminary of Puerto Rico and Candler School of Theology in Georgia. He has authored over one hundred and thirty books and upwards of thirteen hundred articles and adult Bible lessons. (Yes, those numbers are correct!) Among other accomplishments, he is an ordained elder of The United Methodist Church, a co-founder of the first academic journal concerned with Hispanic theology (*Apuntes*), the instigator of multiple programs for Hispanic theology, and—key for our purposes—the author of the Hispanic Creed. See González, "Curriculum Vitae," Princeton, New Jersey: Hispanic Theological Initiative, 2017, https://hti.ptsem.edu/wp-content/uploads/2017/08/Justo_L_Gonz%C3%A1lez_CV.pdf.

Reading the Apostles' Creed in Spanish

Reading the Apostles' Creed in Spanish includes intentionally reading it from the outside in and upside down. It means reading from the borders and in solidarity with those the borders were built to exclude. Indeed, as González says, "a case can be made that the most significant events in the history of the Church have taken place precisely at those edges."[22] Historian Andrew Walls agrees, arguing "cross-cultural diffusion has always been the lifeblood of historic Christianity; that the Christian expansion has characteristically come from the margins more than from the center." The cross-cultural encounter of Jews and Gentiles, Latin Christianity and Germanic peoples, Spanish missionaries and Indigenous peoples, in all their historical complexity, are places where the truth of the gospel is tested and deepened.[23]

Reading the Apostles' Creed from the borders commits one to reading from below. González recalls the curious anecdote shared by Gregory of Nazianzus of how the questions addressed by the Council of Nicaea were on everyone's lips—one could not visit a market or a public bath without running into people asking for one's opinion on whether Jesus was begotten or made. González wonders if one of the reasons why modernist theologians dismiss Nicene faith as a misbegotten, ill-fated, illegitimate adaptation of biblical faith is because they are not reading from below. González writes: "Harnack has said that the Council of Nicaea was 'the apotheosis of Jesus.' Could it be that what was really at stake was the 'carpenterization of God'? Could this be the reason why so many of the Emperors soon came to view the Nicene faith with strong disfavor?"[24]

---

22. Justo L. González, "Towards a New Reading of History," *Apuntes* 1.3 (1981): 4–14, 10.

23. Andrew Walls, "Structural Problems in Mission Studies," *International Bulletin of Missionary Research* 15 (1991): 147.

24. Justo L. González, "Towards a New Reading of History," 12. González's insight into the "carpenterization" of God is rendered concrete in Peter Storey's experience in ministry in South Africa. When his Methodist church in District 6 built a community center they called it the Carpenter's House. On one of the walls, his members hung a placard with a prayer to the "Master Carpenter of Nazareth." Peter Storey, *Protest at Midnight: Ministry to a Nation Torn Apart* (Eugene, OR: Cascade Books, 2022): 27.

As with the Nicene Creed, González reads the Apostles' Creed from below.[25] González locates the composition of the Apostles' Creed in the context of the struggles against Marcion, whose theology separated creation from redemption and separated the Old Testament from the New. Marcion is long dead, but Marcionism lives on. González professes the creed in Spanish by reading it in conversation with the new Marcionism, which separates the sacred from the secular and tells the church not to meddle in political matters like the treatment of refugees.[26]

In affirming that God the Father is *pantokrator* (almighty), the church rejects attempts to circumscribe God's power and care. God is beyond borders. "This was true of the border that Marcion tried to build between the spiritual and the material. It was also true of the barrier that he tried to build between Israel and the Church."[27] It is also true of the creator-creature distinction. "The Jesus Christ of the faith of the church is [the] very God who breaks the barrier that separates God from human."[28] The language is provocative and, if given ontological weight, problematic, but it rightly captures the scandal of the incarnation. If the distinction between creator and creature is real and important and yet the Word nevertheless became flesh, then what are political borders?

Professing faith in Jesus Christ, God-become-flesh—flesh, beautiful and vulnerable—checks against both spiritualizing and secularizing tendencies that privatize the church's witness. Belief in Jesus's life, death, and resurrection sustains Christians working among marginalized peoples with the conviction "that bodies are important; that bodies ought not to go hungry; that bodies ought not to be tortured; that bodies ought not to be killed; but at the same time, that the torturers of bodies and the killers of bodies do not

---

25. For a brief history of the Apostles' Creed and its relationship to the earlier Nicene Creed, see Justo L. González, *The Apostles' Creed for Today* (Louisville, KY: Westminster John Knox, 2007), 1–7 and *The Story of Christianity, Volume 1: The Early Church to the Dawn of the Reformation* (New York: HarperCollins, 2010), 77–79; 189–90.

26. Justo L. González, "The Apostles' Creed and the Sanctuary Movement," *Apuntes* 6.1 (1986): 12–20.

27. González, "The Apostles' Creed and the Sanctuary Movement," 14.

28. González, "The Apostles' Creed and the Sanctuary Movement," 14.

have the last word."[29] This concrete affirmation of belief in the resurrection of the body comes in the third article of the creed because it is only possible by the power of the Holy Spirit.

Metodistas profess faith in the Holy Spirit, who breaks chains, blows beyond borders, and leads the church in its mission. Because the Spirit speaks through the church, Christians can know the truth about God and about what is actually happening in God's world. The 1980s were marked by oppressive Central American regimes and by the US's questionable involvement in and portrayal of Latin America; in this context, González provides an example: "Were it not for the church, I would believe in the newspapers, or I would believe in the Administration, or I would believe in what people who only became interested in Central America last year tell me. But because of the church, because of this One, Holy, Catholic, body, I have sisters and brothers in every Central American country."[30] Because of the Holy Spirit, there is a church, a body, a communion of saints without borders.

Affirming the Fe Viva

The Methodist experience of practical divinity values tradition and translation, ancient and new. Karen Westerfield Tucker notes that for the first North American Methodist congregations, "Innovative practices in worship, therefore, could be evaluated not only in terms of their testimony to Scripture and tradition but also by the witness of the Spirit in human life."[31] The people called metodista faithfully profess the faith in the language passed down from church mothers and fathers in symbols like the Apostles' Creed, and they embrace the freedom to find new symbols that resonate with the experience of being a pilgrim people in solidarity with particular cultural heritages (e.g., Hispanic Creed, Guatemalan Creed) and the experience of marginalized communities (e.g., the Creed of the Immigrant People).

---

29.   González, "The Apostles' Creed and the Sanctuary Movement," 18.

30.   González, "The Apostles' Creed and the Sanctuary Movement," 17.

31.   Karen B. Westerfield Tucker, *American Methodist Worship* (New York: Oxford University Press, 2001), 5.

Affirming the fe viva commits Methodists to value the culture within which that faith is lived. When the early Christians witnessed to the gospel of Jesus Christ among the Greeks, they faced critical questions about how the gospel relates to culture. Must gentiles completely abandon their cultures to follow the way of Christ? Or might gentiles become Christians without abandoning their cultures? If Christians are to offer a reasonable account (*apologia*) of the hope within them (1 Pet 3:15), they must be understood, and this requires them to use the language and cultural conventions of their hearers, even if these are stretched and challenged. According to González, "A culture is, basically, the way in which any group of human beings relates to itself and the surrounding environment."[32] Norman Wirzba contrasts abstract culture with concrete culture. Abstract culture forgets the web of interrelations that make life possible and meaningful, whereas concrete culture grounds a people's worldview in a particular land, language, and story.[33] The Guatemalan Methodist people profess, "We believe God gives us life and the conditions for life. He gives us land, plants, waters, the skies with the multitude of stars, the birds, the fish, and other animals, generating interrelationship, independence, and equilibrium in all forms of life."[34] This is the God who affirms concrete cultures and who is confessed by people who appreciate their concrete culture. This is the God professed in the creed of the Guatemalan Methodist people and in González's Hispanic Creed, which names each person of the Trinity in relation to culture.[35]

God is "the creator of all peoples and all cultures." Contra the Gnostics, creation is not the mistaken act of a lesser and evil God, but a loving expression of generous abundance from a good and wise God. God's

---

32. Justo L. González, *Culto, cultura, y cultivo: Apuntes teológicos entorno a las culturas* (Lima, Perú: Ediciones Puma, 2014), 37.

33. See Norman Wirzba, *The Paradise of God: Renewing Religion in an Ecological Age* (New York: Oxford University Press, 2003), 85–90. Wirzba states, "Another way to describe an abstract culture is to say that its members have undergone a narrowing of vision and sympathy. This narrowing is reflected and abetted in practical living conditions that promote insularity and blindness with respect to the larger contexts of a healthy life" (86).

34. *Cánticos de vida y esperanza*, 4.

35. The Hispanic Creed is found in Spanish and English in both *Mil voces para celebrar*, 69–70 and *Fiesta cristiana*, 269–70.

charge to human beings to "be fruitful and multiply, and fill the earth and subdue it" commits humans to generating many cultures. In the "Table of Nations" of Genesis 10, we read how the multiplication and dispersion of Noah's children across the face of the earth caused a proliferation of families, languages, and nations. Culture communicates a shared cultural memory. Humans share cultural memory in explicit ways, for example, through artistic production, and in implicit ways, such as stories passed down from time immemorial. What is shared and passed down is a fallen good that we should neither romanticize nor demonize. "No doubt there is much evil in the manner in which creation, history, and the cultures which humankind has created operate today. Even so, history and culture exist within the realm of God's creation and beneath the shadow of God's love. Not everything that happens in history and culture is evil because of God's continuous action in them."[36]

The Hispanic Creed professes Jesus Christ as "God made flesh in one culture for all cultures."[37] This affirmation restates the scandal of particularity of Christianity. Jesus is a Jew born in Bethlehem of Judea "while Quirinius was governor of Syria" (Luke 2:2), and he is God's logos, "the true light, which enlightens every one" (John 1:9). As God's word through whom and for whom all things were made, Christ illumines all peoples and cultures and discloses their goodness as historical modes of expression of the richness of human nature. Justin Martyr (c.100–165) affirmed the luminosity of culture, seeing seeds of the Word in the civilizational achievements of Greece. As the redeemer, Christ is also the purifier and perfector of culture, because all peoples are marked by sin and in need of sanctification. Tertullian (c.155–220) emphasized this fallenness of culture, questioning the possibility of reconciling the saving events in Jerusalem with the philosophical schools of Athens. The Hispanic Creed affirms both the continuity of God's work in creation and redemption (like Justin Martyr) and the uniqueness of Christian revelation (like Tertullian), even as it also affirms that Christ's light reaches all dimensions of

---

36. González, *Breve Historia de las Doctrinas Cristianas* (Nashville, TN: Abingdon, 2007), 71.

37. González, "Hispanic Creed," *Fiesta cristiana*, 269.

human existence, not just religious ones. "That is to say, when examining any culture, we should seek signs of the logos not only in their religion, but also in their practice of justice, in their social order, in the structure of their families, in its art, its music, and its ancient legends and myths."[38] In general, European missionaries did not follow this path when they crossed the Atlantic and then the Pacific. Most saw the lands and peoples they encountered as shaded from the light of Christ with only a few glimmers breaking through. Bartolomé de las Casas (c.1484–1566)—who features in this volume's chapter 7—is a notable exception. His *Apologética Historia Sumaria* examines how all aspects of the Indigenous people's culture, from political organization and religious practices to artisanal work, were under the headship of Christ.

The Holy Spirit "makes his presence known in our peoples and cultures."[39] Christianity is always culturally embodied. To think otherwise is to flirt with Docetism. The gospel can only be heard in someone's native tongue. But as we affirm the Holy Spirit's presence in culture, we must avoid cultural idealization. All cultures arise from histories wounded by sin. We must also avoid cultural ossification. All cultures develop by engaging their surroundings. González insists Christians always live in at least two cultures, the surrounding culture and the Christian one.[40] "One aspect of the paradox is clear: simply by virtue of now having faith in Christ, Christians are not plucked from their culture or from their manner of understanding the world, and organizing their lives."[41] At the same time, they will undoubtedly understand some elements of their culture better in the light of the gospel, leading to affirmation in some cases, reformation in others, and rejection in others still. Early church apologists (e.g., the epistles to Diognetus) display a keen awareness of the conflicted nature of these multiple belongings and of the importance of privileging Christian identity. The Holy Spirit's presence in cultures gives these identities an eschatological orientation to the day of the great fiesta, "when all

---

38. González, *Breve Historia de las Doctrinas*, 80.

39. González, "Hispanic Creed," 269.

40. González, *Culto, cultura, y cultivo*, 139.

41. González, *Breve Historia de las Doctrinas*, 70.

peoples will join in joyful banquet, when all tongues of the universe will sing the same song."[42]

"We believe in the Church Universal...where all the colors paint a single landscape."[43] The church and its peoples are one. In this eschatological landscape, the colors join, blend, form new shapes, and lend vibrancy and surprise, engaging in mestizaje (mixing). Mestizo (mixed) historically referred to the children born from the traumatic encounter between Spanish conquistadors and Amerindian women, as well as the broader cultural and religious mixing due to the Spanish conquest. Starting with Virgilio Elizondo's seminal articulations, Hispanic theology has given mestizaje multiple evolving valences.[44] Although the terminology comes with challenges,[45] mestizaje as a theological category pairs its painful history with the hope of better forms of generative togetherness, made possible by the ultimate example and source of mestizaje—the joining of God to humanity in the incarnation. The fe viva finds hope in the shadow of death not by ignoring the shadow but by looking to the God who joins us there and invites us into the bright, multihued landscape of the great fiesta. The fe viva embraces the change that genuine encounter brings us, anticipating how the future is mestiza.

---

42. González, "Hispanic Creed," 270.

43. González, "Hispanic Creed," 269–70.

44. For a thorough overview of mestizaje in Latinx theology, see Néstor Medina, "U.S. Latina/o Theology: Challenges, Possibilities, and Future Prospects," in *Theology and the Crisis of Engagement*, ed. Jeff Nowers and Néstor Medina (Eugene, OR: Pickwick, 2013), 141–60. See also Medina's entry on "Mestizaje" in *Encyclopedia of Christianity in the Global South*, ed. Mark A. Lamport (Lanham, MD: Rowman & Littlefield, 2018), 500–502. For Elizondo's original articulation, see Virgilio P. Elizondo, *Galilean Journey: The Mexican-American Promise* (Maryknoll, NY: Orbis, 2006).

45. Rubén Rosario Rodriquez walks us through one of the challenges that attend the terminology: "Elizondo's emphasis on biological *mestizaje* stems from the fact that his attempts to articulate an alternative to the language of modern racism—which views various human groups as distinct biological entities—can perpetuate an essentialist view of human groups by insisting that *mestizaje* describes a new and distinct biological entity. I support his emancipatory project and strongly believe that *mestizaje* is a vital concept for racial reconciliation, but not as the source of a distinct Latino/a genetic identity. Rather, by emphasizing the universality of *mestizaje* as a more accurate scientific description of human biological diversity, Latino/a theology can resist racism and positively transform racial discourse." Rubén Rosario Rodríguez, *Racism and God-talk: A Latino/a Perspective* (New York: New York University Press, 2008), 68.

Renewing Worship through Creedal Practice

"We believe in the Reign of God, the day of the Great Fiesta."[46] This affirmation from the Hispanic Creed expresses the faith of the people called metodista regarding God's promised future. The end does not look like global pandemics or world war, nor does it resemble the big crunch of cosmic collapse or the long whimper of entropic death. The end looks like the peaceable kingdom of Isaiah 2, the multiethnic choir of Revelation 7, the global dinner party of Matthew 8, and the wedding banquet of Revelation 19. In other words, the future looks like fiesta. The renewal of worship benefits from the gifts metodistas have received while walking the Wesleyan way of salvation in the *cantones* of El Salvador, the barrios of New York, and the side streets of Durham. The gifts of fiesta and the profession of faith in Spanish can reconnect worship to its end: the day of the great fiesta.

The fiesta cristiana has no borders and the fe metodista has no anathemas. True, the day of the great fiesta as announced in Scripture draws a sharp line between those who have been welcomed and those who have been cast off. A universalist account of salvation where all persons, peoples, and cultures are necessarily saved is neither scriptural nor Methodist. However, whereas creeds like the Athanasian Creed and the original Nicene Creed concluded with anathemas[47]—statements that condemn those who do not profess its particular formulation of the faith—the Hispanic Creed ends differently: "Because we believe, we commit ourselves to believe for those who do not believe, to love for those who do not love, to dream for those who do not dream, until the day when hope becomes reality."[48] The day of the great fiesta is precisely the day of hope, and hope renews the fiesta cristiana and the fe metodista.

---

46. González, "Hispanic Creed," 270.

47. For an insightful consideration of anathemas in Christian creeds, see Jaroslav Pelikan, *Credo: Historical and Theological Guide to Creeds and Confessions of Faith in the Christian Tradition* (New Haven, CT: Yale University Press, 2005), 189–95.

48. González, "Hispanic Creed," 270.

Celebrating the fiesta cristiana enlivens the faith. One of the gifts of the Hispanic churches to the church universal is the rediscovery of worship as fiesta and the renewal of Christian anthropology. According to Goizueta, "What lies at the heart of the Latino affinity for festive celebration is not necessarily a happier, warmer, or more easy-going *temperament*, but a fundamentally different *understanding* of the human and, specifically, of the nature of human activity in the world."[49] Human beings are not first and foremost *homo faber* or *homo ludens* but what Cándido Pozo calls *homo festivus*. To be human is to be one "who worships God with a free, gladsome and festive spirit, the human who has a cultic and liturgical posture."[50] This posture contrasts the nihilistic posture powerfully captured in the exhortation, "Let us eat and drink, for tomorrow we die" (Isa 22:13). The posture of *homo festivus* is one of gratitude for the past, commitment to the present, and hope for the future.

The fiesta cristiana embraces all tenses in history. "We celebrate what God has done for and with us. And most especially we celebrate the life, death, and resurrection of Jesus. But above all, we celebrate the great celebration that is still to come, the final fiesta of all ages, the heavenly banquet, the Reign of God."[51] The kingdom-bound celebration of the fiesta cristiana empowers God's people to sing even while walking in the deepest valley and in the darkest shadows. The vision of the end gives contextual worship the catholicity without which it would cease to be Christian. This posture towards the kingdom is only achievable in community. Fiestas are social. One cannot celebrate a fiesta alone. The *homo festivus* is plural and the *homines festivus* a social "we."

Fiesta is a kingdom practice with the power to renew our understanding of the human being as a cultural being made for worship. The fiesta cristiana celebrates the faith in its diversity of concrete cultural expressions. This celebration occurs through doxology. For instance, the popular

---

49.   Goizueta, "Fiesta: Life in the Subjunctive," 90.

50.   Pozo, "La teología de la fiesta," 419.

51.   *Fiesta cristiana*, 11.

corito "Alabaré" expresses the eschatological orientation of the fiesta and the fe.[52]

Alabaré, alabaré, alabaré a mi Señor.	I will praise. I will praise. I will praise my Lord.
Juan vió el número de los redimidos y todos alababan al Señor, unos oraban, otros cantaban, y todos alababan al Señor.	John saw the number of the redeemed and they were all praising the Lord, Some prayed, some sang, and all together praised the Lord.
Todos unidos, alegres cantamos gloria y alabanzas al Señor. Gloria al Padre, gloria al Hijo, y gloria al Espíritu de amor.	All together, we sing joyfully glories and praises to the Lord. Glory to the Father, glory to the Son, and glory to the Spirit of Love.

In charismatic Methodist churches in Peru's Cuzco region, the worship leader often invites the congregation to offer God *tres glorias* (three glories). Although the fe metodista (Methodist faith) finds expression beyond the creeds, the exuberance and mystery of fiesta can protect the creeds from turning into a list of doctrinal propositions abstracted from the way of salvation. Embedded in the density and beauty of fiesta, the creeds can indeed become the confession of faith of a pilgrim people.

---

52.   Alabaré© 1979, Manuel José Alonso and José Pagán. All rights reserved. Exclusive agent in US, Canada and Mexico: OCP. Used with permission. Translated by the author.

Daniel Ramírez connects this chorus of "anonymous authorship" to the Latina/o "subaltern" of the Azusa Street revival, a.k.a. the birth of modern Pentecostalism. According to Ramírez, the corito's emerging popularity traces Pentecostalism's growth, flowing from the "black-brown Pentecostal borderlands" that often go overlooked and spreading across cultural, national, and even religious borders. Daniel Ramírez, *Migrating Faith: Pentecostalism in the United States and Mexico in the Twentieth Century* (Chapel Hill, NC: University of North Carolina Press, 2015), 197.

Professing the fe metodista hallows the fiesta. Reading the Apostles' Creed in Spanish and affirming the fe viva helps Christians live in the subjunctive. The subjunctive mood is fragile. As Goizueta puts it, "Any subjunctive situation has a tendency to revert to indicativity; that is, to lose its ability to celebrate the present *as projected into* a possible future."[53] This tendency toward the indicative and the status quo gives fiestas an ambiguous character. The splurge or *bótate* of a fiesta may be a celebration of the richness of being alive, or an expression of consumerist values that bigger is better. The focus on a young woman in the quinceañera may point to a reversal of social roles that brings a marginalized person to the forefront, or a coming-of-age party that solidifies patriarchal gender roles. Fiestas are structured affairs, a confluence of planning and spontaneity, work and play. At its best, "the fiesta challenges and subverts both an escapist (postmodern) understanding of play and a mechanistic (modern) understanding of work."[54] At its worst, the fiesta becomes romanticized and reduced to mere play. At its best, fiesta is a "royal waste of time" that fires our hope for the transformation of the world.[55]

Creeds help keep fiesta at its best by renewing its roots in the mystery of Christ. As Goizueta asserts, "Jesus' solidarity with and compassion for the outcasts of his society, that is his active celebration of *their* lives, alone makes possible—and credible—the celebration of life as a gift."[56] By professing the fe metodista, we believe in the God who has a special affinity for the cultures of marginalized peoples. The God who became incarnate in Jesus Christ is a God who delivers the oppressed by becoming a victim. Justo González is right. "If being a minority means being subjected and

---

53. Goizueta, "Fiesta: Life in the Subjunctive," 93.

54. Goizueta, "Fiesta: Life in the Subjunctive," 95.

55. See Marva J. Dawn, *A Royal "Waste" of Time: The Splendor of Worshipping God and Being Church for the World* (Grand Rapids, MI: Eerdmans, 1999), 17: "Worship is a royal waste of time that spirals into passion for living as Christians and back into more passionate worship. It is totally irrelevant, not efficient, not powerful, not productive, sometimes not even satisfying to us. It is also the only hope for changing the world."

56. Goizueta, "Fiesta: Life in the Subjunctive," 91.

victimized by forces that one does not control, God is a minority!"[57] This is the scandalous claim at the heart of the fiesta cristiana: the God of the people called metodista, the host of the day of the great fiesta, is a minoritized God who works for the liberation, reconciliation, and sanctification of all peoples and cultures. And to embrace this claim is to provide hope for worship's renewal.

---

57. Justo L. González, *Mañana: Christian Theology from a Hispanic Perspective* (Nashville, TN: Abingdon, 1990), 93.

Chapter Five

Wesleyans and Guadalupans: A Theological Reflection

W hen Elvira Arellano, an undocumented immigrant facing deportation, sought refuge within Adalberto United Methodist Church
in Chicago, she set off a media maelstrom. Probably for most people following the mainstream news coverage, this was a story about church and
state relations. But for Hispanic and Latin American Protestants watching
the numerous television interviews, what caught their eye was not the image of Ms. Arellano valiantly standing by the pulpit of the church where
she had found sanctuary but rather the large statue of the Virgin of Guadalupe prominently displayed next to her.[1] It was this latter image that
stirred profound sentiments of confusion and even resentment among
Spanish-speaking Protestants, particularly Methodists, both in the United
States and abroad.[2] Hispanic Methodist pastors responded to this incident by emphasizing the uniqueness of a Hispanic Methodist identity and
rejecting the use of Roman Catholic popular religiosity as an evangelism
tool. The response from the United Methodist episcopal leadership was

---

1. See Jason Byassee, "Sanctuary," *Christian Century* 123.22 (2006): 10–11. The presence
of the statue of Guadalupe at Adalberto UMC was part of a strategy of congregational development for welcoming Hispanics.

2. The presence of the Virgin of Guadalupe in this United Methodist church in Chicago
prompted some Methodists in Mexico to withdraw their church membership, even though the
Methodist Church of Mexico is autonomous from The United Methodist Church.

more equivocal. While affirming traditional Methodist rejection of the adoration of images, they allowed for the use of the image of the Virgin as a sign of hospitality. In short, the Virgin of Guadalupe could be displayed near the entrance of the church but not near the altar.

For many theologians, the image of the Virgin of Guadalupe is rich in ecumenical potential. In the words of Catholic theologian Virgilio Elizondo, "Guadalupe, properly understood, can become the deepest source of unity not only of Christians but also of people of all religions."[3] Maxwell E. Johnson's work in plowing this ecumenical field has been pioneering.[4] His lead has been followed by Methodists like Paul Barton[5] and Presbyterians like Rubén Rosario Rodríguez, as well as the other contributors to the book *American Magnificat: Protestants on Mary of Guadalupe.*[6]

Nevertheless, as the controversy sparked by the Arellano incident shows, the Virgin of Guadalupe is a sign of contradiction. For many Latino Protestants, the face of this brown-skinned Virgin, *La Morenita*, does not present a maternal image but a sinister specter. At times, the devotees of the Virgin of Guadalupe, the Guadalupanos, have manifested the arrogance of the conquistadors instead of the humility of Juan Diego. In the mid-twentieth century, Mexican Methodist theologian Gonzalo Báez-Camargo linked revivals in Guadalupan fervor with anti-Protestant crusades: "As usual, the feelings aroused about a revival of intolerance.

3. Virgil Elizondo in the preface to Maxwell E. Johnson's *The Virgin of Guadalupe: Theological Reflections of an Anglo-Lutheran Liturgist,* Celebrating Faith: Explorations in Latino Spirituality and Theology (Lanham, MD: Rowman & Littlefield, 2002), ix.

4. See M. E. Johnson, *The Virgin of Guadalupe*; and Johnson, "The Feast of the Virgin of Guadalupe and the Season of Advent," *Worship* 78.6 (2004): 482–99. See also Paul Barton, "Guadalupe in Theology and Culture (panel): A Hispanic Response to Nuestra Senora de Guadalupe," *ATLA Proceedings* 59 (2005): 141–57.

5. Barton, "Guadalupe in Theology and Culture," 142–48. In Barton's opinion, "Guadalupe represents an authentic revelation of the Gospel that has been kept from Latino/a Protestants due to the anti-Catholic message of Protestant missionaries. . . . My belief is that Guadalupe has a message for Latino/a Protestants as well as Catholics and that it is a difficult journey for Latino/a Protestants to arrive at the point of embracing Guadalupe, or being embraced by Guadalupe" (142). His main point is that until Guadalupe is personally encountered, she remains an abstraction that one knows about *(saber)* without knowing intimately *(conocer)*.

6. E.g., see Rubén Rosario Rodríguez, "Beyond Word and Sacrament: A Reformed Protestant Engagement of Guadalupan Devotion," *American Magnificat: Protestants on Mary of Guadalupe*, ed. Maxwell E. Johnson (Collegeville, MN: Liturgical, 2010).

All the windows in a Protestant church, which the pilgrims had to pass on their way to the basilica were broken, and other Protestant chapels in the neighborhood were damaged."[7] As in the days of Father Hidalgo (the "Father of Mexico," d. 1811), Guadalupe served as both an icon of unity and a battle standard. In this fight, Protestants have been far from passive. Hispanic and Latin American Protestants have raised opposition to the Virgin of Guadalupe to something on the level of dogma. In addition to distributing tracts purporting to expose the fraud of Tepeyac, Protestant groups have encouraged conspiracy theories like the one linking Guadalupanismo with Spanish fascism. Given this history, far from promoting the cause of Christian unity, the Virgin of Guadalupe remains a cause of division. As Justo González avers, "The notion that Cuban Catholics and Protestants will come together around the image of Caridad, or Mexicans around Guadalupe, may be very beautiful, but is made less credible by our own stories."[8]

In the present chapter, I propose to engage in a Wesleyan reading of the Virgin of Guadalupe. My ultimate purpose is to suggest that a serious engagement with the sources of Wesleyan theology prepares the way for a Methodist reception of Guadalupe, a Wesleyan Guadalupanismo. Even if my argument is less than convincing on historical and sociological grounds, as long as it clears some of the significant theological obstacles hindering such devotion, then I will consider my work a success. My argument is divided into two parts. First, I will lead us in a very brief historical-theological survey of the state of the Marian question in Methodism. Second, I will engage in a Wesleyan reading of the mission of the Virgin of Guadalupe. I will consider the sending of the Virgin to Juan Diego at Tepeyac by applying a Wesleyan stamp to classic Catholic criteria for judging the authenticity of Marian apparitions. Finally, I will offer some remarks on the prospects for a Wesleyan Guadalupanismo.

---

7.   Gonzalo Báez-Camargo, "Mexico Recrowns Guadalupe Virgin," *Christian Century* 62.47 (1945): 129.

8.   Justo L. González, "Reinventing Dogmatics: A Footnote from a Reinvented Protestant," in *From the Heart of Our People: Latino/a Explorations in Catholic Systematic Theology*, ed. Orlando O. Espin and Miguel H. Diaz (Maryknoll, NY: Orbis, 1999), 217–29, 224f.

Mary among Methodists

Marian reflection was not a significant theme of John Wesley's theology. Unlike Martin Luther, who preached numerous sermons on the occasion of Marian festivals, not one of Wesley's 151 published sermons is based on a Marian text.[9] Wesley knew of Roman Catholic belief in the assumption of Mary, and he was aware of some of the titles bestowed on her like "gate of heaven" and "advocatrix." He knew of these things and was perplexed by the amount of attention that Roman Catholicism gave to one "whose acts on earth, and whose power in heaven, the Scripture doth very sparingly relate, or is altogether silent in."[10]

Wesley sincerely believed that Catholics worshiped Mary along with the saints and holy angels.[11] Commenting on Mark 3:34, where Jesus brushes aside his earthly family's solicitude on his behalf, Wesley states:

> In this preference of his true disciples, even to the Virgin Mary, considered merely as his mother after the flesh, he not only shows his high and tender affection for them, but seems designedly to guard against those excessive and idolatrous honours which he foresaw would in after ages be paid to her.[12]

Wesley knew of the distinction between *dulia* and *latria,* but he saw it as an illicit and inadequate distinction.[13] He was convinced that Catholic devotion to Mary was irredeemably idolatrous.[14] Thus, whenever Wesley

---

9. David Butler, "The Blessed Virgin Mary in the Protestant Tradition," in *Mary Is for Everyone,* ed. William McLoughlin and Jill Pinnock (Leominster, UK: Gracewing, 1997), 64.

10. John Wesley, "A Roman Catechism with a Reply," *Works* (Jackson) 10:103.

11. Wesley, "A Roman Catechism," *Works* (Jackson) 10:103, 105, 107.

12. John Wesley, *NT Notes,* Mk 3:34, 1:155. Significantly, these comments appear to be Wesley's own and not Bengel's, the main source for his commentary on the New Testament. See Butler, "The Blessed Virgin Mary," 64.

13. Wesley, "A Roman Catechism," *Works* (Jackson) 10:110.

14. See Butler, "The Blessed Virgin Mary," 56–67. According to Butler, "The main problem for John Wesley ... with Catholic devotion to the Blessed Virgin is that she is not merely held in reverence but worshipped.... In Nicaea II the distinction was made between 'veneration' and 'adoration' (in the original Greek *'proskunesis'* and *'latreia,'* while confusingly in Latin *'adoratio'* and *'latria'*). One wonders whether the confusion in Wesley and others at this point is not caused by the ambiguous use of *'adoratio'* which looks like 'adoration' and yet is translated 'reverence'" (62).

turned his attention to Mary it was usually for the purpose of giving an admonition: "Little children, keep yourself from idols" (1 John 5:22).

Wesley's views on Mary, conventional for his time and place, were bequeathed to his followers by way of his abridgment of the Anglican Articles of Religion, which stated among other things that:

> The Romish doctrine concerning purgatory, pardon, worshipping, and ado-
> ration, as well of images as of relics, and also invocation of saints, is a fond
> thing, vainly invented, and grounded upon no warrant of Scripture, but
> repugnant to the Word of God.[15]

The assessment of Catholic piety, including its Marian devotion, expressed in this statement remains the dominant view among Spanish-speaking Methodists. For some, anything that gives a whiff of being "liturgical" or "ecumenical" is resisted because it smells Catholic. In fact, in many Methodist churches in Latin America it is by no means clear that even the cross belongs in the sanctuary.[16]

In spite of the overwhelmingly negative tenor of early Methodist Marian thought and devotion, Wesley did make some positive statements about Mary. To begin with, Wesley affirmed the virginity of Mary ante- and postpartum.[17] At times, Wesley spoke appreciatively of the zeal that Catholics showed in their devotion to Mary.[18] For instance, Wesley tells the story of how a penitent drunk professed his newfound faith at a love feast by inviting the congregation to join in singing "Mary's song," the *Magnificat*.[19] Sometimes, Wesley was accused of being a secret Marian

---

15. *The Book of Discipline of The United Methodist Church* (Nashville, TN: United Methodist Publishing House, 2008), 62f.

16. See Diana R. Rocco Tedesco, "Un episodio iconoclasta en la Iglesia Metodista Argentina (abril–setiembre de 1953) y la organización de ALMA (Asociación Laica Metodista Argentina - 1954–1959)," *Cuadernos de teología* 14.2 (1995): 93–109. Rocco recounts the painful cycle of recriminations and membership loss sparked by bringing a cross into a Methodist church.

17. Wesley, "A Letter to a Roman Catholic," §7, *Works* (Jackson) 10:81.

18. Wesley, January 29, 1750, *Journal and Diaries III*, *Works* 20:319.

19. Wesley, June 17, 1763, *Journal and Diaries IV*, *Works* 21:418.

devotee himself, a charge so absurd as to not even merit a rebuttal.[20] Methodists do not worship Mary, but they "honour the blessed Virgin as the mother of the Holy Jesus, and as a person of eminent piety."[21] Wesley does not spell out what kind of practices would honor the Virgin without committing idolatry, but at the very least he allows for the possibility of an authentically Wesleyan Marian piety.

Methodists have not quenched Wesley's generosity of spirit. Side by side with the aforementioned anti-Catholic sentiment so prevalent within early (and not so early) Methodism, there emerged a tradition of theological inquiry that, while fixed on the essentials of Christian orthodoxy, is willing to think and let think on matters not touching the root of Christianity. It was this "catholic spirit" that led The United Methodist Church to adopt an official resolution, which qualified the anti-Catholic Articles of Religion.[22] The United Methodist Church retained the aforementioned Article but underscored its particular historical provenance and insisted that it must be interpreted according to our best ecumenical understanding. Specifically, on the question of Mary, Methodist theologians have meditated on the role of Mary in salvation from an intentionally Wesleyan perspective.[23] A hopeful sign of the vitality of the catholic spirit among Methodists is a joint study of the British Methodist-Catholic dialogue,

---

20.   John Wesley, September 24, 1742, *Journal and Diaries II, Works* 19:298.

21.   John Wesley, "Popery Calmly Considered," *Works* (Jackson) 10:147.

22.   Resolution 97, "Resolution of Intent—With a View to Unity," in *The Book of Resolutions of The United Methodist Church* (Nashville, TN: United Methodist Publishing House, 2004), states "that we declare it our official intent henceforth to interpret all our Articles, Confession, and other 'standards of doctrine' in consonance with our best ecumenical insights and judgments. . . . This implies, at the very least, our heartiest offer of goodwill and Christian community to all our Roman Catholic brothers and sisters, in the avowed hope of the day when all bitter memories (ours and theirs) will have been redeemed by the gift of the fullness of Christian unity" (273).

23.   See David Carter, "Mary—Servant of the Word: Towards Convergence in Ecclesiology," in *Mary Is for Everyone*, 157–70; David Butler, "The Blessed Virgin Mary in the Protestant Tradition," in ibid., 56–67; Geoffrey Wainwright, "Mary and Methodism," in *The Ecumenical Moment: Crisis and Opportunity for the Church* (Grand Rapids, MI: Eerdmans, 1983), 169–88.

titled *Mary, Mother of the Lord: Sign of Grace, Faith and Holiness.*[24] Though brief, this document treats most of the relevant mariological loci: grace, election, the immaculate conception, Mary's *fiat*, Mary's assumption, and significant Marian titles. Curiously, one lacuna in this document and in most ecumenical reflections on Mary is the phenomenon of Marian apparitions. Even a Methodist as open to expressions of Marian piety as Neville Ward (after all, he wrote a book on praying the rosary, which was very popular among English Catholics[25]) has been less than enthusiastic in his attitude toward Marian shrines and visions.[26]

In sum, the state of the Marian question among Methodists varies diachronically and synchronically. From the earliest days of Methodism to the present, anti-catholic sentiments and a catholic spirit have

---

24. British Methodist–Roman Catholic Committee, *Mary, Mother of the Lord, Sign of Grace, Faith and Holiness: Towards a Shared Understanding* (London: Methodist Publishing House, 1995). The statement has not been without its critics. Cf. Edward Ball, "Mary, Mother of the Lord," *Epworth Review* 24.4 (1997): 25–34. At one level, Ball's critique is methodological: "We note a characteristic way these controversial doctrines are handled in this ecumenical document: Methodists, it is said, may not be able to accept the doctrines themselves, but can affirm together with Catholics the 'spiritual truth' underlying them. . . . So how organic, how theologically necessary, is the link to Mary?" At a deeper level, his critique is material: "First, we must ask whether ultimately the emphasis on Mary's role does not betoken a sense of the insufficiency in God's saving work of the *humanity* of Christ himself, not least as the assurance of that work's being brought to completion? . . . This brings us to the second point, which is ultimately, I think, the key to the whole discussion. If, as we have seen, Mary is understood as an 'icon' of the church, then a claim is being made that the church itself already participates fully in some sense in the eschaton. The idea appears in respect of the other Marian doctrines, too" (32). In my judgment, Ball's critique is evidence of an underdeveloped eschatology ill-suited for a Wesleyan theological framework that is built on Christian perfection.

25. J. Neville Ward, *Five for Sorrow, Ten for Joy: A Consideration of the Rosary* (Cambridge, MA: Cowley, 1985).

26. See Neville Ward, "Mary: Intercessor," *One in Christ* 19.3 (1983): 282–90. While arguing for an intercessory role for Mary, Ward confesses his own sense of alienation from at least this aspect of popular Marian piety. He admits, "I wish I could be more excited about visions like those of Lourdes and Fatima than I am. It may well be that inhibition inherent in the tradition in which I have learned Christianity slows me down. I am quite ready to acknowledge the possibility of genuine glimpses into the unseen, though I would certainly expect inadequacies and various kinds of spiritual and intellectual clumsiness in the attempts to describe them. On the other hand, I can easily imagine the possibility of someone being so stirred by the image of our Lady that love and longing should produce hallucinatory satisfaction of one sort or another" (288).

coexisted, but their respective intensity has waxed and waned throughout geography and history. Openness to Marian reflection is a relatively new experience for Methodists, and it is largely localized in the English-speaking world. Openness to Guadalupan reflection is at a different stage altogether, and it is to the consideration of the Virgin and Juan Diego that we now turn.

A Wesleyan Reading of the Virgin of Guadalupe

Wesley betrays no knowledge of the events surrounding the apparition of the Virgin of Guadalupe. With one significant exception to which I will return later, Wesley is not very interested in the happenings of Mexico during the time of the conquest. For this reason, a Wesleyan reading of Tepeyac cannot start with Wesley. Instead, I wish to engage in an ecumenical exercise where I attempt to listen to what God might be saying through Guadalupe. Through long experience with these matters, Roman Catholics have developed criteria for answering these questions. According to the eminent Mariologist René Laurentin, in assessing the authenticity of an apparition the church considers the adequacy of information concerning the event itself, the orthodoxy of the message, the evidence of supernatural signs, and the fruits of the event.[27] I intend to apply these criteria in order to discern the veracity and significance of Guadalupe from a Wesleyan perspective.

First, assessing the historical evidence for the apparition of Guadalupe is of primary importance. The historical-critical study of the textual and oral sources of the Guadalupan story and the scientific examination of the image, even when inconclusive, play a vital and necessary role in theological reflection on Guadalupe. Whether one agrees with his conclusions or not, no theologian can ignore the kinds of questions raised by Stafford Poole on the dating and origins of the Guadalupan

---

27. René Laurentin, *The Apparitions of the Blessed Virgin Mary Today* (Dublin: Veritas, 1990), 39–42.

tradition.[28] Nor can one ignore discussions on the genre of the apparition narratives. Theologians would do well to heed Maxwell Johnson's comments on Miguel Sánchez's *Imagen de la Virgen María* and Luis Laso de la Vega's *Nican Mopohua* and treat these as theological portraits rather than as eyewitness, scientific accounts.[29] Yet even if the Guadalupan traditions share more in common with the genre of gospel than with newspaper columns, the search for the historical Juan Diego, so to speak, is indispensable. Theological appreciation for Guadalupe will not be compelling if it easily elides questions of history and practice as if these were in some secondary position to the beautiful message of Guadalupe. Among various contemporary appraisals of the Virgin of Guadalupe (from Catholics and Protestants alike) there lurks a regrettable tendency to separate the authenticity of the apparition from the significance of its message. Appreciation for the liberationist themes in the Virgin's appearance to Juan Diego is coupled with indifference about this event's actual historic basis. The result of such an approach is that Guadalupe becomes an abstract symbol unrecognizable to Guadalupanos and Methodists. Rapprochement between these two groups will not be attained without careful study of the documentary evidence.

A firm judgment concerning the authenticity of the sending of the Virgin of Guadalupe to Juan Diego on Tepeyac, however, exceeds the competence of the theological task. What theologians can do is reflect a posteriori on the appropriateness or fittingness of an event occurring in a

---

28. See Stafford Poole in *Our Lady of Guadalupe: The Origins and Sources of a Mexican National Symbol, 1531–1797* (Tucson: University of Arizona Press, 1995). For a contrasting account, see Eduardo Chávez, *Our Lady of Guadalupe and Saint Juan Diego: The Historical Evidence*, Celebrating Faith: Explorations in Latino Spirituality and Theology (Lanham, MD: Rowman & Littlefield, 2006).

29. Johnson's argument is persuasive and instructive: "Hence, for example, if Archbishop Juan Zumárraga (whose own writings, to be fair, have not all survived) did not, in fact, play historically the central episcopal role accorded to him in the official Guadalupan narratives, this does not need to be any more of a problem than the equally problematic worldwide census under Emperor Augustus narrated as part of the birth of Jesus in Luke 2 or other similar questionable historical details throughout the New Testament writings" (M. E. Johnson, *The Virgin of Guadalupe*, 54).

certain way, at a certain time and place.[30] For example, since according to Thomas Aquinas one of the main purposes of apparitions is the stirring of hope,[31] how appropriate that these events took place in 1531, a time when conscientious Christians despaired of the future of the church's mission in the Americas! How fitting that the Virgin who sang about how God had scattered the proud appeared to Juan Diego rather than to Bishop Zumárraga! How proper that she manifested herself as mestiza and that she participated in the birth of Mexico as a mestizo people! Wesley himself did not shy away from engaging in these kinds of explorations in theology of history. One need only read his remarks on Methodism's providential purpose to see that Wesley considered the theological interpretation of historic events as a legitimate theological exercise. As a Wesleyan theologian, I can appreciate the efforts of the early Guadalupan theologians in interpreting the encounter in Tepeyac; their work should inspire Methodists to humbly plow the field of theology of history in order to discern God's purpose in raising the people called *metodista*.

Second, can a Methodist read the message of Tepeyac as orthodox? In a real sense, the theological coherence of the revelation of Guadalupe with traditional Christian doctrine is more fundamental than the evidence of historic documents, miraculous signs, or changed lives. Is the message of the Virgin in accord with the message of Jesus Christ? For, to quote Paul, "even if we or an angel from heaven should proclaim to you a gospel contrary to what we proclaimed to you, let that one be accursed!" (Gal 1:8).

---

30.   See Francisco Raymond Schulte, *Mexican Spirituality: Its Sources and Mission in the Earliest Guadalupan Sermons* (Lanham, MD: Rowman & Littlefield, 2002). Schulte's study of the earliest Guadalupan sermons uncovers a profound theology of history that seeks to answer the question of the timing of Guadalupe by arguments from fittingness or *convenientia*. In the words of the Dominican Fray Juan de Villa y Sanchez, from a sermon preached in 1733 and quoted by Schulte, "Do you know, O Mexico, why God did not send Apostles to these lands before? Because the Most Holy Virgin who appeared at Guadalupe, and is portrayed in this her miraculous Image, had to be—as indeed she was and is—the Missionary of this entire new World. Say now: It was actually advantageous that the lights of the Gospel took so long to reach our America, if they were meant to dawn in the Dawn *[Aurora]* of Mary" (35).

31.   René Laurentin, *Pilgrimages, Sanctuaries, Icons, Apparitions: A Historical and Scriptural Account* (Milford, OH: The Riehle Foundation, 1994), 91.

The message of Guadalupe is not simply the words of the Virgin but her very appearance at Tepeyac.[32] Can a Methodist read the appearance of the Virgin as a sign (*semeia*) from God or must it be automatically dismissed as a lying wonder (*terata pseudos*) of the devil? Wesley believes that in the communion of saints, "it is certain human spirits swiftly increase in knowledge, in holiness, and in happiness, conversing with all the wise and holy souls that lived in all ages and nations from the beginning of the world."[33] In heaven, saints grow in happiness as they commune with each other, but the communion of saints is not merely a heavenly club. The communion of saints above increases in holiness and happiness as it interacts with the communion of saints below. For this reason, Wesley muses: "May we not probably suppose that the spirits of the just, though generally lodged in paradise, yet may sometimes, in conjunction with the holy angels, minister to the heirs of salvation?"[34] Indeed, "how much will that add to the happiness of those spirits which are already discharged from the body, that they are permitted to minister to those whom they have left behind!"[35] God does not need the help of creatures in order to accomplish God's purposes. By means of divine almighty power, God spreads the gospel to all lands and brings all the nations into God's fold. And yet it pleases God to work through the participation of secondary agents. As Wesley explains, "The grand reason why God is pleased to assist men by men, rather than immediately by himself, is undoubtedly to endear us to each other by these mutual good offices, in order to increase our happiness both in time and eternity."[36]

Applying Wesley's logic to the issue at hand, may we not suppose that the Blessed Virgin Mary, "though generally lodged in paradise, yet may

---

32.   Salvatore M. Perrella, "Le 'mariofanie': presenza segno e impego della Vergine glorificata nella storia," *Marianum* 67 (2005): 51–153, citing De Luna: "Il *messaggio*, spesso orale, non si limita a una semplice comunicazione verbale della Vergine al veggente o ai veggenti the dovranno poi trasmetterla al popolo. L'apparizione é di per sé un messaggio: incarnando la realtà invisibile dell'ordine soprannaturale, ne rivela l'esistenza" (117).

33.   John Wesley, Sermon 132, "On Faith," §6, *Works* 4:192.

34.   Wesley, "On Faith," §6, *Works* 4:191.

35.   Wesley, "On Faith," §12, *Works* 4:197.

36.   John Wesley, Sermon 71, "Of Good Angels," II.10, *Works* 3:15.

sometimes, in conjunction with the holy angels, minister to the heirs of salvation"? Is she not, at the very least, a just spirit? Would it not add to her happiness to be permitted to be a mother to someone like Juan Diego? From a Wesleyan perspective, the sending of Mary to Juan Diego is a theologically intelligible event. I deliberately use the word "sending" because no saint in heaven is an independent agent acting on her or his own initiative.[37] From the beginning of the gospel, "The 'acts of Mary' are the Acts of the Spirit."[38] Hence, any authentic Marian apparition must originate from a divine mission. Obviously, that God could send the Blessed Virgin to Juan Diego does not mean that God in fact did. But the message of her appearance need not be summarily dismissed, by a Wesleyan, as a lying wonder. Instead, given the theological coherence of a divine sending of Mary, we need to consider the content of her mission.

Ostensibly, the purpose of the Virgin's mission is the building of a Marian shrine on the hill of Tepeyac. This message is not exactly congenial to Methodist ears. A shrine is a container for the sacred and as such a point of destination for a pilgrimage. However, Jesus's ministry devalued the spiritual significance of geography. God is not bound to the temple in Jerusalem (John 4:21). The true Christian temple is not "made with human hands" (Acts 7:47-50). Christian life is indeed a pilgrimage, but one whose final destination is heaven. And yet, Methodists cannot completely dismiss the role of shrines in Christianity because Jesus was not above making pilgrimages himself. From the time he was a child to the time of his crucifixion, Jesus joined his people in their yearly processions to Jerusalem; he made the psalms of ascent his own. What does this mean for the orthodoxy of the Lady's request for a shrine? It means, at the very least, that the request is not irredeemably heterodox. Granted, Wesley did not have anything good to say about Muslim pilgrimages to Mecca or

---

37. Richard Rutt, "Why Should He Send His Mother? Some Theological Reflections on Marian Apparitions," in McLoughlin and Pinnock, *Mary Is for Everyone*, 274–91. As Rutt helpfully observes: Mary is sent. "Common parlance tells of our Lady as though she appears of her own volition. I have deliberately spoken of her as being sent. As a saint in eternal glory her will must be so united to the Will of God, and so far beyond the space-time continuum, that she can appear only if God wills it; and since God's will is prior to ours in all things good, it is better to speak of her as being sent by God" (280).

38. *Mary, Mother of the Lord*, 9.

Catholic ones to Loreto.[39] He feared that on the way of salvation, earthly shrines are distractions or even temptations. This fear is not without its basis. Opportunities for abuse abound. A shrine can upset the balance of centripetal and centrifugal forces in Christianity. The church exists for mission, not for pilgrimages. Nevertheless, *abusus non tollit usum.*[40] Hans Urs von Balthasar's judgment on the role of shrines in Christianity offers a helpful correction to the abuses while preserving the possibility of right uses: "Catholic shrines have the grace of sending pilgrims away with the certainty that this grace is not bound to any one place. Having established their credentials, they efface themselves."[41] The Basilica of Our Lady of Guadalupe as a place of sending is a message that a Methodist could appreciate. From this perspective, the shrine would serve as a landmark along the way of salvation, a place to get one's bearings before moving on. If the message of Guadalupe is heard in this way, then the pilgrimage to Guadalupe for the feast of December 12 might be interpreted as something analogous to "watchnight" services, which Methodists celebrate on December 31. The purpose of the gathering is for the sake of being sent back into the world with a renewed commitment to walk in holiness. Such an interpretation of the message of Guadalupe would dovetail nicely with David Chapman's suggestions for a Methodist approach to Marian piety.[42] Mary's *fiat* sums up the Methodist covenant prayer, she fully embodies the promises and petitions that Methodists make during the "watchnight" services. As such, Mary can be approached as an icon of the covenant that Methodists are trying to live into, and if an icon, then "Mary is both an inspiration to follow and a worthy re-

---

39. John Wesley, *A Farther Appeal to Men of Reason and Religion, Part III*, I.2, *Works* 11:273.

40. This is a distinction Wesley knew and employed when considering the authenticity of the violent physical phenomena associated with some conversions (Wesley, November 25, 1759, *Journal and Diaries IV, Works* 21:234ff.).

41. Hans Urs von Balthasar, *In the Fullness of Faith: On the Centrality of the Distinctively Catholic* (San Francisco, CA: Ignatius, 1975), 116ff.

42. David Chapman, "Mary, Icon of the Covenant: A Methodist Perspective," *One in Christ* 33.1 (1997): 55–66.

cipient of our devotion and veneration (*dulia*)."[43] Such bold statements require that we consider another aspect of the Guadalupan message—the image of the Virgin on Juan Diego's cloak or *tilma*.

Often it is said that the medium is the message. This is very much the case when it comes to the message of Tepeyac. The Guadalupan cult is built around an image that was not made by human hands. The Virgin's request for a shrine is precisely for the sake of the integrity and preservation of this message. Theologians like Virgil Elizondo have helpfully discussed how the rich message written on Juan Diego's *tilma* is born from the mestizaje of Aztec and Christian symbols.[44] Like the woman of Revelation 12, she appears clothed with the sun and standing on the moon. Like the people of Mexico, the Virgin is brown-skinned. And she wears a band around her waist like that worn by pregnant Mexica women. In brief, Mary appears as the Theotokos who offers Christ to Juan Diego. Much more could be said about the symbolism of the image. I mention these few details in passing to illustrate the thickness of this message.

Wesley's understanding of the role of images in the church is more limited than that affirmed by other Christian traditions. Images have a legitimate place in the church when they bear a gospel message.[45] Some images have been commissioned by God, and God works miracles through some images. Think of the seraphs resting on top of the ark of the covenant or of Moses's bronze serpent. But the role of images in Christianity has become confused throughout church history. "What were at first designed as monuments of edification, became the instruments of superstition."[46] Not that want of images immunizes one to the dangers of idolatry. Wesley is careful to warn Protestants about the perils of spiritual idols.

---

43. Chapman, "Mary, Icon of the Covenant," 65.

44. E.g., see Elizondo, *Guadalupe*.

45. John Wesley, "The Origin of Image Worship among Christians," *Works* (Jackson) 10:175.

46. Wesley, "The Origin of Image Worship among Christians," *Works* (Jackson) 10:175–77.

> Let the blind sons of Rome bow down
> To images of wood and stone;
> But I, with subtler art,
> Safe from the letter of thy word,
> My idols secretly adored,
> Set up within my heart.[47]

Nevertheless, Wesley saves his sternest remarks for the images of wood and stone. Even in the case of images through which miracles were worked, the moment that an image or relic becomes an object of worship, it should be destroyed in the same way that King Hezekiah destroyed Moses's bronze serpent when the Israelites began to make offerings to it.[48]

In spite of these negative comments on images, I do not think being a Wesleyan means being an iconoclast. Images can serve as *libri laicorum*. Whatever else it may be, the image of Guadalupe is a book that tells a story. Thus, one Wesleyan response to this image would be to engage in a patient reading of its message. If the message is orthodox and edifying then the viewing of this image could be considered a prudential means of grace, but the image must not be confused with grace itself. The image is at most a means, and as such it cries *noli me tangere*. On this point, we would do well to listen to Balthasar's comments on the place of relics and images in Christian life: "The relics of the saints are entrusted to us only conditionally: they are more properly part of their resurrection reality and, like the Lord, they tell us not to hold on to them. At best they are a memento of the Spirit who indwelt them and who is as alive as ever in the Lord's Eucharist."[49]

Third, can a Methodist acknowledge miracles at Tepeyac? The Guadalupe story overflows with supernatural signs from the apparition of the Virgin to the out-of-season flowers to the image on Juan Diego's *tilma*. The healing of Juan Bernardino is the first of many miracles associated

---

47. John Wesley, "A Word to a Protestant," *Works* (Jackson) 11:193.

48. John Wesley, "Popery Calmly Considered," §5, *Works* (Jackson) 10:147.

49. Balthasar, *In the Fullness of Faith*, 116.

with Guadalupe.[50] Whether this event is a genuine miracle is not something I can competently adjudicate as a theologian. What I can do is offer a Wesleyan perspective on the theological significance of miracles.

Contrary to the views expressed by some of his contemporaries, Wesley believed God still worked miracles even in eighteenth-century England. Indeed, Wesley claimed to have witnessed cures that came about in supernatural ways and also recorded the visions witnessed by some of his followers.[51] Yet, whereas in the early church the purpose of miracles was to make manifest the holiness of the apostolic community, in the eighteenth century these signs made manifest the sovereignty of God. In other words, the purpose of miracles in the modern era is to confound deists who deny that God still acts in the world. Surprisingly, Wesley found such signs of the supernatural in tales of ghosts and witches. As Wesley states, "With my latest breath will I bear my testimony against giving up to infidels one great proof of the invisible world; I mean, that of witchcraft and apparitions, confirmed by the testimony of all ages."[52]

Nonetheless, Wesley found evidence of the invisible realm not only in its infernal manifestations but also in a more hopeful phenomenon—miracles at shrines. In his journal, Wesley recounts the story of Montgeron, a deist miraculously converted to Christianity during a visit to a Jansenist shrine in Paris:

> I read, to my no small amazement, the account given by Monsieur Montgeron both of his own conversion and of the other miracles wrought at the tomb of Abbé Pâris. I had always looked upon the whole affair as a mere legend, as I suppose most Protestants do, but I see no possible way to deny these facts without invalidating all human testimony. I may full as reason-

---

50. See Fernando de Alba Ixtilxóchitl, *Nican Motecpana* in *La Protohistoria Guadalupana,* ed. Lauro López Beltrán (México: Editorial Jus, 1966), 173–91.

51. John Wesley, "The Principles of a Methodist Farther Explained," *Works* 9:214. See also Wesley's account of the vision of the crucified Jesus experienced by a young woman of his acquaintance (August 29, 1748, *Journal and Diaries III, Works* 20:246). Wesley records other visions in his journals but withholds judgment on their authenticity or significance (e.g., September 7, 1755, *Journal and Diaries IV, Works* 21:28).

52. John Wesley, "Preface to a true Relation of the Chief Things which an Evil Spirit did and said at Mascon, in Burgundy," *Works* (Jackson) 14:290. Cf. his journal entry of May 25, 1768, *Journal and Diaries V, Works* 22:135.

ably deny there is such a person as Mr. Montgeron, or such a city as Paris in the world. Indeed in many of these instances I see great superstition as well as strong faith. But the "times of ignorance God does wink at" still, and bless the faith, notwithstanding the superstition.[53]

Wesley is aware that Montgeron's account is not free from superstitions and defects. Yet, Wesley is not willing to close his mind to the evidence of miracles at a Catholic (Jansenist) site. The insistence on the importance of supernatural phenomena for the coherence and confidence of Christian witness places Wesley on the same side as Laurentin and over against ecclesial deists who confine miracles to the primitive church. True, Christians walk by faith and not by sight, but miracles and apparitions play a vital role in keeping the church from closing in on itself.[54] In short, there is a need to find a golden mean between a radical skepticism that, as Laurentin states, "leads to asphyxia of the faith" and a credulous simplicity that "leads to superstition, illuminism and distortion of focus."[55]

Consider for a moment, what if God never sends anyone? What if there is no intercourse of humans and spirits (separate or otherwise)? Is not closing the door on Guadalupe giving up "one great proof of the invisible world"?[56] Should we allow "this weapon to be wrested out of our hands" because some people have mishandled it?[57] If the evidence of

---

53.   Wesley, January 11, 1750, *Journal and Diaries III, Works* 20:317–18.

54.   René Laurentin, "Fonction et statut des apparitions," in *Vraies et fausses apparitions clans l'Eglise*, ed. Bernard Billet (Paris: Editions P. Lethielleux, 1973), 149–96. According to Laurentin, miracles and apparitions matter. "C'est important, pour que la liberté de la communication avec Dieu ne se trouve pas remplacée par un système clos forme d'éléments et organisations terrestres" (160).

55.   Laurentin, *The Apparitions*, 31. Wesley was aware of the need to steer between this particular Scylla and Charybdis. As his remarks on the genuineness of spiritual manifestation show: "The danger was to regard extraordinary circumstances too much, such as outcries, convulsions, visions, trances, as if these were essential to the inward work, so that it could not go on without them. Perhaps the danger is to regard them too little, to condemn them altogether, to imagine they had nothing of God in them and were an hindrance to his work." Wesley, November 25, 1759, *Journal and Diaries IV, Works* 21:234.

56.   John Wesley, "Preface to a true Relation of the Chief Things which an Evil Spirit did and said at Mascon, in Burgundy," *Works* (Jackson) 14:290.

57.   Wesley, May 25, 1768, *Journals and Diaries V, Works* 22:135.

witchcraft, ghosts, and demons is enough to storm the bastions of deism, atheism, and materialism, what could the evidence of Marian intercessions accomplish?

Fourth, can a Methodist enjoy the fruits of Tepeyac? What are the fruits of the mission of Guadalupe? In Marian apparitions, the fruits test usually examines the transformation of the lives of those who encountered the Virgin (or her shrine). The first fruits of Guadalupe are the faith, hope, and love of Juan Diego. As I said earlier, Wesley seems to be wholly ignorant of the apparition of Mary in Mexico. The closest that Wesley comes to the Guadalupana is through his reading of the life of Gregory López. Wesley regarded López as a prime exemplar of the doctrine of Christian perfection. So highly did he think of this poor, Catholic mystic that Wesley published an abridgment of López's biography for the meditation and imitation of the Methodist people. From this abridged work, we learn that Gregory López's resolve to travel to Mexico in 1542 followed a miraculous encounter with Christ during a visit to the shrine of the Virgin of Guadalupe in Extremadura, Spain. It is unlikely (though not impossible) that López became a Guadalupano in New Spain. We do know that one of Wesley's points of contention with López is that his Catholic biographer "ascribed all [López's] virtues to the merits and mediation of the Queen of heaven."[58] Little wonder that Wesley referred to Gregory López as "that good and wise (though much mistaken man)."[59]

What would it take for a Methodist to say at least that much about Juan Diego? From a Methodist viewpoint, Juan Diego's biography is full of problematic beliefs and practices. But is Gregory López's case much better? López was a Spanish Catholic solitary mystic—all damning descriptions for an eighteenth-century Anglican. And yet Wesley held up López as an example of holiness because holiness is more a matter of the heart than of the head. We call people saints not because they are right but

---

58. Wesley, August 31, 1742, *Journal and Diaries II*, *Works* 19:294.

59. Wesley, August 31, 1742, *Journal and Diaries II*, *Works* 19:294.

because they are good. As Wesley affirms, "Without holiness, I own, no man shall see the Lord; but I dare not add, 'or clear ideas.'"[60]

A Methodist need not gloss over troublesome aspects of Juan Diego's biography to find aspects of his life that are worthy of imitation. Juan Diego's willingness to approach Bishop Zumárraga with the Lady's request demonstrates a holy boldness, with which early Methodists could have identified. His willingness to give up on a future family and earthly goods for the sake of serving in the shrine at Tepeyac is an act of self-denial, which though incongruent with Methodism's missional priorities is still admirable in its complete dedication to the work of God. If Methodists patiently read and meditated on the life of Juan Diego, they might be able to join one of his biographers and exclaim, "May we serve [Christ] as he did and withdraw from all the distracting things of this world so that we might also attain the eternal joys of heaven!"[61] If Juan Diego could be recognized by Methodists as an exemplar of Christian perfection, then much of the way would be paved for an authentically Wesleyan Guadalupanismo. A Methodist life of Juan Diego "that good and wise (though much mistaken) man" might be the best remedy for the bitter taste left in the mouth of Methodists from the years of abuse suffered from "Guadalupanos."[62]

60.　Wesley, Sermon 130, "On Living without God," §15, *Works* 4:175. Internal quotation marks added for clarity.

61.　Fernando de Alba Ixtilxóchitl, *Nican Motecpana* in *La Protohistoria Guadalupana*, 191. The original Spanish reads: "¡Ojala que así le sirvamos y que nos apartemos de todas las cosas perturbadoras de este mundo, para que también podamos alcanzar los eternos gozos de los cielos!" It is not clear from the Spanish whether the antecedent to "le sirvamos" is Christ, the Virgin, or even Juan Diego. But for a Methodist, the best way to read the text is to make Christ the antecedent.

62.　In the nineteenth century, Guadalupanismo sparked murderous rampages such as the execution of twenty-two Anglicans in Puebla on December 12, 1879. Allegedly, the executioners' cry was: ¡Viva la *Guadalupana*! (See Cody C. Unterseher's essay, "Mary in Contemporary Protestant Theological Discourse," above, pp. 29–50). In this connection, one might recall the wisdom of George Lindbeck's words on the necessity of an intrasystematic coherence for a statement to be true: "The crusader's battle cry *Christus est Dominus*, for example, is false when used to authorize cleaving the skull of the infidel (even though the same words in other contexts may be a true utterance)" (*The Nature of Doctrine: Religion and Theology in a Postliberal Age* [Philadelphia, PA: Westminster, 1984], 64). In other words, the persons who cried '¡Viva la *Guadalupana*! as they martyred the Anglican congregants lied.

Wesleyan Guadalupanismo

The contradictory responses to the presence of the Virgin of Guadalupe at Adalberto United Methodist Church in Chicago signal the need for further reflection. I believe that the range of Methodist responses to *La Morenita* is not limited to outright rejection, naïve acceptance, or, worst of all, cynical tolerance. In this essay, I have attempted to begin clearing the ground for a different kind of response. I have sought to plow the fields of Methodist history and theology in order to discern a Wesleyan way to honor Juan Diego and Our Lady. Admittedly, the fields are not exactly ripe for the harvest. The obstacles that have to be removed to make way for a possible Wesleyan Guadalupanismo are considerable. One of the chief difficulties facing the appropriation of Guadalupe in a Hispanic Methodist context is that Catholic-Protestant injuries are not "of old, unhappy, far-off tales and battles long ago" but freshly inflicted wounds.[63] No essay can overcome this painful living record. Instead, I have directed my efforts to clearing some of the theological obstacles to a Wesleyan reception of Guadalupe.

Followers of Wesley should have no problem in acknowledging the possibility and benefit of apparitions, miracles, and visions. It pleases God to work in these ways to confound the proud and also to keep Christianity from turning into a closed system. Of course, Methodists would want to insist that the most important visitation is the invisible indwelling of the Holy Trinity and the most important miracle conversions. The graces that Christians are to seek earnestly and pursue are the sanctifying graces. We are to aspire not only for those gifts that inform us about God (prophecies, miracles, and tongues) but also for those that conform us to God (faith, hope, and love).

For a Methodist, the clearest way into the Guadalupan mystery is through Juan Diego and hymnody. On the one hand, if Charles Wesley could write a hymn about Mary Magdalene being sent to disciple the apostles of humankind, is it completely unimaginable that a Wesleyan could write a hymn about Juan Diego being sent to disciple the Span-

---

63. Resolution 97, "Resolution of Intent—With a View to Unity," in *The Book of Resolutions,* 273.

ish missionaries?[64] On the other hand, if John Wesley could learn about Christian perfection from Gregory López, could not Methodists learn about the universality of God's call to holiness from Juan Diego? Sadly, the difficulty of discerning genuine exemplars of holiness from aspirants and counterfeits has led many Methodists to abandon the attainment of sanctity as impracticable. My point is that only a Methodist church capable of recognizing saints like Juan Diego will be capable of welcoming miracles like Guadalupe.[65]

This is not to say that all Latinos must be Guadalupanos. For Roman Catholics, even when the most careful, judicious investigation is conducted and the Catholic Church renders a positive judgment on the status of an apparition like Guadalupe, the "yes" is neither infallible nor universally binding.[66] Catholics are free to dissent from the church's judgment on an apparition as long as their dissent is marked by humility and respect. Methodists should not be held to a higher standard. If one can be a faithful Mexican Catholic without being a Guadalupano, then surely one can be an authentically Hispanic Protestant without being devoted to *La Morenita*. Still, some Methodists might find that the way of salvation leads them through Tepeyac.

---

64.   See Charles Wesley, *Hymns for Our Lord's Resurrection*, Hymn 3.

65.   For Roman Catholics, the status of canonizations and apparitions are related but distinct. "Si le Saint-Siège a solennise les canonisations, il ne les impose pas sous peine d'anathème, mais les propose plutôt comme une fête accordée aux souhait des fidèles. Quant aux apparitions, le Saint Siège a pris soin de déclarer de manière plus nette et plus explicite qu'il ne les imposait pas, mais les proposait seulement à l'adhésion des chrétiens" (Laurentin, "Fonction et statut des apparitions," 186).

66.   Laurentin, "Fonction et statut des apparitions," 149–96. According to Laurentin, "En ce qui concerne les apparitions (auxquelles, encore une fois, la théologie classique n'a jamais accordé la même certitude qu'aux canonisations), la garantie du magistère s'entend de même: le jugèrent autorise porte, au premier chef, sur l'orthodoxie du message, en second lieu sur l'authenticité du mouvement collectif de prière et de conversions qui en découle, en fin sur les miracles, dont on juge selon un processus analogue a celui des canonisations" (185). "Bref, les encouragements que des papes ont prodigues avec ferveur à Lourdes et a d'autres sanctuaires d'apparitions ne semblent pas changer le statut fondamentalement précis par Benoit XIV: un statut qui propose les apparitions a la liberté, a la générosité, a l'engagement du croyant, mais ne l'impose pas comme prescription et obligation" (188).

Chapter Six

Singing Wesley in Spanish

"O for a thousand tongues to sing." Thus begins Charles Wesley's most famous hymn. The inspiration for these words is variously attributed to Peter Böhler's exclamation, "Had I a thousand tongues, I would praise him with them all," and to a hymn by Johann Mentzer that began, "O dass ich tausend züngen hätte."[1] In either case, the origin of the phrase is far removed from the context of the Hispanic ministry that I was appointed to start when I graduated from Duke Divinity School. I had read John Wesley's sermons and I had sung Charles Wesley's hymns, but was it possible to read, sing, and ultimately live Wesley in Spanish? As I went deeper into the life of the Hispanic community in Durham, North Carolina, I was both asked and asked myself the question: What does being both Methodist and Hispanic mean?

As it happened, right around the time that I was starting in Hispanic ministry, I became involved in the production of *Obras de Wesley*, the critical translation into Spanish of a significant amount of John and Charles Wesley's works. The impetus for this publication came from Latin American Methodists struggling with questions of denominational identity in a context where the two principal religious options are Catholicism and Pentecostalism. Many Methodists arrived at the conclusion that the answer to these questions would not be found apart from an intentional retrieval of

---

1. *The United Methodist Hymnal* (Nashville, TN: United Methodist Publishing House, 1989), 56–57.

the Wesleyan heritage of the people called metodista. By providing a fresh translation of the Wesleys' works into Spanish, it was hoped that the way would be paved for evangelical renewal in the Wesleyan spirit.

As I have traveled throughout Latin America in the past few years, I have had the opportunity of seeing the firstfruits of the renewal sparked by reading Wesley in our native tongue. However, I have become convinced that the renewal largely neglects the Wesleyan hymnody. Even among those of us who want to ground the Methodist identity of our ecclesial communities in the Wesleyan revival of eighteenth-century England, our energies are more focused on retrieving John Wesley's sermons than Charles Wesley's hymns. It is as if we expect to relive the faith of the early Methodists without their spirituality, their *lex credendi* without their *lex orandi*.

In order to elucidate this claim, I want us to examine the Wesleyan roots of Methodist worship among Spanish speakers by attending to three translations of "O for a Thousand Tongues to Sing." From this brief historical survey I infer that Wesley's hymns have never played a significant role in the worship life of the people called metodista. I propose that until more of Charles Wesley's hymns are known and sung by his heirs south of the border (and north too), all attempts at Wesleyan, theological renewal will be one-sided and self-limiting: all prose, no verse.

O for a Thousand Tongues

The hymn "O for a Thousand Tongues to Sing" was written by Charles Wesley in 1739 to commemorate the anniversary of his conversion on Pentecost Sunday 1738. Originally, the hymn consisted of eighteen stanzas, the first of which began with a doxology.

> Glory to God, and praise and love
> Be ever, ever given,
> By saints below and saints above,
> The church in earth and heaven.

After this stanza, the hymn unfolds the principal loci along the way of salvation. Stanzas 2 through 6 are inward-looking. They commemorate Charles's Pentecost day experience when the Sun of Righteousness shone "on my benighted soul" (stanza 2). "'Twas then I ceased to grieve" (stanza 3). Then "with my heart I first believed" (stanza 4). "I felt my Lord's atoning blood" (stanza 5). "I found and owned his promise true" (stanza 6). A shift occurs in the seventh stanza, as the focus moves outward: "O for a thousand tongues to sing." "My gracious Master and my God, assist me to proclaim" (stanza 8). The singer goes on to proclaim the glories of Jesus's name. The name of Jesus is "music in the sinner's ears" (stanza 9) because "He breaks the power of canceled sin" (stanza 10), a reference to Christian perfection. Moreover, "He speaks and listening to his voice, new life the dead receive" (stanza 11). All people regardless of their condition are invited to come to Christ in their own way. The sick are invited: "Hear him ye deaf" (stanza 12). The peoples of the earth are invited: "Look unto him ye nations" (stanza 13) and "See all your sins on Jesus laid" (stanza 14). The most notorious sinners, "Harlots and publicans and thieves" (stanza 15), "Murderers and all ye hellish crew" (stanza 16) are called to "awake from guilty nature's sleep" (stanza 17) and join the author, the chief of sinners, in anticipating heaven here below "and own that love is heaven" (stanza 18). In sum, the hymn does not simply celebrate Charles's deliverance from sin but God's mighty deeds on behalf of humanity. In relating his own experiences, Charles is seeking to evoke a sympathetic "amen" from other believers. Hence, the use of the first-person pronoun in this and other Wesley hymns is not meant to be individualistic, but representative and invitational.[2]

Since it was first published in the 1740 collection of *Hymns and Sacred Poems*, this hymn underwent several significant adaptations. First, the hymn was placed at the beginning of the 1780 *Collection of Hymns for the Use of the People Called Methodists*, known as the "Large Hymn Book," that was the most extensive hymnal published during the time of the Wesleys. This collection was deliberately organized along the schema of the

---

2. On the question of Charles's use of personal pronouns in his hymns, see J. Ernest Rattenbury, *The Evangelical Doctrines of Charles Wesley's Hymns* (London: Epworth, 1941), 28–31.

Wesleyan *via salutis* (way of salvation), beginning with an exhortation for sinners to return to God.

In the 1780 book, Charles's hymn was no longer a poem celebrating the anniversary of his conversion experience but a universal invitation to join in the praise of Jesus Christ, the redeemer of humankind. Second, and probably on account of its location in the "Large Hymn Book," the hymn began with what was originally the seventh stanza, "O for a thousand tongues to sing." The force of the hymn became centripetal. It was less a personal testimony than a heraldic proclamation of the triumphs of Christ's grace in the world. Third, the more colorful verses describing harlots and murderers were cut from the poem. In all likelihood, while these descriptors were accurate for many of the earliest Methodists (one thinks of the Wesleys' work in the prisons of Oxford), they seemed less pertinent for the settled, respectable Methodists of the late eighteenth century.[3]

As the hymn crossed the Atlantic, several smaller revisions occurred. A few minor textual changes were introduced (for instance, changing "my dear redeemer's praise" to "my great redeemer's praise," a change that John Wesley would have endorsed given his dislike for his brother's occasional lapse into excessively familiar language for God). Also, the trend to trim from the original 1739 poem continued. Stanzas 1 through 6 of the 1780 version (7 through 12 of the 1739 version) were the ones most commonly printed. The concluding stanza of the 1739 version was added as a seventh stanza in the 1992 hymnal of The United Methodist Church with one key modification. Instead of ending the hymn by invoking the solidarity of forgiven sinners ("with me, your chief, ye then shall know"), worshipers are led to seek their one accord in Jesus: "In Christ, your head, you then shall know."

Hymnbooks of the nineteenth century (and beyond) continued the precedent of the 1780 hymnal in beginning their collections of hymns with "O for a Thousand Tongues to Sing." However, as the nineteenth century wore on, the original organization of Methodist hymnals along the schema of the *via salutis* gave way to a more dogmatic structure that

3. See Helmut Renders, "Mil linguas eu quisera ter," in *Mil vozes para celebrar: Tricentenário do nascimento de Charles Wesley*, ed. Luis Carlos Ramos (São Bernardo do Campo: Editeo, 2008), 177.

ordered hymns according to classical theological loci.[4] For example, instead of beginning as in the 1780 hymnal by "exhorting, and beseeching to return to God" and "describing the pleasantness of religion," the newer hymnals began with "the existence of God" and "the character of God." These hymnals still included the Wesleyan soteriological emphases on repentance, justification, and sanctification, but within a broader creedal structure. In most cases, the adoption of this new schema did not dislodge "O for a Thousand Tongues" from its place at the beginning of the collection, but it nudged it into the category of general worship. However, in some cases, the new schema meant moving "O for a Thousand Tongues to Sing" to the section dealing with justification and the new birth.[5] In short, the adoption of a creedal, catechetical schema, though a gain from a theological standpoint (one cannot live on soteriology alone) added stress to an already fragile Methodist identity.

Wesley Goes South

Missionaries from the various branches of the Methodist family began working among the Spanish-speaking populations of the Southwest of the United States, Mexico, and South America from the middle of the nineteenth century. As might be expected, the Methodism that was introduced into Latin America reflected that practiced in North America. At the danger of oversimplification, one could say that the people called metodista owed more to the camp meeting than to the Methodist society. Their worship practices were more revivalist than sacramental, and more American than Wesleyan. In any case, Methodist missionaries valued the role of music in shaping Christian identity and produced hymn books for Spanish speakers.

In 1875, the Methodist Episcopal Church, South, published the *Himnario de la iglesia metodista del sur* for the use of Methodists in Mexico

---

4. Karen Westerfield Tucker, *American Methodist Worship* (New York: Oxford University Press, 2001), 162–72.

5. See Hymns 349–350 in *A Collection of Hymns and Tunes for Public, Social, and Domestic Worship* (Nashville, TN: Southern Methodist Publishing House, 1885).

and the US Southwest.[6] The table of contents is organized according to the theological loci that became popular in the nineteenth century, but, curiously, the hymns themselves are organized according to their meter, beginning with those that are written in Long Meter (88.88), followed by Common Meter (86.86), Short Meter (66.86), and so forth. I do not know what the reasoning was for adopting this schema, but it is similar to that used for books of hymn tunes.[7]

The first hymns in Spanish were sung to the same tunes as they were in the United States. The result was a form that was alien to the receiving culture. The melodies were not culturally Indigenous but reflected the styles and preferences reigning in nineteenth-century North American Methodism. Of course, one would not expect it to be otherwise. The missionaries were going to pass on what they in turn had received. Nevertheless, there is a darker side to the story. North American missionaries had serious misgivings about the suitability of Latin American culture. These lands seemed to them to be much more conducive to the growth of syncretism and Catholicism than to the true gospel. They thought it better to keep the message in its original container. Spanish worship music was to be sung as much as possible to the same meter and melody as in the United States. So successful was the introduction of these musical forms into the piety of Latin American Protestants that many came to regard the tunes and styles brought by the missionaries to be the only real sacred music. Popular, Indigenous musical forms were rejected as "worldly."[8] Well into the middle of the twentieth century, Spanish-language hymnals were being published without a single example of a song set to a non-Euroamerican form. Even when new hymn texts were written by Latin American Christians, they were set to tunes that owed more to the Sunday school movement in North America than to the history and culture of Latin America.

---

6. *Himnario de la iglesia metodista del sur* (Mexico: Methodist Episcopal Church, South, 1875).

7. See Tucker, *American Methodist Worship*, 160.

8. Pablo Sosa, "Himnodia Metodista—Los Wesley EE.UU y América Latina," in *La tradición protestante en la teología latinoamericana. Primer intento: lectura de la tradición metodista*, ed. José Duque (San José, Costa Rica: Departamento ecuménico de investigaciones, 1938), 311.

Back to the 1875 *Himnario*, of the more than 100 hymns included in the collection, only five were written by Charles Wesley. One of these, "Con cánticos Señor," is of doubtful authorship. Incidentally, the translation of hymns to Spanish can make it very difficult to discover the original English text in order to ascertain authorship. In any case, the other 4 hymn texts are Wesley's: "Cariñoso Salvador" ("Jesus, Lover of My Soul"), "Oíd un son en alta esfera" ("Hark! the Herald Angel Sings"), "Yo tengo que guardar" ("A Charge to Keep I Have"), and "Tocad trompeta ya" ("Blow Ye the Trumpet"). "O for a Thousand Tongues" is conspicuous by its absence from this and other early Spanish hymnals. For example, the 1908 *Himnario cristiano para uso de las iglesias evangélicas* included 7 Wesley hymns (two of these of doubtful authenticity) among its 250 hymns and songs, but "O for a Thousand Tongues" was not one of these.[9]

One of the earliest translations of Charles's conversion hymn into Spanish was done by Henry Godden Jackson. Jackson was a missionary who supervised Methodist efforts in Buenos Aires from 1868 to 1878. In 1876, he published a collection of hymns titled *Himnos evangélicos para uso de las congregaciones cristianas*.[10] Of the 101 hymns in that collection, 57 are Jackson's own translations including "O for a Thousand Tongues to Sing." Since I have not been able to look at a copy of that 1876 collection, I cite the text as it appears in an 1890 Sunday school resource called *Himnos evangélicos para escuela dominical*.[11] Incidentally, it is the only Wesley text in that collection of hymns.

¡Mil voces para celebrar
(A thousand voices to celebrate)
De Jesús-Cristo el honor!
(The honor of Jesus Christ)
¡Mil voces para ensalzar
(A thousand voices to extol)

---

9. *Himnario cristiano para uso de las iglesias evangélicas* (Nashville, TN: Smith and Lamar, 1908). All translations from Spanish and Portuguese are my own.

10. Cristián Guerra Rojas, "La música en el movimiento pentecostal de Chile," http://www.scribd.com/doc/16313368/La-musica-en-el-pentecostalismo-chileno.

11. *Himnos evangélicos para escuela dominical* (Montevideo: La Oriental, 1890).

Los triunfos de mi redentor!
(The triumphs of my redeemer.)

¡Oh maestro mío! Dios de amor,
    (Oh, my teacher! God of love,)
Ayúdame a proclamar
(Help me to proclaim)
Las glorias de mi redentor;
(The glories of my redeemer)
Su dulce nombre a cantar.
    (His sweet name to sing.)

¡Jesús! el nombre encantador
(Jesus! The charming name)
Que inspira amor y gratitud,
    (That inspires love and thankfulness)
Es vida para el pecador,
(Is life to the sinner.)
Es paz, y gozo, y salud.
(It is peace, joy, and health.)

Al preso libertad, perdón,
(To the prisoner, liberty, forgiveness)
Al penitente da Jesús;
(To the penitent Jesus gives.)
Y él la plena redención
    (And he the full redemption)
De todos, hizo en la cruz.
(Of all accomplished on the cross.)

Jackson continues the trend of abridging the hymn, translating only the first four stanzas of the 1780 version. A few features of the Spanish text are worth noting. First, Jackson changed the meter of the original from Common Meter (86.86) to Long Meter (88.88). Second, he doubled the phrase *mil voces*. The imagery of a "thousand voices" is polyvalent. It can carry the sense of the German phrase at the root of the English, "O dass ich tausend züngen hätte" ("O, if I had a thousand tongues"). As such it is an expression of the believer's desire to give herself wholly to the worship of Christ. On the other hand, the phrase *mil voces* can refer to the number of people praising God. In this case, the phrase has a strong missional directive. In other words, in the first instance, the believer longs for more capacity to praise God ("increase my faith"). Notice the explicit allusion to sanctification in the fourth verse, which speaks of *plena redención* ("full redemption"). In the second, the singer longs for more choristers, mission ("increase the faithful"). These twin emphases, sanctification and mission, are not in competition but constitute the core of Methodist identity.

The second translation of "O for a Thousand Tongues" I want us to consider is the one done by J. N. de los Santos, a Presbyterian minister from Texas. Unfortunately, I have not been able to ascertain the date of publication for this hymn or its role in Methodist hymnody in the first half of the twentieth century. What is certain is that this version was popular among Mexicans and Mexican Americans. De los Santos's translation was placed as the first hymn in the 1973 *Himnario metodista* prepared for the Rio Grande conference of The United Methodist Church.[12] This is also the version of "O for a Thousand Tongues" still found today in the hymnal of the Methodist Church of Mexico, though in that collection it is not placed at the beginning but in the section on "Salvation and Liberation."[13] It is worth noting that the number of Wesleyan hymns in these two collections, though larger than in early twentieth-century hymnbooks, is still relatively small. In the *Himnario metodista* of the Rio Grande conference, 15 out of 394 hymns are attributed (questionably in two cases) to Charles Wesley, 8 out of 331 in the Mexican hymnal.

> Quisiera yo poder cantar
> (I wish that I could sing)
> Las glorias de mi Rey,
> (The glories of my king)

---

12. *Himnario metodista* (Nashville, TN: United Methodist Publishing House, 1973).

13. *Himnario metodista* (México: Casa Unida de Publicaciones, 2006).

Su dulce gracia proclamar,
(His sweet grace to proclaim)
En medio de su grey.
(In the midst of his flock.)
Mi gran maestro y mi Dios
(My great teacher and my God)
Quisiera proclamar
(I wish that I could proclaim)
Tu nombre con celeste voz
(Your name with heavenly voice)
A todos sin cesar.
(To all without ceasing.)
Al dulce nombre de Jesús
(At the sweet name of Jesus)
Las penas huirán,
(Afflictions will flee,)
Pues el da paz, salud, y luz,
(For he gives peace, health, and light)
Y calma a nuestro afán.
(And calms our anxieties.)
Destroza las cadenas Él,
(He breaks the chains)
Y libertad nos da;
(And gives us liberty.)
Las culpas todas del infiel,
(All the faults of the impious)
Su sangre lavará.
(his blood will wash away.)

Like Jackson, de los Santos translated the first four stanzas of the 1780 version. The omission of the word "thousand" in the first stanza is striking and gives the opening words of the hymn a decidedly less exuberant tone. Also, the use of the conditional tense in the first two stanzas (*quisiera poder cantar* and *quisiera proclamar*) introduces an element of reserve lacking in the original. In this version, the proclamation of Christ's grace occurs in the midst of the congregation (*su grey*) rather than in "the earth abroad."

Another feature of this translation is the muted sanctification motif in the fourth stanza. The blood of Christ washes away all our guilty stains (justification), but no mention is made of "breaking the power of canceled sin" (the eradication of inbred sin) or *plena redención* (entire sanctification). Now, it is altogether possible that I am reading too much into the use of verb tenses and the omission of certain words; after all, unlike Jackson, de los Santos is trying to keep to the meter of the original and he should be allowed some poetic license. However, the overall impression one is left with from this translation is that Christ's work of redemption is both more individual and less far-reaching in scope than what Charles Wesley envisioned.

The final translation of "O for a Thousand Tongues" I want to consider is Federico Pagura's. Pagura, a Methodist bishop in Argentina and an accomplished hymn writer, is by far the most assiduous translator of Wesley's hymns into Spanish. Of the 65 Wesley hymns that are compiled in *Obras de Wesley*, Pagura was involved in the translation of all but 22. *Cántico Nuevo*, a hymnal produced in 1962 for Protestants in South America, included 17 hymns attributed to Wesley (out of 476 total), possibly making it the most Wesleyan hymnal published in Spanish.[14] Of these 17 Wesley hymns, 10 were translated by Federico Pagura, including "O for a Thousand Tongues to Sing."

Mil voces para celebrar
(A thousand voices to celebrate)
A mi libertador;
(my liberator)
Las glorias de su majestad,
(The glories of his majesty)
Los triunfos de su amor.
(The triumphs of his love.)
El dulce nombre de Jesús
(The sweet name of Jesus)
Nos libra del temor;
(Frees us from fear)

---

14. *Cántico Nuevo: Himnario Evangélico* (Buenos Aires, Argentina: Methopress Editorial, 1962).

En las tristezas trae luz,
(In sadness he brings light,)
Perdón al pecador.
(Forgiveness to the sinner.)

El habla y al oír su voz,
(He speaks and listening to his voice)
El muerto vivirá;
(The dead will live)
Se alegra el triste corazón,
(The sad heart rejoices,)
Los pobres hallan paz.
(The poor find peace.)

Although not the opening hymn of *Cántico nuevo*, this text is found in the first section of the hymnal under the subject of praise to God the Father, a strange choice given that the hymn's praise is more explicitly oriented to the Son. Pagura's translation appears to be textually indebted to Jackson's translation as far as the first opening phrase, which is identical in the 1876 and 1962 versions: *Mil voces para celebrar*. But here the resemblance ends. In Pagura's translation, the original meter is kept, but only two stanzas of the 1780 version (1 and 3), along with stanza 11 of the 1739 version, remain. Moreover, the translation of "redeemer" as *libertador* (liberator) in the first stanza is startling. Pagura appears to be tipping his hat to the concerns of liberation theology. Jesus as liberator evokes a set of images of social justice and preferential option for the poor that are of great relevance in the Latin American context. Also, in retaining Jackson's translation of the word "praise" as *celebrar* ("to celebrate") and eliminating the more archaic *ensalzar* ("extol"), Pagura underscores the dimension of fiesta to the act of worship. In raising her voice, the believer invites a thousand other voices to join in throwing God a party.

The success of this translation and Pagura's stature as a hymnodist and Methodist leader prompted The United Methodist Church to commission him to translate stanzas 2, 4, 5, and 9 of the 1780 version for inclusion in the present United Methodist hymnal.[15] That he was satisfied with the accuracy of his first translation is evident in that he did not make any changes to the verses that he had published previously.

Mi buen Señor, maestro y Dios,
(My good Lord, teacher and God)
Que pueda divulgar
    (May I be able to proclaim)
Tu grato nombre y su honor
(Your gracious name and your honor)
En cielo, tierra y mar.
(In heaven, earth and sea.)

Destruye el poder del mal
(He breaks the power of evil)
Y brinda libertad;
(And grants liberty;)
Al más impuro puede
    (To the most impure he is able)
Dar pureza y santidad.
(To give purity and holiness.)

Escuchen, sordos, al Señor;
(Listen, deaf, to the Lord;)
Alabe el mundo a Dios;
    (The world praises God)
Los cojos salten, vean hoy
(The lame leap, and today behold)
Los ciegos al Señor.
    (The blind, the Lord.)

En Cristo, pues, conocerán
(In Christ, then, you shall know)

---

15. Carlton R. Young, *Companion to The United Methodist Church Hymnal* (Nashville, TN: Abingdon, 1993), 482.

La gracia del perdón
(The grace of forgiveness)
Y aquí del cielo gozarán,
(And here heaven you shall enjoy)
Pues cielo es su amor.
(Because heaven is his love.)

Pagura's translation restores the emphasis on sanctification to the hymn as well and conveys the generosity and exuberance of the invitation to praise Christ. The staying power of this translation is evident from the fact that the new Spanish version of the United Methodist hymnal (which in effect took the place of the 1973 *Himnario metodista*) was named *Mil voces para celebrar*, and that this hymnal opens not with de los Santos translation of "O for a Thousand Tongues to Sing" but with Pagura's version. The fact that a new translation of this hymn could be introduced to Spanish-speaking United Methodists at this late date is possibly a sign of both the tenuous hold of de los Santos's version and more generally of the status of Wesley's hymns among Hispanic Methodists.

Singing Wesley in Spanish

As we have seen, the journey of Charles Wesley's conversion hymn into Spanish is a circuitous one with false starts and dead ends. It is sobering to consider that of the more than nine thousand hymns written by Charles Wesley, fewer than seventy have ever been translated into Spanish, and that no one hymnal has carried even twenty of these.

Compare the pace of translation of Wesley's hymns with that of Wesley's sermons. By 1892, Primitivo Rodríguez had published a Spanish edition of Wesley's fifty-two "standard sermons."[16] This version was widely used until the publication of *Obras de Wesley* beginning in 1994. Even at its best, the Wesleyan heritage in Latin America (and indeed in the United States too) has been more homiletical than hymnic, prose rather

---

16. See Justo González's introduction to *Obras de Wesley, Tomo 1* (Franklin, TN: Providence House, 1996), 16–17.

than verse. Of course, Spanish-speaking Methodists honor the memory of Charles Wesley as hymnodist. Everyone knows he wrote thousands of hymns and that Methodists are a singing people. Yet, as we have seen, even Charles Wesley's most famous hymns are virtually unknown and unsung among his heirs. Charles Wesley is admired. John Wesley is studied.

Why does this matter? What is at stake in singing Wesley in Spanish? In brief, a Wesleyan spirituality. The songs we sing in worship both shape and are shaped by our common life. S. T. Kimbrough's statement is right on the mark: "If the hymns/songs one sings are shallow, there is a strong possibility that the spirituality from which they emerge is shallow, and the spirituality they spawn will likely be the same."[17] It is not that Methodists should only sing Wesley hymns; John and Charles included hymns from other authors in their collections (John even translated a hymn from Spanish to English). However, Wesley's hymns have a unique contribution to make to the formation of Christians. S. T. Kimbrough observes that Charles Wesley's hymns arose from a particular spiritual ethos.[18] Consider Charles's daily reading of the Scriptures in the original languages, the praying of the Psalter, his devotion to the Eucharist, weekly fasts, and service to the poor. A life ordered by these practices and oriented toward the sanctification of believers is the wellspring of Wesleyan hymnody. As J. H. Nelson, a Methodist missionary to Brazil, averred, translating Charles Wesley's hymns "made it now possible to sing in Portuguese the 'full salvation' from all sin."[19] The same is true in Spanish. Wesley's hymns celebrate the possibility of attaining Christian perfection in a way that is unmatched in nuance and intensity by virtually any other Christian hymn writer. Ultimately, the most important issue at stake in singing Wesley in Spanish is not Wesley but the formation of a people whose motto is *santidad* (holiness). To accomplish this goal, more translations of Wesley's hymns would be a good first step, but other steps would be needed.

---

17. S. T. Kimbrough, "Lyrical Theology: Theology in Hymns," *Theology Today* 63 (2006): 22–37, esp. 37.

18. S. T. Kimbrough, "Lyrical Theology."

19. Omir Wesley Andrade, "Os Hinos de Charles Wesley e sua Influência na Hinologia do Metodismo Brasileiro," in *Mil vozes para celebrar: Tricentenário do nascimento de Charles Wesley*, ed. Luis Carlos Ramos (São Bernardo do Campo: Editeo, 2008), 223.

In the words of D. T. Niles, "The gospel came to us as a potted plant. We have to break the pot and set the plant in our own soil."[20] Charles's hymns arrived to Latin America in English planters. Newer settings of Wesley's hymns and Wesleyan motifs are necessary. Admittedly, breaking the pot carries the risk of damaging the plant. However, if the plant is to thrive and grow roots in the culture, then the risk must be taken. Taking the risk might mean breaking "O for a Thousand Tongues" loose from the pot of its Common Meter and shaking loose the soil of Azmon (the melody with which it is most commonly associated in the United States) in order to plant it in the soil of Mexican cumbia or Caribbean salsa. Taking the risk might mean following the example of Charles Wesley, who turned the prose of theological books by Daniel Brevint and biblical commentaries by Matthew Henry into verse. Taking the risk might also mean composing a series of hymns on Virgilio Elizondo's book *The Future Is Mestizo*. What would this sound like? It might sound like Pablo Sosa's setting of Charles Wesley's hymn "Stranger Unknown" to a melody written in the Argentine gaucho style.[21] It might sound like Federico Pagura's original hymn "Tenemos esperanza" ("We Have Hope") sung to a tango. In any case, it would sound Latin and feel Wesleyan.

---

20. Cited by C. Michael Hawn, "The Fiesta of the Faithful: Pablo Sosa and the Contextualization of Latin American Hymnody," *The Hymn* 50 (1999): 32.

21. Pablo Sosa, "Wesley gaucho: un poema olvidado de Charles Wesley," *Cuadernos de teología* 22 (2003): 383–89.

Chapter Seven

Evangelizing During the Eclipse: Wesleyan and Lascasian Reflections

The Great Ecclesial Eclipse

Some members of the media described the solar eclipse of August 21, 2017, as the "Great American Eclipse."[1] The buzz generated by the astronomical event was tremendous. Stores sold out of solar viewing glasses. From west to east, people took vacation days and travelled to places where the eclipse would be total. The blocking of the light, the path of totality, and other similar descriptors likewise apply to Christianity in North America, which is undergoing the "Great Ecclesial Eclipse."

Signs of the Great Ecclesial Eclipse abound. The demographic decline of mainline Christianity; the sexual abuse crisis in the Roman Catholic Church; the increasing secularization of US society; the growing schisms in United Methodism—these all signal an eclipse loud and clear. The church still looms large in the North American landscape, but as a

---

1. E.g., see Edward Steed, "The Great American Eclipse of 2017," *The New Yorker* (September 4, 2017) and Sean Lakind, "The Great American Eclipse and Its Effect on Retail Traffic," *Forbes* (September 12, 2017).

shadow of itself, its light often a mere afterglow. The effects of the Great Ecclesial Eclipse on the social fabric of the United States have been the subject of much writing.[2] Instead of focusing on the signs and effects of Christian decline, this chapter explores one cause for the dimming of the light—what the Uruguayan Methodist theologian Mortimer Arias calls "an eclipse of the kingdom," which obscures the church's announcement of God's reign.[3] In other words, the Great Ecclesial Eclipse is a crisis of evangelism.

In what follows, I bring Mortimer Arias's Wesleyan reflections into conversation with those of the Spanish Dominican missionary Bartolomé de las Casas, with the intent to seek guidance on how to practice evangelism when the church itself obscures the light of the gospel.

To Spread Scriptural Holiness over the Land

The Wesleyan movement began with the conviction that God intended them "to reform the nation, and in particular the Church, to spread scriptural holiness over the land."[4] Given this originating impulse, evangelism has been the subject of concerted theological reflection, missional experience, and even ecclesial handwringing among the people

---

2. E.g., Ross Douthat suggests the collapse of mainline Christianity cleared the way for fringe—even heretical—views to flourish: "You can't have fringes without a center, iconoclasts without icons, revolutionaries without institutions to rebel against. We have always been a nation of heretics, but heresy has never had the field to itself." Ross Douthat, *Bad Religion: How We Became a Nation of Heretics* (New York: Free Press, 2012), 6. Timothy Carney argues the church played a key role in fostering a sense of communal belonging. After studying voting patterns in the early Republican primaries in 2016, Carney found a correlation between declining congregations and the sense of alienation that moved voters toward Donald Trump when the field of Republican candidates presented several more conventionally conservative choices. "To explain Trump's core supporters, many commentators pointed to the factories that were closing, but they should have been pointing to the churches that were closing." Timothy P. Carney, *Alienated America: Why Some Places Thrive While Others Collapse* (New York: HarperCollins, 2019), 12.

3. Mortimer Arias, *Announcing the Reign of God: Evangelization and the Subversive Memory of Jesus* (Eugene, OR: Wipf & Stock, 1999), 12.

4. John Wesley, "The 'Large' *Minutes,* A and B (1753, 1763)," Q.4, *Works* 10:845.

called Methodists and metodistas.[5] The work of Mortimer Arias expresses an abiding concern for the heirs of Wesley and their call to evangelism.[6]

In *Announcing the Reign of God*, Arias argues, "Jesus had only one theme, only one gospel…the kingdom of God."[7] The language of the kingdom of God marks Jesus's preaching and parables. Through words and actions, he announces the good news of God's jubilee, where debts are forgiven and prisons are emptied. Jesus's acts of healing, exorcisms, and miraculous feedings are signs of the immanence and imminence of God's reign. God's reign is a holistic reality, both personal and social, present and future. Jesus's mission was "kingdom evangelization,"[8] and this mission became the apostles' commission.

> The christocentric apostolic proclamation is about the kingdom—the presence of the kingdom with a name and a face: Jesus from Nazareth. *There*, in Jesus Christ himself, is where we have the indispensable and indestructible link between Jesus's evangelization and apostolic evangelization.[9]

In interpreting Arias's work, Philip Meadows distinguishes between two paradigms for evangelism: the soteriological and the missiological.[10] The traditional soteriological paradigm promotes preaching aimed at conversions, focusing on personal salvation. This paradigm can be overly individualistic, anthropocentric, and mechanistic, privatizing faith and

---

5. E.g., see Jack Jackson, *Offering Christ: John Wesley's Evangelistic Vision* (Nashville, TN: Abingdon/Kingswood, 2017); James C. Logan, ed., *Theology and Evangelism in the Wesleyan Heritage* (Nashville, TN: Abingdon/Kingswood, 1994); William J. Abraham, *The Logic of Evangelism* (Grand Rapids, MI: Eerdmans, 1989); Mark R. Teasdale, "The Contribution to Missiology by United Methodist Scholarship on Evangelism," *Missiology: An International Review* 41.4 (2013): 452–61.

6. Arias, *Announcing the Reign of God*, xiv.

7. Arias, "The Kingdom of God," *Wesleyan Theological Journal* 23.1–2 (1988): 33–45, 35.

8. Announcing the kingdom was central to Jesus's ministry, as was evident to all who encountered Jesus. As Arias notes, even the devil implicitly acknowledges the importance of the theme by tempting Jesus with the kingdoms of the world. Arias, *Announcing the Reign of God*, 3.

9. Arias, *Announcing the Reign of God*, 58.

10. Philip R. Meadows, "The Journey of Evangelism," *Oxford Handbook of Methodist Studies*, ed. William J. Abraham and James E. Kirby (New York: Oxford University Press, 2009): 413–30.

narrowing the scope of evangelism to counting converts by inducing decisions for Christ. The missiological paradigm seeks to correct these errors by making discipleship the goal of evangelism, in which disciples are initiated into Christian community. This paradigm—promoted by Arias—focuses on God's eschatological kingdom as inaugurated in Christ. Despite its pitfalls, the soteriological paradigm nevertheless has its place in a healthy Wesleyan approach to evangelism. As Meadows avers, "Wesley can easily be taken as a champion of personal salvation with its logic of proclamation and conversion. On the other hand, he claimed that the movement was raised up to spread scriptural holiness, not merely to make converts."[11]

The Wesleyan paradigm is both soteriological and missiological. Wesley's sermon "The Way to the Kingdom" displays the soteriological aspect. Here, Wesley connects Mark 1:15 with Romans 14:17, identifying the kingdom of God with "true religion," which, according to Paul, is not found in outward observances but in joy and holiness in the Holy Spirit.[12] He writes:

> This holiness and happiness, joined in one, are sometimes styled in the inspired writings, "the kingdom of God," (as by our Lord in the text), and sometimes, "the kingdom of heaven." It is termed "the kingdom of God" because it is the immediate fruit of God's reigning in the soul. So soon as ever he takes unto himself his mighty power, and sets up his throne in our hearts, they are instantly filled with this "righteousness, and peace, and joy in the Holy Ghost." It is called "the kingdom of heaven" because it is (in a degree) heaven opened in the soul.[13]

The missiological paradigm shines in Wesley's understanding of the commission of the Methodist movement to reform the church and spread scriptural holiness across the land. This paradigm also animates Wesley's decision to preach outdoors at George Whitefield's request, including his choice of text:

---

11. Meadows, "The Journey of Evangelism," 415.

12. John Wesley, Sermon 7, "The Way to the Kingdom," I.1, *Works* 1:218.

13. John Wesley, Sermon 7, "The Way to the Kingdom," I.12, *Works* 1:224.

At four in the afternoon I submitted to "be more vile," and proclaimed in the highways the glad tidings of salvation, speaking from a little eminence in a ground adjoining to the city, to about three thousand people. The Scripture on which I spoke was this (is it possible any one should be ignorant that it is fulfilled in every true minister of Christ?): "The Spirit of the Lord is upon me, because he hath anointed me to preach the gospel to the poor. He hath sent me to heal the broken-hearted, to preach deliverance to the captives and recovery of sight to the blind, to set at liberty them that are bruised, to proclaim the acceptable year of the Lord."[14]

Methodism's original evangelistic impulse is both soteriological and missiological. Laceye Warner furthers this understanding, arguing the Wesleyan movement is called to be both centripetal (pressing in, or inviting) and centrifugal (pressing out, or proclaiming). The Methodist movement of spreading of scriptural holiness cannot simply be centrifugal, for "a merely centrifugal understanding of evangelism does not offer a comprehensive representation of biblical foundations or life in communities of faith in which disciple-making is a defining characteristic."[15] On the other hand:

> The centripetal approach has its problems and challenges. The authenticity of our Christian life becomes essential and decisive. As many as are attracted may be repelled by our style of life and our attitudes. It is one thing to go "out there" and tell the people "the old, old story"; it is another thing to bring them here and show them how Christians live.[16]

In other words, Wesleyan evangelism includes going out and gathering in, apostolicity and hospitality.[17]

Wesleyan evangelism's soteriology and missiology is fundamentally christological. As Wesley says, "We are not ourselves clear before God

---

14.   John Wesley, April 2, 1739, *Journal and Diaries II*, *Works* 19:46.

15.   Laceye C. Warner, *The Method of Our Mission* (Nashville, TN: Abingdon, 2014), 27.

16.   Mortimer Arias, "Centripetal Mission, or Evangelization by Hospitality," in *The Study of Evangelism: Exploring a Missional Practices of the Church*, ed. Paul W. Chilcote and Laceye C. Warner (Grand Rapids, MI: Eerdmans, 2008), 433.

17.   Mortimer Arias, "Centripetal Mission or Evangelization by Hospitality," *Missiology* 10 (January 1982): 69–71.

unless we proclaim Christ in all his offices,"[18] which means Wesleyan evangelism centers on announcing Christ in his offices as priest, prophet, and king. This christological vision of soteriology and missiology has been obscured by the Great Ecclesial Eclipse, diminishing the radiance of our witness to the gospel.

The Eclipse of Evangelism

Eclipses are not confined to northern latitudes or to the people called Methodists. The people called metodista have also walked in the path of totality as they sought to "spread scriptural holiness over the land."[19] Arias quips that theological curricula include Christology (the study of Christ) and pneumatology (the study of the Pneuma, the Spirit) but not basileialogy (the study of the *basileia*, the kingdom).[20] Magali do Nascimento Cunha notes that many churches in Brazil aspiring to reach great multitudes dream of having a TV channel or radio program. "There is a tendency here to transform the religious content into one more commercial product because it receives the same treatment (logic of production and broadcast) as any other spread by the media."[21] José Duque laments how Wesley's vision of seeing the world as his parish has not been clearly perceived by the people called Methodists or metodistas. Wesley imagined all places and communities as beloved by God, touched by prevenient grace, and in need of pastoral accompaniment. Too many times, Wesley's heirs have understood their mission in parochial terms with demarcated boundaries that separate the sacred from the secular.[22]

---

18.   John Wesley, Sermon 36, "The Law Established through Faith, II," I.6, *Works* 2:37.

19.   John Wesley, "The 'Large' *Minutes,* A and B (1753, 1763)," Q.4, *Works* 10:845.

20.   Mortimer Arias, "The Kingdom of God," 36.

21.   Magdali do Nascimento Cunha, "Comunicação, mídia e riligião: Lições do movimento wesleyano," in *Teologia wesleyana, latino-americana e global: Uma homenagem a Rui de Souza Josgrilberg* (San Bernardo do Campo, Brazil: Editeo, 2011), 269–79, 276.

22.   José Duque, "El mundo es mi parroquia porque otro mundo es posible," *Teologia e prática na tradição wesleyana: Uma leitura a parti da América Latina e Caribe* (San Bernardo do Campo, Brazil: Editeo, 2005), 205–17, 208.

Eclipses are not new. In its pilgrimage through history, the church has experienced all kinds of eclipses. The light of the face of Jesus Christ has been blocked by powers and principalities enthroned in the world and the church. Its holistic view of God's work of transfiguring the world has been narrowed to saving souls. Its immanence has been reduced to new social structures. Its imminence has been dimmed to ominous apocalyptic visions inspiring terror rather than hope. If, as the church mothers and fathers taught, the church is God's "lesser light to rule the night" (Gen 1:16),[23] then, at times, the eclipses have been lunar: the world has interfered with the light of the gospel. The evangel has been absorbed by the realities of a culture that is antithetical to the vision of Christ. At other times, the eclipses have been solar: the light of the gospel has been blocked by the church itself. This happened during the conquest of the Americas, when the cross was weaponized and employed as an instrument for nation-building.

Even when shrouded in the deepest darkness, the church has never failed to twinkle with the light of Christ. Arias states: "The message and perspective of the kingdom of God has always been there in the biblical record, in the memory of the church, and in the mission of the people of God. It has been a subversive memory."[24] The subversive memory of Jesus informed the ministry of Bartolomé de las Casas. When the expansionist and extractivist dreams of Spain and the church in the Americas eclipsed the vision of God's reign announced in the Gospels, Las Casas presented an alternative. By considering Las Casas's understanding of how the gospel

---

23. The symbol of the moon has been used as an apt expression for the mystery of the church throughout the centuries, from St. Augustine to Hugo Rahner. Augustine writes, "The moon is understood to be the Church, because she has no light of her own, but is lighted by the only-begotten Son of God, who in many places of holy Scripture is allegorically called the Sun." St. Augustine, *Exposition on the Book of Psalms*, Ps. XI §3, in *Nicene and Post-Nicene Fathers*, Series 1, vol. 8, ed. Philip Schaff (Grand Rapids, MI: Eerdmans; Christian Classics Ethereal Library, 2009), 91. Hugo Rahner sees the lunar figure as a helpful way of summing up the mystery of the church's life cycle. *Symbole der Kirche: Die Ekklesiologie der Väter* (Salzburg: Otto Müller Verlag, 1964), 92–93.

24. Arias, *Announcing the Reign of God*, 12.

brings people into God's reign, we can learn lessons for evangelizing during our Great Ecclesial Eclipse.

Bartolomé de las Casas and *The Only Way*

Few ecclesial eclipses have been as great as that which resulted from the church's expansion across the Atlantic to what came to be known as the Americas. The depth of the darkness was far from obvious to the Spanish and European colonizers who ranked the "discovery" of the lands and their peoples as an event whose historic and theological significance was only inferior to God's creation of the cosmos and the saving events of the Incarnation.[25] Such hyperbolic language was common but not universal. No doubt, the first cries of protest came from the Indigenous persons whose lands and lives were being consumed, but these cries found an echo among Dominican missionaries such as Bartolomé de las Casas.

The story of Las Casas is complex and summed up by his own admission of being "good but blind."[26] In this section, I engage Las Casas's reflections on evangelism during the great ecclesial eclipse of the conquest. In particular, I draw attention to a treatise he wrote during a period of theological reflection on the island known as Quisqueya by its Indigenous inhabitants, which the Spanish later named La Hispaniola. The title of the treatise was *De unico vocationis modo*. The backdrop for the treatise was the forced conversions and *en masse* baptisms of Indigenous people.

In *De unico*, Las Casas mounts an extensive and rigorous scholastic rebuttal of these evangelistic approaches adopted by fellow missionaries, in particular the Franciscans, and he argues instead for a peaceable proclamation of the gospel. A refrain encapsulates the argument:

---

25. See Alain Milhou, "Las Casas: Prophétisme et millénarisme," *Études* (March 1992): 398–99.

26. Carlos Castillo Mattasoglio, *Libres para creer: la conversión según Bartolomé de las Casas en la Historia de las Indias* (Lima, Perú: Fondo Editorial de la Pontificia Universidad Católica del Perú, 1993), 27, 73.

> The one and only way to instruct human beings in the true religion was instituted by divine providence for all the world and for all times, namely, that way which is persuasive of the intellect with reasons and is gently alluring and encouraging of the will.[27]

Indigenous people cannot be forced into faith because they are human beings with understanding, will, and freedom. The gospel cannot be announced in a credible fashion if the audience is not "free to believe"—which is also the apt title of a book by Carlos Castillo Mattasoglio, Archbishop of Lima.[28] In *De unico*, Las Casas offers a Thomistic account of the dynamics of the saving encounter of God and humans from the perspective of the Americas. God's actions toward the Indigenous and the response of the Indigenous are noncompetitive. In what follows, I offer an abridgment of Las Casas's synthesis.[29]

Las Casas's argument has a strong teleological orientation. There is only one way to lead human beings to Christianity because humanity only has one end: eternal communion with God. God creates human beings for this purpose and constitutes them with the capabilities and principles needed to respond to the summons of this end. In the journey toward their goal, human beings are moved and self-moved. Because the goal of eternal communion with God transcends human capacities, God gifts human beings with a constitution ready to respond to grace.

The end is supernatural, but the way is not unnatural; quite the contrary, the way to union with God entails the full flourishing of humanity. According to Thomistic theology, human beings achieve union with God

---

27. Bartolomé de las Casas, *Obras Completas, Vol. 2: De unico vocationis modo*, §3, ed. Paulino Castañeda Delgado y Antonio García del Moral (Madrid: Alianza Editorial, 1990), 16; hereafter *De unico*. All translations are my own. For more information on composition dates and textual problems in *De unico*, see Jesús Ángel Barreda, "Ideología y pastoral misionera en el 'De unico vocationis modo,'" *Studium* 21 (1981): 186–354, and his introduction to *Obras Completas, Vol. 2: De unico vocationis modo*, i–xvi.

28. Carlos Catillo Mattasoglio, *Libres para creer: La conversión según Bartolomé de las Casas en la Historia de las Indias* (Lima: Pontificia Universidad del Perú, 1993).

29. My analysis of Las Casas's *The One and Only Way* appears in an earlier form in Edgardo Colón-Emeric, "Thomas's Theology of Preaching in Romans: A Lascasian Application," in *Reading Romans with St. Thomas Aquinas*, ed. Michael Dauphinais and Matthew Levering (Washington, DC: Catholic University of America Press, 2012), 83–100.

"by knowledge and by love."[30] Thus, the one and only way into communion with the Father, Son, and Holy Spirit requires the movement of the intellect (by the persuasiveness of the truth) and of the will (by the attractive presentation of the good). The acts of the intellect and the acts of the will are specified by different objects: the acts of the intellect are elicited by *truth*, whereas the acts of the will are drawn towards the *good*. And these hang together. In the words of Augustine, *credere est cum assensu cogitare*—to believe is to think with assent—and assent involves the will.[31] Faith, therefore, is a joint act of the intellect and the will. Las Casas writes:

> For those who do not know what pertains to faith and religion to come to believe, it is necessary for their reason and understanding to be quiet and still, and in this way, kept from any nuisance and from all that could disturb them. Furthermore, it is necessary that these have more than a little bit of time for reason to run freely and fully. This being the case, it is necessary for the understanding to judge and admit that that is true, and that the will does not experience any violence or anything repulsive, but delights in listening to what has been proposed regarding faith and religion and adheres to it and loves it and desires it as a pleasing good.[32]

The great ecclesial eclipse of the sixteenth century obscured the only way of evangelism. For Las Casas, the eclipse does not overshadow the *content* of the proclamation—the catechetical works of his fellow missionaries are orthodox—rather, Las Casas opposes the unorthodox *way* in which they share the catechism. He denounces his Spanish peers' method of spreading the gospel, calling it new, irrational, unnatural, and anti-catholic. The colonial way runs contrary to good pedagogy, philosophical methodology, and the biblical witness. It runs contrary to the nature of rational creatures, which should move freely—not violently—toward their end. It runs contrary to the nature of the mind, which requires time

---

30. Thomas Aquinas, *Summa Theologiae* 3.2.10. See also Michael Sherwin, *By Knowledge and By Love: Charity and Knowledge in the Moral Theology of St. Thomas Aquinas* (Washington, DC: Catholic University of America Press, 2005).

31. Las Casas, *De unico* 7, 28.

32. Las Casas, *De unico* 12v, 43.

and tranquility to think matters over. It runs contrary to the nature of the will, which is attracted by the good. For Las Casas, reason is the source of freedom, and whatever disturbs reason limits freedom.

> Like the stars that usually give us light and germinate the ground cease to do so when dark clouds block them, thus is the case with the understanding and reason, which shine and lighten human beings for the understanding of truth when they are impeded by the haze of disturbances.[33]

A forced faith is a theological impossibility. Will the survivors of genocide cogitate with delight the teaching of their captors? Will their hearts be strangely warmed by the cry of their orphaned children? Las Casas insists Christians should be bearers of peace, not instruments of war. They should preach deliverance to the captives, not consign them to colonial subjugation on earth and eternal damnation in hell. The colonial way of evangelism is worse than a dead end; it is a gaping maw. By contrast, the only way is life and light, because that is who Christ is.

> It was not seemly for the goodness of Christ and his royal dignity to acquire, propagate, or preserve his reign with weapons of war or physical slaughters, devastations, violence, pillaging, and similar calamities. On the contrary, he accomplishes these things through the sweetness of doctrine, the sacraments of the church, by forgiving and showing compassion, with gifts, peace, meekness, charity, and beneficence.[34]

Christ is the chief evangelist in *De unico* and the way incarnate. Jesus is "the eternal law, the art and wisdom of the Father, the Word dressed in mortal flesh, through whom God the Father spoke to the world. All that he said conformed to the mind and will of the Father and, thus, to the most high Trinity."[35] Jesus's words and deeds have weight because he is the Father's wisdom, so "all that Christ established and ordained while living in the mortal flesh was established and ordained by divine

---

33. Las Casas, *De unico* 11v, 38.

34. Las Casas, *De unico* 192, 478.

35. Las Casas, *De unico*, 79, 214.

providence."[36] The great ecclesial eclipse of the sixteenth century eclipsed Christ's light—and without this light, the difference between the sword and the cross was hard to see.

Evangelism under a Starless Sky

The Methodist theologian Elsa Tamez describes the situation of Christianity in Latin America as walking "bajo un cielo sin estrellas" (under a starless sky).[37] The metaphor evokes absence and mystery. The absence results from the social conditions of Latin America, where millions are abandoned and cast off as irrelevant. The mystery is that lights yet shine in the night. Christians are called to seek lights "at home, in the street, in institutions and organizations, in oneself and the other, for they must exist."[38] The starry cloak of life has been torn in the Latin American context, but it still shines. The subversive memory of Jesus persists. The only way remains passable.

When asked for general guidance on preaching, John Wesley extended the following counsel: the best way to preach is "1. To invite. 2. To convince. 3. To offer Christ. 4. To build up: and to do this in some measure in every sermon."[39] We can extend his guidance on preaching to evangelism, and the movements of evangelism track with the movement of grace along the Wesleyan way of salvation: to invite (prevenient grace), to convince (convincing grace), to offer Christ (justifying grace), and to build up (sanctifying grace). Evangelism is thus God's work, but not without human participation. In this section, I point to lights twinkling along the Lascasian way that illumine Wesley's counsels for announcing God's reign under a starless sky.

---

36. Las Casas, *De unico* 57v, 161.

37. Elsa Tamez, *Bajo un cielo sin estrellas: Lecturas y meditaciones bíblicas* (San José, Costa Rica: Departamento Ecuménico de Investigaciones, 2001).

38. Tamez, *Bajo un cielo sin estrellas*, 20.

39. John Wesley, "The 'Large' *Minutes*, A and B (1753, 1763)," Q.44, *Works* 10:859.

To Invite

The only way to announce the reign of God is to invite all people by pointing out the signs of its presence in the world and in the church. In the history of the Americas, the church has obscured its invitation to the reign of God via its collusion with oppressive regimes. In certain places and historical periods, the church has instead been a sign of the kingdom's absence. The use of biblical passages like Luke 14:23 ("compel them to come in") as justifications for conquest hid the nature of the kingdom of God. "Forced conversions," which, as Las Casas taught, were both a historical reality and a theological impossibility, may lack for modern apologists, but softer forms of cultural and economic power are still employed to invite people to Christian faith.

Shockingly, the flawed community so horribly struggling to fulfill its commission to "invite" is nevertheless part of the gospel message. The church and the kingdom may not be identical, but they are inseparable. Its commission is not an endorsement for imperialistic expansion but an invitation to participate in God's new reality. This reality has taken root throughout the world, not as an invasive species but as a testament to the surprising fertility of native soils in which seeds of the gospel thrive. As Arias explains,

> To disciple the nations does not involve the sending of transcultural missionaries from a given center to the rest of the world. In our world of migrations, both forced and voluntary, the seed of the gospel is carried by disciples around the earth, and new missionary frontiers are opened up in the most unexpected places, both in the old missionary centers or in islands of peripheries of the Christian world.[40]

The church is commissioned to invite all people because God's grace is for all. No human being is a blank slate waiting to be written upon. Christians can presuppose all people bear at least seeds of knowledge.[41] In

---

40. Mortimer Arias, "Church in the World: Rethinking the Great Commission," *Theology Today* 47.4 (1991): 410–18, 417.

41. Drawing on Aquinas's "praeexistunt in nobis quaedam scientiarum semina" ("seeds of knowledge pre-exist in us") as found in Aquinas, *Disputed Questions on Truth* 11.1.

the words of Paul, ever "since the creation of the world, God's invisible qualities—his eternal power and divine nature—have been clearly seen, being understood from what has been made" (Rom 1:20). Of course, the mystery of sin has obscured this knowledge with superstitions and fables. However, genuine knowledge of God lies within or underneath these stories, serving as a special kind of principle or preparation for the gospel.[42] Grace illumines the truth that there is only one human nature created for one common purpose: eternal communion with God. When it comes to the call of God, there is no difference between people living in one land or another, one culture or another, one age or another.[43]

The Lascasian way calls for inviting people to see the signs of God's kingdom in our midst. In this connection, Las Casas speaks of the importance of miracles in the apostolic preaching:

> It is clear that those great and wondrous benefits which the apostles did miraculously for those who welcomed or heard them, were most effective in winning the love and pleasure of the hearers, and naturally apt at making them kind, meek, and attentive, disposing them to hear and receive the doctrine that was being preached and believed.[44]

Las Casas's words should not be heard as a summons to lulling naive people into belief by pulling miracles out of the hat. Instead, signs help introduce people to the kind of kingdom being announced. To invite all people to welcome the in-breaking of God's kingdom calls for highlighting signs of its presence. Evangelism therefore depends on miracles for its confirmation, whether by performing miracles or recounting them.

---

42. Las Casas, *De unico* 20v, 60: "quasi principium quoddam speciale," or "as a special principle."

43. Las Casas, *De unico* 145–45v, 368.

44. Las Casas, *De unico* 63, 174–76: "It was sufficiently attractive, animating and suitable to gain the interest of hearers to heal the sick without price, to raise the dead, to cleanse the lepers and cast out demons from possessed bodies. For nothing, in general, do people receive with as much pleasure and gratitude great gifts and benefits from others, for to these they are obliged to respond with gratitude without any forcing of the will."

Wesley likewise spoke of miracles, even claiming to have witnessed "supernatural" cures.[45] Indeed, he believed the rise of Methodism itself was a sign.

> At this day the gospel leaven—faith working by love, inward and outward
> holiness, or (to use the terms of St. Paul) "righteousness, and peace, and joy
> in the Holy Ghost"—hath so spread in various parts of Europe, particularly
> in England, Scotland, Ireland, in the islands, in the north and south, from
> Georgia to New England and Newfoundland, that sinners have been truly
> converted to God, throughly changed both in heart and in life; not by tens,
> or by hundreds only, but by thousands, yea, by myriads! The fact cannot
> be denied: we can point out the persons, with their names and places of
> abode. And yet the wise men of the world, the men of eminence, the men
> of learning and renown, "cannot imagine what we mean by talking of any
> extraordinary work of God"! They cannot discern the signs of *these times*!
> They can see no sign at all of God's arising to maintain his own cause and
> set up his kingdom over the earth![46]

These wondrous signs of the reign of God are signs that point to cracks in plausibility structures of the present age. Miracles are signs, not proofs, of God's favor and God's promised kingdom.[47] Miraculous signs need not accompany each and every act of evangelism, but without signs, the spread of scriptural holiness is simply unimaginable.

---

45.   Wesley, "The Principles of a Methodist Farther Explained," V.1, *Works* 9:214.

46.   John Wesley, Sermon 66, "The Signs of the Times," II.4, *Works* 2:527.

47.   For Wesley, not all miracles are from God, e.g., the devil's lying wonders (τέρατα ψεύδος) (Wesley, "The Principles of a Methodist Farther Explained," V.5, *Works* 9:219). In addition to demonic signs, there are also the lies of charlatans and the superstitions of the credulous. These false signs call into question the self-attesting character of true signs and highlight our need for spiritual discernment. However, even authentic miracles are ambiguous in their effects. Pharaoh's heart was not softened by Moses's wondrous works. The Pharisees were not persuaded by Jesus's healing of the blind man. Miracles cannot convert the person; only the convicting grace of God can accomplish this mighty work. As Wesley argues, for the unbeliever, "Nothing will ever be an effectual proof to these of the holy and acceptable will of God, unless first their proud hearts be humbled, their stubborn wills bowed down, and their desires brought, at least in some degree, into obedience to the law of Christ" (Wesley, "The Principles of a Methodist Farther Explained," V.4, *Works* 9:218).

To Convince

The only way to announce the reign of God calls for convincing people of the truth of this gospel. Grace, whether prevenient, convincing, justifying, or sanctifying, is God's gift to give. However, God commissions the church to be an instrument of grace by telling the story of Scripture in a way that is "persuasive of the intellect with reasons and is gently alluring and encouraging of the will."[48] Historical and philosophical movements have questioned the universal hospitality of this story, obscuring the vision of human beings as creatures capable of God. This obscurity casts shadows, two of which dominate in the history of the Americas: the ranking of peoples on a scale of human development, and dividing the intellect from the will—or, differently said, the independence of what we know from what we love.

Under the starless sky of the Americas, Las Casas draws attention to the integration of the mind and the will in the act of faith. Faith is an act of the intellect, and announcing God's reign requires giving people thoughts to ponder. Thinking precedes believing. Not everyone who thinks believes, but all who believe think.[49] Las Casas's confreres insisted on producing catechisms and preaching guides that presented and exposited the truths of the Apostles' Creed and the Lord's Prayer in the Indigenous languages.[50] Only after a clear presentation of the gospel in their native language could the Indigenous people properly exercise their reason in community and deliberate over what they heard before deciding whether to give their assent. This last point highlights another significant aspect of the light of faith: faith is an act of the will. The attractiveness of the gospel, the goodness of its promises, induce the will to direct reason to accept what has been proposed and cling to it as credible.

---

48. Las Casas, *De unico* 3, 16.

49. Las Casas, *De unico* 7, 28: "credere … est cum assensu cogitare," drawing on Augustine's phrasing in *De praedestinatione sanctorum*, cap. 2.

50. See Miguel Ángel Medina, *Los dominicos y América: Doctrina cristiana para instrucción de los indios* (Salamanca: Editorial San Esteban, 1987); Ramón Hernández, Gregorio Celada, Brian Pierce, et al., *El grito y su eco: El Sermón de Montesino* (Salamanca: Editorial San Esteban, 2011).

The credibility of the teaching is connected to the credibility of the teacher. According to Aquinas, "To believe always means: to believe some-one and to believe something."[51] In this connection, Las Casas emphasizes the importance of holiness. Preachers should be holy: holy in their way of living, holy in their way of preaching. If preachers are wolves among sheep, if they proclaim captivity to the free, or if they preach war instead of peace, then, barring some great miraculous intervention from God, people will not believe.

Underscoring the significance of holiness for convincing people of the gospel's truth is not an excuse for intellectual indolence. If Christians are going to stimulate the minds of their communities with reasonable argu-ments for—and credible examples of—the salvific uniqueness of Christ, then they need to know their subject matter well. The reign should be announced in a winsome fashion that both exercises the mind and moves the will. Christian evangelists thus benefit from the study of rhetoric and pedagogical methods. That said, intellectual formation and technical ex-pertise are insufficient for proclaiming the gospel persuasively. Holiness matters, particularly when evangelizing under a starless sky.

Holiness persuades reason with the truth of a life transformed. And holiness moves the will by presenting the hearer with the possibility of being equally transformed. The holiness of the message and the holiness of the messenger belong together. God can bring faith about without any messenger whatsoever, but this is not the usual way. Only a person who is gentle, humble, meek, and peaceful will earn the trust necessary for the gospel to gain a joyful hearing. The fact that many Indigenous persons believed the gospel despite the unholy way in which it was introduced is a sign that God has intervened in wonderfully unexpected ways.[52] The Catholic tradition offers an example of this kind of divine intervention:

---

51. Josef Pieper, *Faith, Hope, Love*, trans. Clara Winston, Richard Winston, and Mary Frances McCarthy (San Francisco: Ignatius, 1997), 29, discussing Aquinas's "Ad fidem pertinet aliquid et alicui credere" as found in *Summa Theologiae*, 2-2.129.6.

52. As Las Casas puts it, "nisi per magnum miraculum," or "except by some great mira-cle." Las Casas, *De unico* 174v, 439.

the apparition of the Virgin of Guadalupe offering Christ in a new way to Juan Diego.[53] This leads us to the next point.

To Offer Christ

The only way to announce the reign of God calls for offering Christ. In the words of Las Casas, "It is clear that to preach the kingdom of heaven or the kingdom of God means that Christ himself is the kingdom."[54] Christ is the kingdom in person, wisdom incarnate, and the fountain of all grace. He is the evangel and the evangelizer. Under a starless sky, evangelism follows an encounter with the risen Christ in the peripheries.

The lands known to Las Casas as the Indies presented challenging contrasts of light and darkness. On the one hand, the cultures of the Taínos, the Incas, and the Aztecs were quite different from European cultures. On the other hand, these very cultures showed signs of the grace of God at work among them, and none were as prepared to receive the gospel as the Indigenous peoples of these lands. This receptivity presented a great opportunity for announcing the gospel to a mass of humanity who had never heard it, but this opportunity accompanied the violent expansion of Europe and the subjugation of new peoples to the Spanish crown. Amid these complexities and contradictions, Las Casas learned to discern Christ in the bodies of the Indigenous. He confesses, "I leave Jesus Christ our God in the Indies being flogged, afflicted, struck, and crucified, not once, but thousands of times."[55]

Evangelism under a starless sky calls for a movement that starts from the periphery. As Arias says, "In Christian terms, to reach is to be reached. To evangelize is to be evangelized."[56] Through the practice of evangelism,

---

53. See chapter 5, "Wesleyans and Guadalupans: A Theological Reflection," for more on the Virgin of Guadalupe and the possibilities for a Wesleyan Guadalupanismo, which includes recovering Wesley's appreciation of miracles and saintly holiness.

54. Las Casas, *De unico* 58, 162.

55. Bartolomé de las Casas, *Historia de las Indias*, ed. André Saint-Lu (Caracas: Biblioteca Ayacucho, 1986), 3.138.

56. Arias, "Centripetal Mission, or Evangelization by Hospitality," 434.

the church does not only offer Christ but encounters and receives Christ anew.[57] Christians should proclaim the gospel to all nations, but the poor—the "little ones"—should receive priority.[58] This prioritization is Christological: "Everything we do for our neighbor is not merely activism, social service or social action; it is a service to Christ himself."[59]

To offer Christ from the margins is to affirm the prevenience of God's grace and God's preferential option for the poor. God's love is universal, but the way is preferential. It is not top down but bottom up. As de Souza puts it, for Wesley, "The offer of universal salvation during an age that discriminated against the wretched and the disinherited of the earth was an affirmation of the unconditional love of God for the excluded."[60] Wesley found greater openness to the message of the gospel among people living on the margins of society than among those at the center. After preaching to an affluent congregation, he expected little good to come from it, "For we begin at the wrong end. Religion must not go 'from the greatest to the least,' or the power would 'appear to be of men.'"[61]

---

57. Joerg Rieger argues that Las Casas's identification of Christ is momentous. "Las Casas finds a fresh encounter with the Amerindians. The people are not merely the recipients of the gospel, they also participate in the reality of Christ to some degree." Joerg Rieger, *Christ and Empire: From Paul to Postcolonial Times* (Minneapolis, MN: Fortress, 2007, Kindle Edition, Loc 2626). That said, Rieger argues this identification has its blind spots, and the two-way street for evangelism promoted by Arias and others is underdeveloped by Las Casas (Loc 2565–71).

58. Arias, "Rethinking the Great Commission," 417.

59. Arias, "Rethinking the Great Commission," 414.

60. José Carlos de Souza, *Leiga, ministerial e ecumênica: A igreja no pensamento de John Wesley* (San Bernardo do Campo, Brazil: Editeo, 2013), 143.

61. John Wesley, Friday, May 25, 1764, *Journal and Diaries IV, Works* 21:465–66. Wesley's language evokes Hebrews 8:11, which speaks of the new covenant: "They shall not teach one another or say to each other, 'Know the Lord,' for they shall all know me, from the least of them to the greatest" (NRSV). Commenting on this verse, Wesley applies this promise to "all real Christians" and explains how "in this order the saving knowledge of God ever did and ever will proceed; not first to the greatest, and then to the least. But 'the Lord shall save the tents,' the poorest, 'of Judah first, that the glory of the house of David,' the royal seed, 'and the glory of the inhabitants of Jerusalem,' the nobles and the rich citizens, 'do not magnify themselves,' Zech. xii, 7." Wesley, *Explanatory Notes Upon the New Testament, Volume II* (London: Thomas Cordeux, 1813), 271.

Christians amplify the power of truth by embracing Christ's poverty in solidarity with his marginalized little ones. Gustavo Gutiérrez notes that Las Casas's encounter with Christ in the Indigenous helps him see in a new way, a more Indigenous way. Gutiérrez writes, "It is not a mere question of the importance of a *direct knowledge* of a particular state of affairs. It is also a matter of adopting the *perspective of others*, other persons, in order to experience and understand from within the situations and events in which those persons are caught up."[62] Truth, poverty, and vulnerability connect. In the words of Joseph Ratzinger, "Poverty is the truly divine manifestation of truth: thus, it can demand obedience without involving alienation."[63] Poverty is an eloquent witness of truth. By voluntarily taking nothing, the apostles gained credibility. By giving up the props of colonial power, Lascasian missionaries were sent "as poor, yet making many rich; as having nothing, yet possessing everything" (2 Cor 6:10). The light of Christ shines for the life of the world. However, during times of ecclesial eclipse, his light shines from the social margins with a distinctive glow. This glow is evident, as Arias writes in song, in the midst of life: "You are in the work of the field and the city . . . in joy and also in pain, . . . to turn this world into the jewel of your reign."[64]

---

62. Gustavo Gutiérrez, *Las Casas: In Search of the Poor of Jesus Christ* (Maryknoll, NY: Orbis, 1993), 87.

63. Joseph Ratzinger, *Many Religions—One Covenant: Israel, the Church and the World* (San Francisco: Ignatius, 1999), 109. In writing on the relationship of Christianity to other religions, Ratzinger reflects on how the incarnation of the Word, the *kenosis* of God the Son, opens a path that acknowledges confidence in divine revelation while preserving humility before God's mystery—namely, the path of poverty. Ratzinger offers the classic example of Plato's account of the trial of Socrates. Socrates considers himself a gadfly sent to arouse the city of Athens from its philosophical slumber. As one might expect, the Athenians asked him for proof. What evidence did Socrates have to substantiate such a bold—even boastful—claim? To which Socrates replied, "I have a sufficient witness that I speak the truth, namely, my poverty" (*Apologia*, 31c).

64. Mortimer Arias, "En medio de la vida," in *Mil voces para celebrar: Himnario metodistas*, ed. Raquel Martinez (Nashville, TN: Abingdon, 1996), 375. The translation is my own.

To Build Up

The only way to announce the reign of God calls for building a community modeled not after New Spain or New England, but the new creation. The Great Commission in Matthew envisions a catechetical mission: evangelism as disciple-making. Evangelism entails forming citizens of the kingdom—not colonial subjects or consumers—and this formation includes culture.

When Las Casas tested the argument of *De unico*, he commissioned Dominican missionaries who worked with Indigenous people to translate biblical stories and catechetical lessons into song in the native languages. Custom is like nature.[65] Through repetition, certain practices assume the character of a habitus. Custom is like a second nature, rendering some actions easy to perform.[66] The opposite is also true: new acts are unfamiliar, are difficult to perform, and feel unnatural. A new teaching, precisely as unknown, appears alien and less credible than a familiar saying. Because the gospel message introduces previously unknown doctrines, preaching should repeat that message, making it familiar and generating receptivity among listeners. According to Las Casas, frequently repeating what Christians believe causes in the listener an almost natural disposition toward the truths of the faith. Generating this habit or custom requires time and the patient goodwill of the listener. For Las Casas, songs served this purpose, and the results were extraordinary. Within months of the arrival of the missionaries, the Indigenous people had composed new verses of

---

65. As Aquinas argues, repeated acts form dispositions and justify calling custom a "second nature." In the original Latin: "Cum multoties inclinatur, determinatur ad idem a proprio movente, et firmatur in eis inclinatio determinata in illud, ita quod dista dispositio superinducta, est quasi quaedam forma per modum naturae tendens in unum. Et propter hoc dicitur, quod consuetudo est altera natura." Aquinas, *Disputed Questions on Truth* 1.9.

66. Las Casas, *De unico* 34–35, 94: "non est natura, sed est quasi natura" ("it is not nature, but it is like nature").

their own, abolished sacrifices, built a church, and become evangelists to neighboring populations.[67]

Las Casas, like the Wesley brothers, found that persuading the intellect with reason and gently alluring the will called for both prose and poetry, as well as forming societies and institutions. In effect, announcing the reign of God for Las Casas and the Wesleys requires forming a new culture, a culture that aims to prepare people as witnesses of the new creation, as heralds of the reign of God. Arias argues, "Christian education is the evangelization of each generation, learning the way of the kingdom at each stage of life and through all human experiences."[68] Studying Scripture, praying, and serving as a community of disciples prepare the people called metodista to be witnesses of the kingdom.

Eschatology informs our understanding and practice of evangelism. Our vision of the end fuels our motivations for announcing the gospel. When Wesley preached outdoors, he aimed to "follow the blow" of the sermon with discipleship in small groups. George Whitefield's evangelism emphasized justification to the near exclusion of sanctification. After Wesley observed the results of Whitefield's work in places like Pembrokeshire, he foreswore evangelism that did not "follow the blow" of the sermon with induction into Christian society[69]:

> I was more convinced than ever that the preaching like an apostle, without joining together those that are awakened and training them up in the ways of God, is only begetting children for the murderer. How much preaching has there been for these twenty years all over Pembrokeshire! But no regular societies, no discipline, no order or connection. And the consequence is that nine in ten of the once awakened are now faster asleep than ever.[70]

---

67. See Lewis Hanke's masterful account in *Del único modo de traer a todos los pueblos a la verdadera religion*, ed. Agustín Millares Castro (Pánuco, México: Fondo de Cultura Económica, 1942), xxxiii–xxxviii, which I consider in more depth in Edgardo Colón-Emeric, "Thomas's Theology of Preaching in Romans: A Lascasian Application," 100.

68. Arias, "Rethinking the Great Commission," 412.

69. John Wesley, March 13, 1763, *Journal and Diaries II, Works* 19:318.

70. John Wesley, August 25, 1763, *Journal and Diaries IV, Works* 21:424.

Methodists were instructed to preach both God's commands and God's promises. A divine indicative leads to a divine imperative. "Christ died for you: therefore die to sin. Christ is risen: therefore rise in the image of God. Christ liveth evermore: therefore live to God, till you live with him in glory."[71] The interplay of indicative and imperative has an eschatological direction that marks the way Methodists should participate in God's mission. As Wesley observes, "So we preached; and so you believed. This is the scriptural way, the Methodist way, the true way."[72]

The eschatological vision of the kingdom guides Methodist doctrine, worship, and mission. Its originating vocation to reform nation and church by spreading scriptural holiness envisages a radical transformation of persons and structures. Moreover, to speak of the world as his parish is different from an ecclesiastical empire encompassing the world. The purpose of evangelism is not the "churchification" of the world,[73] but to announce God's reign by inviting all, convincing by the persuasive power of truth and goodness, offering the poor Christ, and building up holy communities. Arias adds, "The World Parish, the church in the world, is not the kingdom, but she is at the service of the kingdom as witness and sign."[74]

Given its eschatological orientation, evangelism is an expression of hope. Announcing the reign of God calls for what Pablo Neruda calls *ardiente paciencia* (burning patience). This virtue is not a problem for those schooled by the Spirit in the ways of holiness—for as another Pablo affirms, "Love is patient" (1 Cor 13:4).[75]

---

71.   John Wesley, Letter to an Evangelical Clergyman (Dec. 20, 1751), *Letters II*, ¶31, *Works* 26:488.

72.   Wesley, Letter to an Evangelical Clergyman (Dec. 20, 1751), *Letters II*, ¶32, *Works* 26:488–89.

73.   Arias, *Announcing the Reign of God*, 87.

74.   Arias, "The Kingdom of God," 44.

75.   In his acceptance speech for his Nobel Prize in literature, Pablo Neruda said, "Al amanecer, armados de una ardiente paciencia, entraremos a las espléndidas ciudades." Cited in Eldin Villafañe, *Seek the Peace of the City: Reflections on Urban Ministry* (Grand Rapids, MI: Eerdmans, 1995), 43. As Pablo Neruda notes, the phrase comes from the poet Arthur Rimbaud. See https://www.nobelprize.org/prizes/literature/1971/neruda/25206-pablo-neruda-nobel-lecture-1971/.

Conclusion: Dreaming from the Shadowlands

The Great Ecclesial Eclipse has turned the Americas into shadowlands. Contemporary readers criticize Las Casas as another face of empire.[76] In their view, the only way of evangelism is really an act of epistemic conquest. The postcolonial critique of Las Casas clarifies the nature of the eclipse that he tracked and did not altogether escape. Signs of the eclipse of the kingdom are everywhere. Some identify the kingdom with church growth, others with social reform. In some cases, the kingdom has been understood as an abstract metaphysical reality; in others it has been collapsed into apocalyptic, cataclysmic events. At times, some look for the kingdom in communities that serve as "islands of the kingdom in the ocean of a world contaminated by sin."[77] All of these visions of the kingdom are reductive. They are not altogether wrong; they are simply incomplete.

Christians need not fear the darkness of the shadowlands. The eclipse is not total and will not last because, in spite of it all, the church and its subversive memory of Jesus persevere. The mission of the Methodists and metodistas "to reform the nation, and in particular the Church, to spread

---

76. "Las Casas cannot see beyond the Eurocentric view of the Americas, in which the highest generosity and charity would be bringing Amerindians under the control and tutelage of the true religion and its culture. The natives are the underdeveloped potential Europeans." Michael Hardt and Antonio Negri, *Empire* (Cambridge, MA: Harvard University Press, 2000), 116. For a counterpoint in thoughtful dialogue with the decolonial critique, see David M. Lantigua, "The Freedom of the Gospel: Aquinas, Subversive Natural Law, and the Spanish Wars of Religion," *Modern Theology* 31.2 (2015): 312–37. For more, see Daniel Castro, *Another Face of Empire: Bartolomé de Las Casas, Indigenous Rights, and Ecclesiastical Imperialism* (Durham, NC: Duke University Press, 2007) and Juan Comas, "Historical Reality and the Detractors of Father Las Casas," in *Bartolomé de las Casas in History: Toward an Understanding of the Man and His Work*, ed. Juan Friede and Benjamin Keen (DeKalb: Northern Illinois University Press, 1971), 506.

77. Arias, "The Kingdom of God," 42. Arias terms this the monastic reduction. For a contemporary example, see Rob Dreher's *The Benedict Option: A Strategy for Christians in a Post-Christian Nation* (New York: Penguin Random House, 2017). Alasdair MacIntyre's closing thoughts in his influential *After Virtue*, in which he calls for "another—doubtless very different—St. Benedict," famously fit this pattern. MacIntyre, *After Virtue: A Study in Moral Theory, Third Edition* (Notre Dame, IN: University of Notre Dame Press, 2007), 219.

scriptural holiness over the land"[78] remains pressing precisely when the church itself is blocking the light. As Arias sates, "We are getting out of the shadow cone. We are beginning to see the shining edge of the sun, and soon we will be in daylight."[79] The church is a lunar mystery. Only one of its sides is visible. We can see those who gather, the buildings, the ministries. Sometimes these shine brightly and cast soft radiance on their surroundings, sometimes they fade into darkness.[80] However, an entire side goes unseen: grace, the elect, the saints and angels in heaven. Even the unseen can have a powerful effect. The prayers of the saints, the ministry of the angels, and, above all, the grace of God are invisibly at work in the life of the church. As a lunar mystery, the church's light is borrowed: it reflects the light of Christ, the sun of righteousness. He alone is light from light. Without the sun's light, the moon is simply a big, barren rock. With the sun, it serves as the brightest light in the firmament. Like the moon, the church in its pilgrimage through history goes through phases. It waxes and wanes. But it is precisely then—when it appears to be gone—that the potential for rebirth is greatest.

Evangelism testifies to and participates in this lunar mystery. Announcing the reign of God by night is challenging. The lights are few and dim. However, night is not only the time of darkness; it is when we dream. The time of the Great Ecclesial Eclipse is also the season of dreams. With that in mind, Arias offers wise counsel for evangelism under our starless sky:

> We need to recover the capacity to dream. The reign of God is God's own dream, his project for his world and for humanity! He made us to be dreamers, and he wants us to be seduced by his dream and to dream with him.[81]

---

78. John Wesley, "The 'Large' *Minutes*, A and B (1753, 1763)," Q.4, *Works* 10:845.

79. Arias, *Announcing the Reign of God*, 121.

80. Augustine likewise plays with multiple lunar metaphors, as when he suggests "the moon in allegory signifies the Church, because in its spiritual part the Church is bright, but in its carnal part is dark: and sometimes the spiritual part is seen by good works, but sometimes it lies hid in the conscience, and is known to God alone, since in the body alone is it seen." Augustine, *Enarrationes in psalmos*, 11.3.

81. Arias, *Announcing the Reign of God*, 116.

Chapter Eight

The Word of Reconciliation: A Wesleyan Perspective on Public Theology

The Immigration Question: Does This Church Fix Papers?

Some years ago, a friend of mine who served as a United Methodist pastor in Siler City, North Carolina, baptized a family of recent immigrants from Mexico. Many Methodists baptize children in birdbaths masquerading as fonts, but on this occasion, for reasons unknown to me, they gathered by the river. The family, dressed in white, went down into the water, and the pastor dunked them three times while invoking the triune name. They came out of the water, the pastor handed the newborn Christians their baptismal certificates, and everybody went back to the church for a party. What none of the participants knew at the time was that they were being watched by two men. These men turned up at the church office the following day to ask the pastor a very important question: Is this the church that fixes papers? The men were undocumented immigrants who thought that the baptismal certificates were immigration documents. Hence, the question: Is this the church that fixes papers?

This question touches on matters of great ecclesial importance. Does immigration status make a difference for baptism? Is the undocumented status of a person an impediment to baptism? Should one encourage such a person to first repent of this crime? But then, does repentance mean leaving the country? Or should one instead encourage them to be baptized and become citizens of heaven? Conversely, does baptism make a difference for immigration status? Does the local congregation assume responsibility over their continuing residence in this country? Does the congregation fight a deportation order? At a deeper level, the question that these two men asked is ecclesiological and missiological. What kind of community is the Methodist church? What is the church's response to the broken immigration system? Or to state it a different way: What has Aldersgate to do with Washington?

What Has Aldersgate to Do with Washington?

In posing this question, I am evoking the famous question of Tertullian: What has Athens to do with Jerusalem?[1] By this question, Tertullian was calling into question the role of philosophy in Christian faith. According to him, we do not believe because the content of Christian faith makes sense. We believe because it is absurd. In other words, there is no relation between Athens and Jerusalem. I am not rejecting the relationship between Aldersgate and Washington by raising this question. Instead, I am calling attention to the magnitude of the distance. A helpful, if perhaps controversial, guide to this transatlantic journey is Stephen Long; the final chapter of Long's book *John Wesley's Moral Theology: The Quest for God and Goodness* examines the manner in which the Methodist founder entered the public square, by way of Ernst Troeltsch.

---

1. See Tertullian, *The Prescription Against the Heretics*, 7.

In *The Social Teachings of the Christian Churches*, Troeltsch asks the question: "What role does theology have in the public realm?"[2] According to Stephen Long, this question has come to define the agenda for contemporary Christian engagement in society. The framing power of Troeltsch's question is at work in the deployment of the word *social* by early-twentieth-century theologians. From the promulgation of a "social gospel" by Walter Rauschenbusch and the crafting of a "social creed" by Methodism, one cannot help inferring that previous gospels and creeds were at best "asocial" and hence in need of supplementation.[3] The introduction of the adjective *social* in the early twentieth century or *public* in the twenty-first denotes attempts to find the relevance of creed and gospel in a secularized society.

Troeltsch's question finds one of its most persuasive answers in the theology of Reinhold Niebuhr. Long draws attention to the role of fallibilism in Niebuhr's theological vision. Our faith's search for understanding is always going to be led astray by self-interest. Questions of power will always lurk behind assertions of truth. Hence, all knowing and loving are tinged by the tragic. Reality is a sea of gray—*simul Justus et peccator* is the norm of human existence in history. Unintended consequences follow upon all human action. Answering Troeltsch's question with Niebuhr entails abandoning a world created for beatitude for one that is tragic all the way down. Long states, "Christian realism, contra the Wesleyan holiness movement, dogmatically knows that perfection, deification, and a participation in God's goodness are impossible. There is only the will to power, and all we can do is minimize its inevitable evil consequences."[4]

Troeltsch's question and Niebuhr's answer cede too much of the ground from which Christian discourse arises. The question presupposes

---

2.   Ernst Troeltsch, *The Social Teachings of the Christian Churches*, trans. Olive Wyon (New York: The Macmillan Company, 1931). According to Stephen Long, the social problem that Troeltsch addresses is not really the relation between church and state but the church's contribution to social phenomena not directly regulated by the state, like the family and the market. See D. Stephen Long, *John Wesley's Moral Theology: The Quest for God and Goodness* (Nashville, TN: Abingdon/Kingswood, 2005), 213.

3.   See Walter Rauschenbusch, *A Theology for the Social Gospel* (Louisville, KY: Westminster John Knox, 1997).

4.   Long, *John Wesley's Moral Theology*, 222.

that there is some extra-ecclesial realm (e.g., society, the nation-state) that is more universal, more catholic, than the church. The question, far from a neutral or innocent query, carries an implicit renunciation of the catholicity of the church and advances a new catholicity—that of the nation-state into whose public square the church may perhaps approach, but only as a private entity. Instead, Long proposes that "the church is that social reality than which nothing more universal or more public can be conceived."[5] The eschatological dimension of the church makes it the most catholic and public realm imaginable.

One does not have to agree with every detail of Long's analysis of the social question to see that he is on to something. His judgments are echoed by Charles Mathewes: "Typically, 'public theologies' are self-destructively accommodationist: they let the 'larger' secular world's self-understanding set the terms, and then ask how religious faith contributes to the purposes of public life, so understood."[6] Simply put, Troeltsch's question is not Wesley's question. The question that has guided the Methodist ministry of reconciliation has not been: "What role does theology have in the public realm?" This is a question that Methodists take up, because it was asked of them, but the more primitive and important question was phrased in a different way.

"What may we reasonably believe to be God's design in raising up the preachers called 'Methodists'?" God raised the Methodists not to form any sect but to "reform the nation, and in particular the Church, to spread scriptural holiness over the land."[7] The divine design for Methodism is not bound to tragedy. Those who have felt their hearts strangely warmed at Aldersgate can have hope for Washington, a hope that is based on a gift and a responsibility: the word of reconciliation.

Paul, the apostle of reconciliation, writes to the Corinthians that "God was in Christ, reconciling the world unto himself, not imputing

---

5. Long, *John Wesley's Moral Theology*, 210.

6. Charles T. Mathewes, *A Theology of Public Life* (New York: Cambridge University Press, 2007), 1.

7. John Wesley, "The 'Large' *Minutes*, A and B (1753, 1763)," Q.4, *Works* 10:845. The imagery of Wesley's declaration echoes the words of Isaiah 11:9, "The earth will be full of the knowledge of the LORD as the waters cover the sea."

their trespasses unto them; and hath committed unto us the word of reconciliation" (2 Cor 5:19 KJV). The "word of reconciliation" belongs to the core of John Wesley's message.[8] The passage from 2 Corinthians 5 was one of the axles around which his preaching revolved.[9]

A brief overview of how Wesley understands this word may be helpful. The need for reconciliation stems from the Fall of humanity. Sin has introduced enmity into all human relations, starting with the relation with God. Wesley derides William Law's treatise on "The Spirit of Prayer" as a false gospel. "For if God was never *angry* (as this tract asserts) he could never be *reconciled*. And consequently the whole Christian doctrine of *reconciliation by Christ* falls to the ground at once."[10] The effects of sin extend beyond the divine-human relation to all other dimensions of human existence.[11] Human disobedience binds all creation to futility. Instead of being channels of blessing for creation, the "human shark" devours and destroys.[12] The stain of sin can be as invisible as the stain of unholy

---

8.   John Wesley, August 10, 1738, *Journal and Diaries I*, *Works* 18:271.

9.   See Wesley's journal entries for May 28, 1749 (*Works* 20:277), October 2, 1749 (*Works* 20:306), May 4, 1761 (*Works* 21:318), June 6, 1787 (*Works* 24:35), August 29, 1787 (*Works* 24:56), October 28, 1788 (*Works* 24:113), June 10, 1789 (*Works* 24:142), and August 26, 1789 (*Works* 24:152).

10.   Wesley, July 27, 1749, *Journals and Diaries III*, *Works* 20:292–93 (emphasis original). Wesley does worry the manner in which some theologians interpret Christ's atoning sacrifice as mere metaphor undermines the Pauline gospel of reconciliation. E.g., Wesley condemns Andrew Michael Ramsay's *The Philosophical Principles of Natural and Revealed Religion, Unfolded in a Geometrical Order* (Glasgow: Robert Foulis, 1768) for this very reason. In response to Chevalier Ramsay's statement that "pure Divinity is impassible, and unsusceptible of anger, wrath, vengeance, grief and horror" (Ramsay, 393), Wesley retorts, "I demand the proof. I take anger to have the same relation to justice as love has to mercy." Wesley, Letter to Dr. John Robertson (Sept. 24, 1753), *Works* 26:521. Wesley is not unaware of the analogical character of theological speech. However, he does not read Ramsay's work or the reception of his work as a call for careful theological speech but as a call for accommodating the gospel to the reasoned expectations of the age. For Wesley, "If God was never angry, his anger could never be appeased; and then we may safely adopt the very words of Socinus, *Tota redemptionis nostrae per Christum metaphora;* seeing Christ died only to 'show to all the celestial choirs God's infinite aversion to disorder'" (ibid., 522). This language cannot be pushed too far. After all, "God was in Christ, reconciling the world unto himself" (2 Cor 5:19). The triune God is at work in the salvation of humanity. Only the second person of the Trinity was made to be sin (a "sin-offering," as Wesley adds), but not without the Father and the Spirit.

11.   See John Wesley, Sermon 60, "The Great Deliverance," *Works* 2:437–50.

12.   John Wesley, "The General Deliverance," II.6, *Works* 2:445.

tempers upon the soul and as visible as the naked bodies of African people sold in the marketplaces. In all cases, Wesley's account of reconciliation is christocentric. Reconciliation with God in Christ is the basis for reconciliation with the neighbor and creation. Wesley is wary of any theology that would privilege reconciliation with neighbor either temporally or logically over reconciliation with Christ.[13] To Wesley's ears, any muting of the priority of Godward reconciliation smacks of Pelagianism or even atheism. At the same time, he is adamant in his refusal to spiritualize the semantic range of the word of reconciliation.

The word *reconciliation* (καταλλαγή, transliterated as *katallagé*) was used in Greek society to name the coming together of an estranged or separated couple, and also for the signing of peace treaties. Reconciliation was not originally a religious term; it was a political one. Paul stretches this word when he applies it to the work of salvation, but he never abandons the original political usage; instead, he resituates it within the politics of the kingdom of God. Wesley follows Paul in this reorientation of the political. The ministers of reconciliation are ambassadors for Christ. In this connection, Wesley underscores the fact that Scripture lists peace among the fruit of the Spirit expected from the person who is in Christ. In his reading of European history, Wesley appears to buy into the narrative (some say myth) of religious violence. The divisions among Christians have contributed to wars among nations, making the restoration of peace every Christian's desire and task, even if it seems impossible. Wesley states, "And suppose we cannot 'make these wars to cease in all the world,' suppose we cannot reconcile all the children of God to each other; however, let each do what he can, let him contribute if it be but two mites toward it."[14]

What does the word of reconciliation that I have just outlined have to do with the relationship between Aldersgate and Washington? Simply put, the reformation of the nation and the church is an expression of the ministry of reconciliation. The call for reformation stems from the reality

---

13. "Nay, but first believe. Believe in the Lord Jesus Christ, the propitiation for thy sins. Let this good foundation first be laid, and then thou shalt do all things well." John Wesley, Sermon 6, "The Righteousness of Faith," III.1, *Works* 1:214.

14. John Wesley, Sermon 20, "The Lord Our Righteousness," §2, *Works* 1:449.

of their present deformation. It is as a community reconciled with God in Christ by the power of the Holy Spirit that Methodists are agents of reconciliation in the world. On one occasion, Wesley describes his understanding of the essentials of Methodist doctrine by means of the metaphor of a house. He says, "Our main doctrines, which include all the rest, are three, that of repentance, of faith, and of holiness. The first of these we account, as it were, the porch of religion; the next, the door; the third is religion itself."[15] The admission by grace into this house leads Methodists to the practices of confession of sin, repentance, conversion, and forgiveness, all for the sake of communion with the triune God and all other creatures. By reconciling people with God, creation, neighbor, and self, this Methodist House is forming reconcilers who can then reform the nation—neither as technocrats nor as theocrats but as witnesses.

Spanning the ocean separating Aldersgate from Washington with the ministry of reconciliation will strike some as problematic. There is a terminological challenge; the word *reconciliation* has a history of co-option and guilt by association, rendering its usage suspect. The Argentine Methodist theologian José Míguez Bonino worries that the Church has sometimes misunderstood its service of reconciliation as one of pacification, thereby ignoring the need for conversion.[16] It is "in Christ" that there is neither Jew nor Greek, slave nor free, male nor female. The denunciation of errors, sins, and idols is necessary for reconciliation. On the other hand, Míguez Bonino calls us to test the authenticity of the language of peace that the Church has used in responding to conflicts in the world. In the words of Uruguayan Methodist theologian Emilio Castro: "The reconciling word, the Church's act of drawing near can only be credible when it is accompanied by the marks of the cross; it is credible when the Church has not kept its distance from the conflict but has shared the fate of the most vulnerable sectors."[17]

---

15. John Wesley, "Principles of a Methodist Farther Explained," VI.4, *Works* 9:227. For more on Wesley's house metaphor, see this book's introduction, pages 11–21.

16. José Míguez Bonino, "Unidad cristiana y reconciliación: Coincidencia y tensión," *Cuadernos de teología* 2.2 (1972): 109–23.

17. Emilio Castro, "Conflicto y reconciliación," *Cuadernos de teología* 3.3 (1974): 125–33, 130.

Methodists' record as peacemakers is checkered. At times, Methodists have spoken the word of reconciliation prematurely and covered up conflicts. At times, Methodists have betrayed their vocation and served as ambassadors for the present age. But at other times, the Methodist church's diplomatic credentials have been stamped with the suffering of the crucified, and its simplest acts of gathering, singing, and praying were transformed into powerful symbols of a liberating reconciliation. The Methodist ministry of reconciliation gains in power to the extent that it lives into the eschatological tension of its vocation and sees its life from this end.

In order to examine how one lives into the Christian tensions of the public space, I turn to the example of Óscar Romero, the martyred bishop of El Salvador.

What Does Aldersgate Have to Do with El Salvador?

Why Óscar Romero? It seems an unlikely choice. Romero's contact with Methodists during his pastoral ministry was virtually nonexistent. Yet Romero did enjoy fraternal relations with many Protestants. He rhapsodizes about his experiences worshipping alongside them in Protestant churches during the celebrations of the Week of Prayer for Christian Unity. But the Methodist Church was not established in El Salvador until 1994, so Romero could not have visited a Methodist congregation in El Salvador.

The contacts between Romero and the Methodists are somewhat indirect. I mention two. First, one of Elsa Tamez's books, *La hora de la vida: Lecturas bíblicas*, is found in Romero's personal library.[18] Ownership does not necessarily suggest familiarity, but Tamez's thinking is representative of a line of socially engaged Protestant theology of which Romero knew and approved. Second, there is an odd story circulated by one of Romero's

---

18.   Elsa Tamez, *La hora de la vida: Lecturas bíblicas* (San José, Costa Rica: DIE, 1978).

opponents, Freddy Delgado.[19] In his tale, José Míguez Bonino was a liberation theologian and former Catholic priest who travelled to El Salvador to work with the Jesuits in a campaign to position Romero as the successor to Archbishop Chávez y González. While in El Salvador, Míguez Bonino enrolled in the Universidad Centroamericana (UCA) and became Minister of Tourism (ISTU). After the election, Míguez Bonino left El Salvador, satisfied they had elected a bishop who could be easily "handled" by the liberationists. Obviously, Delgado is mistaken about Míguez Bonino's ecclesial history, and the role he is assigned in engineering Romero's election beggars the imagination. Even so, it would be interesting to explore if there was any contact between the Argentine Methodist theologian and the Salvadoran Jesuits during this period that could have served as the particle of truth for this flaky tale.

Why Romero, then? I offer two reasons. First, the choice is made in the catholic spirit. When Wesley looked for exemplars of holiness, he never turned to a looking glass but turned to stained glass, to the church around him. One cannot live on Wesley alone. That Wesley could find a witness to Christian perfection in Gregory López, that "good and wise (though much mistaken man),"[20] inspires me to look beyond Wesley to Romero for an exemplar of a public theologian. In Romero, I find an exemplar of the practical divinity Methodists aspire to embody. Like Wesley's, Romero's theology is grounded in the life of the church and has a popular orientation. He spoke at academies, but he did not speak for the academy. Moreover, like Wesley's, his theology has a theological end, namely, reconciliation and communion with the triune God. Romero was a stranger to the dialectical "either/or" theology of some Protestants and Catholics and instead embraced the kind of "both-and" that Wesley modeled at his best: theology and holiness, the pastoral and the prophetic, tradition and liberation, love for God and for the country, fidelity to the hierarchy and to the people.

---

19. Santiago Mata, *Monseñor Óscar Romero: Pasión por la Iglesia*, Colección Testimonios (Madrid: Ediciones Palabra, 2015), Kindle locations 4039–53.

20. John Wesley, August 31, 1742, *Journal and Diaries II*, *Works* 19:294.

Second, the theology and life of Romero have contributed to the theological formation of Methodists in Central America through the work of the Methodist Course of Study. There are good reasons for this. The contexts in which these Methodist pastors serve are similar to Romero's, and they have been impacted by him. Also, the clarity of his theological vision and the transparency of his life to the gospel make him sound very evangelical. By the time students graduate from this coursework, they have spent time reading from and about Romero and visited key sites of his ministry (including the cathedral where he preached, the house where he lived, and the Chapel of the Hospitalito where he died).

Óscar Romero was familiar with the public square. As archbishop, he played the role of a prophet who gestured to the coming kingdom with large sign acts. The One Mass (*Misa única*) is perhaps the most famous of these. Following the murder of his friend Father Rutilio Grande, the priests of the archdiocese called for the con-celebration of a single mass for the entire archdiocese at the cathedral of San Salvador. After deliberation, and over the protests of several important church officials, Romero agreed. By means of the *Misa única*, Romero gathered his flock together in solidarity and hope, pointing to the final day when there would only be one congregation gathered in peace around one common altar. In the words of William Cavanaugh, "Romero intended the one eucharist to be an anticipation of the kingdom, of the day when rich and poor would feast together, of the day when the body of Christ would not be wounded by divisions."[21] Romero's foes blamed him for fanning the flames of the conflict in El Salvador, but Romero rejected such characterizations. The sign pointed out, but did not cause, the problem.

Romero also played the role of a diplomat. He attempted to use the venerable place of the archbishop in civil society for the benefit of his suffering people. Perhaps the most famous of these interventions was the

---

21. William Cavanaugh, "Dying for the Eucharist or Being Killed by It? Romero's Challenge to First-World Christians," *Theology Today* 58.2 (2001): 185.

letter he wrote to President Carter on February 17, 1980.[22] In this letter, Romero calls for a halt to the US government's efforts in arming and training the Salvadoran armed forces. Romero details how the weapons sent by the US were being turned not against Marxist rebels but against the people of El Salvador. He mentions the particular case in which gas masks and bulletproof vests valued at $200,000 were sold by six Americans to the Salvadoran security forces. He ends his letter in the same fashion in which he began—with an appeal to the Christian and humanitarian sensibilities of President Carter.[23]

Óscar Romero was first and foremost a pastor. He did not primarily understand himself as a theologian or as an expert in political matters. In Salvadoran society, bishops had an ex officio role in the public square as priests of the state and sanctifiers of the status quo. Romero could not play this role, but neither could he abandon the public square; too much was at stake. Instead, he sought to transform it into a space of reconciliation and expand it to include voices not typically allowed to contribute to the national conversation. As an example of how Romero sought to reconstitute the public square, I consider his homily from March 16, 1980, with its descriptive if ungainly title of "The reconciliation of human beings in Christ, project of true liberation."[24]

---

22. For Óscar Romero's homilies, I am consulting *Homilías: Monseñor Óscar A. Romero*, Vols. I–VI, ed. Miguel Cavada Diez (San Salvador: UCA Editores, 2005–2009). All translations are my own. Romero read this letter to his church in the Sunday homily of February 17, 1980, in order to inform his congregation about this action and to seek their judgment *(Homilías* VI, 293f). The frequent interruption of the reading of the text by congregational applause is good evidence that the people approved.

23. Carter's Secretary of State, Cyrus Vance, replied to the letter on March 1, 1980. Vance expresses appreciation for the manner in which Romero is trying to lead his people through the difficult social situation in which they find themselves, but he believes that without US military assistance to the government a civil war may start, which will destabilize the entire Central American region. In brief, Vance disagrees with Romero's reading of the situation while agreeing on key principles guiding action in Central America. Incidentally, Carter's response to the news of the assassination of Romero gives ample evidence of the deep respect he had for the martyred archbishop. He wrote, "Archbishop Romero spoke for the poor of El Salvador, where their voices had been ignored for too long. He spoke for change and for social justice, which his nation so desperately needs" (http://www.presidency.ucsb.edu/ws/index.php?pid=33182). The show of respect did not, however, have any real policy consequences.

24. *Homilías* VI, 391.

As a Roman Catholic pastor, Romero was a lectionary preacher, and the texts for the fourth Sunday of Lent 1980 focused his attention on the theme of reconciliation. The word for that day included the parable of the Prodigal Son, one of the most well-known stories of reconciliation in the Bible; the passage from 2 Corinthians 5 in which Paul speaks of the message of reconciliation in Christ; and the lesser-known but very important account of Joshua celebrating the entrance to the Promised Land at Gilgal.

Following his usual practice, Romero begins with a catechesis of the liturgical season. He likens Lent to an ecclesial springtime; it is a season when the church's spiritual pilgrimage is marked by the sacramental signpost of penance and reconciliation. The journey culminates at the Easter Vigil, when the church baptizes its catechumens and renews its own baptismal configuration to the death and resurrection of Jesus. The word of reconciliation is liturgically in season. The penance of Lent (penance and reconciliation being inseparable for Romero) prepares the way for the renewal of Easter.

The word of reconciliation is timely liturgically and also historically. In 1980 the people of El Salvador find themselves in desperate need of reconciliation, indicated by the polarization prevalent in the nation. Surveying the jockeying for power among the leaders of the right and the left, Romero declares: "Each one thinks to possess the truth and blame the other. . . . Each has placed himself in a pole, incapable of being reconciled."[25] The polarization has become so powerful that the previous Sunday someone placed a bomb close to the altar of the church where Romero was preaching. Thankfully, the timing mechanism failed to detonate. Romero himself is accused of being an agent of polarization, but he dismisses the charge by explaining that "the word of the Church is not making up the evils that are already present in the world, it illumines them." With the light of the Scriptures, Romero illumines the journey of reconciliation that the people of God and the people of El Salvador need to walk. What becomes clear in light of the Scriptures is the need for agrarian reform.

---

25. *Homilías* VI, 390.

Romero tells his congregation that "in this time when the land of El Salvador is the subject of conflicts, we must remember that the land is very tied to the promises of God."[26] In the Old Testament lesson from the book of Joshua for that Sunday morning, the people of Israel's Lenten journey has ended. They have entered the Promised Land. The need for manna is over. God's people can now work with their own hands to gather the fruit of the land, and the first thing they do with this harvest is to celebrate a Passover in Gilgal.

The purpose of the land in Romero's theology is paschal. Those who understand that the goods of the earth have a Eucharistic orientation would "use these as in the ceremony of the Passover of Gilgal. They would cut the sheaves and praise God who has given them land and has given them the fruit of the land; and they would share with their brothers in a true paschal feast, in the reconciliation of human beings with respect to the fruits of the earth; in reconciliation instead of struggle."[27] The ultimate purpose of agrarian reform, then, is to spread scriptural holiness across the land. If you want to grow saints, you must first defend humans. Romero's apologetic ministry is an application of the Thomistic principle that grace presupposes nature. The Eucharist presupposes bread and wine; the new creation presupposes the old. But the importance of the land goes beyond supplying matter for sacraments or providing subjects for grace. By receiving and sharing the gifts of below, like the land, the Salvadorans learn to receive and share the gifts of above. Agrarian reform is not simply a politically prudent measure—it is a theological necessity.

The second part of the sermon is devoted to the parable of the Prodigal Son. The vision of integral reconciliation, presented in the Old Testament vision of people offering God a paschal feast, one harvested from the fruit of the land that they now call home, is personalized in what Romero calls the parable of reconciliation. In proclaiming this text, the archbishop hopes to lead his congregation in an examination of their own personal contribution to the problems in El Salvador. Each person has contributed to the polarization of the country by blaming the other for the troubles

---

26. *Homilías* VI, 393.

27. *Homilías* VI, 393ff.

facing the nation: "We need to break these dams; we need to feel that there is one Father who loves all of us and is waiting for us."[28] The call of reconciliation requires abandoning postures of moral superiority that blind us to our own culpability, acting as "the ones who feel pure and clean, the ones who think that they have the right to present others as the cause of the injustices and are not capable of looking within and seeing that they too have contributed to the national chaos."[29]

Romero's final thought from this Sunday homily is that the ministry of reconciliation is the Church's most important service in the world. A beautiful articulation of this ministry is found in 2 Corinthians 5—the epistle read on that day. The narration of the life of the church and the reading of the events of the week are located within this third movement of the sermon, and they account for two-thirds of the homily. This section of Romero's homilies serves at once as parish announcements, investigative news reports, and a reading of the signs of the times. These comments are usually located at the end of the sermon in order to highlight that such realities can be understood in light of the dominical readings. However, on this occasion, Romero integrates into the third point of the homily a kind of exercise in a narrative ecclesiology and missiology of reconciliation. The Church of El Salvador has lived out the ministry of reconciliation, with many signs to serve as proof: the peace prize that Romero received from the church of Sweden, the progress of the repairs being made on the archdiocesan radio station YSAX after it was destroyed by a bomb, the police search of a parsonage on the made-up charge that the priests living there were supporting terrorists, the failed attempt to blow up the church where Romero was celebrating mass the previous Sunday. All these events and more point to the price that the Church is paying for being in the service of reconciliation—this is the gospel of reconciliation. This is the word that the Church bears to the oligarchy, the government, the social activists, and even the guerrillas: be reconciled.

---

28.   *Homilías* VI, 399.

29.   *Homilías* VI, 399.

Listening to Romero's Word with Wesleyan Ears

What should Methodists, who are historically concerned with finding our voice in the public square, hear in Romero's preaching and ministry? What can we learn from Romero's proclamation of the word of reconciliation that can help norm our services as ambassadors for Christ?

First, the word of reconciliation bursts forth from an encounter with Christ. The Christian activist, like any Christian, must follow the words of Wesley: "First believe. Believe in the Lord Jesus Christ, the propitiation for thy sins. Let this good foundation first be laid, and then thou shalt do all things well."[30] The centrality of Christ is the reason why Romero energetically rejects any politicization of Christian worship. He knows that many tune in to his masses out of curiosity about what the archbishop will say about the latest deaths or about the government's inept attempts to usher in banking reform. He insists that these words are necessary but they are not the main speech event. The national and ecclesial realities of which he speaks in the homily are not the core of his proclamation; the core is Christ. The mass is not a political party in prayer; it is a gathering of the people of God walking with the God of the people—the God who sets up God's tent along the margins of society. The more the bodies pile up in the roadside ditches, the less people are willing to speak in the police station. A neighbor is dragged away on trumped-up charges, and then no one dares to testify to his or her innocence. But by faith, the discarded Savior can be seen in the discarded bodies of the Salvadorans, and this recognition has the power to move Christians to speak the truth to power with power.

Second, the word of reconciliation gives theological necessity to some social reforms. The Bible teaches Romero that landlessness is the wages of sin. The truth of this assertion is grounded in the story of Israel, and it is experienced also in the story of El Salvador. In El Salvador, the unequal distribution of land is no accident. The greed of some has led to the misery of many. The commodification of the land—its absolutization as private property—prostitutes it; the goods of the land are enjoyed not by those who are united to it by memory of its history and hope for its future

---

30. John Wesley, Sermon 6, "The Righteousness of Faith," III.1, *Works* 1:214.

but by those who can place the highest bid. For Romero, the unbridled expansion of one's landholdings without consideration for those who are now left landless is a form of what Wesley calls practical atheism. People are acting as if there were no God. Romero exclaims: "Ah, if only they understood that God gives being to the farms, the haciendas, the cattle, they would not use these as instruments of exploitation!"[31] The goal of agrarian reform is not simply land redistribution but the creation of the conditions of possibility for a new vision that sees traces of the Trinity in the land and the *imago Dei* in the human. In other words, Romero preaches agrarian reform for the sake of holiness. John Wesley shared similar concerns. Christians care for the just use of the land because they are appointed by God as stewards of God's creation.[32] In the fulfilling of this vocation, the Methodists were to be particularly attentive to the needs of the most vulnerable. Methodist advocacy for abstinence from spirituous beverages and simplicity in clothing were not simply prudish practices but a call for the gifts of the land to be shared by all and not commodified for the few.[33]

Third, the word of reconciliation judges all social reforms. The church is not the only actor on the national stage, nor does it seek to be. Romero never tires of insisting that he is not a politician and that the church does not want to grab the levers of power. He believes that it is important for the church not to supplant the work of grassroots organizations and government agencies in working for justice and peace. These social bodies have their own parts to play in the reform of the nation. They may have expertise the church lacks or play particular political roles the church can-

---

31. *Homilías* VI, 394.

32. John Wesley, Sermon 60, "The General Deliverance," I.3, *Works* 2:440. Wesley speaks of human beings as serving a priestly role with respect to creation. Through human beings' stewardship, many of God's blessings are conveyed to the rest of creation.

33. In one treatise, Wesley attributes the high costs of basic food items to the manner in which the land is used to serve the needs of the rich. The demand for horses to pull coaches and run races increased fourfold in his time. Consequently, more land was being set aside for the raising and feeding of horses than for people. Related to this ill, Wesley points to the monopolizing of farms: "The land which was some years ago divided between ten or twenty little farmers, and enabled them comfortably to provide for their families, is now generally engrossed by one great farmer" ("Thoughts on the Present Scarcity of Provisions," I.6, *Works* (Jackson) 11:56). Admittedly, Wesley does not propose a plan for land redistribution, but his call for restraining luxury and limiting the size of estates points in this direction.

not assume. The church does not offer the country a blueprint for social reform—it offers the light of the gospel, which has the power to illumine realities often unseen by those in authority, along with guiding principles or criteria for evaluating the justice of the reforms. The church can collaborate with these groups when their work aligns with the church's mission of spreading scriptural holiness across the land. What the church cannot do is give any social or political organization a blank check. Romero asserts "the autonomy of the church to lift up whatever is right in all organizations and to denounce, also, the unjust acts of violence and immaturity of those who mobilize themselves and which can turn their organization into an idolatrous one and into an abuse of power."[34] The light of the gospel brings into focus the end of human existence, sharing in the good that is God, and from this end it evaluates the trajectory set out by the various national plans for reconciliation.

Fourth, the word of reconciliation invites all reformers to self-reflection. The hour of reconciliation is the hour of prayer when all Salvadorans must join in praying, "Forgive us our sins, as we forgive those who sin against us." The parable of reconciliation was told to the scribes and the Pharisees, but Romero invites his congregants to read themselves into the parable and therefore examine themselves. Each person has also contributed to the polarization by seeing herself or himself as the sole solution to the national predicament. The concerns that Romero raises are echoed by Cathleen Kaveny in her book *Prophecy without Contempt: Religious Discourse in the Public Square*. She writes: "The greatest danger to moral character associated with the practice of prophetic indictment is arrogance. It is all too easy for its practitioners to assume not only that they stand in right relation with God but also that they are fully knowledgeable about God's purposes and endeavors."[35] There is a time for public deliberation and a time for prophetic speech, but never a time for public humiliation. One of the points of contact between Wesley and Romero is their profound love for their nation and particularly for the church. Reform is motivated by

---

34. *Homilías* VI, 396.

35. Cathleen Kaveny, *Prophecy without Contempt: Religious Discourse in the Public Square* (Cambridge, MA: Harvard University Press, 2016), 9.

love, patriotism toward the country, filial love for the church. However, Romero warns against an unduly high evaluation of one's patriotism or filial duty. He says:

> Be careful that the manner in which you love the country is so deep that you set yourself in opposition to those who love it in a different way. Do not feel as if you were the sole owner of the solutions and as if you were the sole owner of the country. All have the right to speak. Let us respect this.[36]

Fifth, the word of reconciliation has the power to create its own public square. The standard view of the relationship between the church and the public square is that the former needs to divest itself of ecclesial trappings in order to have a voice in the latter. As Kevin Vanhoozer and Owen Strachan explain, "Public theology is therefore theology that addresses common concerns in an open forum, where no particular creed or confession holds pride of place."[37] John Wesley's *Thoughts upon Slavery* becomes Exhibit A in the case for presenting Wesley as public theologian. Indeed, this case has been advanced with power and clarity by David Field. A similar argument could be made for the public theologian credentials of Óscar Romero on the strength of his letter to President Carter. These approaches to the public square have their value, but they cannot be absolutized. There are other ways of witnessing the gospel of reconciliation with God in Christ to the world. The church itself is a public square, or in the words of Vanhoozer and Strachan, "a public spire . . . the public truth of Jesus Christ, and not only truth, but also the public goodness and public beauty of God's plan of redemption."[38] Wesley's field preaching and Romero's *Misa única* did not enter into the public square, cap in hand, begging for a hearing; they worked indefatigably to reform the nation, because the word of reconciliation they proclaimed created a new public out of a crowd, a new nation, the people of God.

---

36. *Homilías* VI, 402.

37. Kevin J. Vanhoozer and Owen Strachan, *The Pastor as Public Theologian: Reclaiming a Lost Vision* (Grand Rapids, MI: Baker Academic, 2015), 17.

38. Vanhoozer and Strachan, *The Pastor as Public Theologian*, 21.

The Church as Public Square

With these reflections on the word of reconciliation in mind, let us return to our original story and consider again the baptism that those two men witnessed.

First, they would have seen people like themselves renouncing sins and confessing their faith. They would not have been asked to produce a US birth certificate, a green card, or a visa. They would not have heard any questions about when or how they arrived in the United States. Instead, they would have heard questions like, "Do you renounce the spiritual forces of wickedness, reject the evil powers of this world, and repent of sin?" Now sin, according to Wesley, is a voluntary transgression of a known divine law. Hence, these men may have been led to reflect on how they have trespassed against others. Regardless of whether simply being undocumented is per se sinful, these men might have examined the moral consequences of their unauthorized entry. It is not that they are bad hombres, but being undocumented can dispose one to certain sinful acts such as lying about one's immigration status, identity theft, healthcare fraud, and the like. Moreover, being undocumented can increase the likelihood of adultery and divorce, as borders separate spouses and divide families. Whatever sins they might have pondered in their hearts and professed with their lips, their confession would have been to God, not to ICE. The primary and fundamental movement in conversion is a turn from darkness to light, from confession of sin to confession of faith in Christ, not a trip to Washington or a return to Mexico.

Second, our two men would have seen water poured and heard the name of the triune God invoked. The same element that was used to exclude some from one country, because a river divided one piece of soil from another, was now being used to bond different people together. The rite of water and the Spirit conditions the reach of the right of soil (*jus soli*); the baptized are kin and they bear the same surname—Christian. The forgiveness of sins and people's adoption as children of our Father in heaven has social implications: they are "no longer strangers and aliens"; they are "citizens with the saints and also members of the household of

God" (Eph 2:19). The invocation of the name of the Holy Trinity creates a public square, a new republic.

Third, our two men would have seen the people clothed in white being welcomed into the congregation. This is the conclusion of the act of baptism. The local congregation commits itself to "surround these persons with a community of love and forgiveness." Now it might be argued that these promises are largely symbolic, yet symbols have an underlying reality upon which they are grounded. So unless our congregational vows are mere air vibrations without signification, they must mean something. At bare minimum, the congregation should not itself initiate deportation proceedings. However, such a minimalist approach does not rule out richer interpretations of these promises (political advocacy, employment, sanctuary); interpretations that take seriously Paul's commendation in Galatians 6:10: "Do good unto all people, especially unto those who belong to the household of faith." Moreover, it is significant that the reception of the baptized into the congregation becomes the occasion for the congregation to renew its own membership vows. In welcoming the stranger as brother or sister, the church revitalizes its own identity as constituted of ambassadors for Christ who are entrusted with the ministry of reconciliation.

Perhaps those two men, those undocumented immigrants, saw more clearly than most of us what the church is and is called to be: a *paroikia*, a community of aliens who have no abiding home here on earth because, as Paul says, "our citizenship is in heaven" (Phil 3:20).

Conclusion

Rediscovering the Heart of Methodism

In 2021, Duke Divinity School launched a course series called Rediscovering the Heart of Methodism.[1] The course grew out of conversations with United Methodist denominational leaders and was inspired by the conviction that at the heart of Methodism lay a Christian social entrepreneurship that was surprisingly effective in the eighteenth century and could be again in the twenty-first century.

Longing for the rediscovery of the heart of Methodism affirms that Methodism has a heart. Its essential core and coherent vision distinguish it from other Christian communities and movements. As addressed in this volume's introduction, Wesley presented the heart of Methodism using the metaphor of a house.[2] The house centers around the formation of a holy people; its blueprint derives from the key doctrines that Methodists preached: the porch of repentance, the door of justification, and the interior of sanctification. These doctrines are themselves grounded in the apostolic faith and embodied in practices of piety and mercy. The people called Methodists have a doctrinal, liturgical, missional heart, a heart that

---

1.   See   https://divinity.duke.edu/events/rediscovering-heart-methodism-nurturing
-entrepreneurial-mindsets.

2.   See this volume's introduction, pages 11–21, for a thorough discussion of the Methodist House.

beat strong from the rediscovery of biblical Christianity in Wesley's time, a heart that has grown weak among many of Wesley's heirs.

The rediscovery of the heart of Methodism begins with acknowledging and repenting for what has been lost. The heart of Methodism is troubled, and nowhere is this heartsickness more evident than among English-speaking Methodists in the Northern Hemisphere. The statistics on membership and average worship attendance tell a tale of decline. The news of infighting and division paint a dispiriting portrait of a people who have lost their bearings.[3]

In this book, I have explored how the witness of the people called metodista promotes the renewal of Methodism and, indeed, Christianity. Renewal and reform are not simply marks of failure but marks of a living ecclesial body. The Dominican theologian Yves Congar is right: "The church is constantly reforming itself; it can really live only by doing so, and the intensity of its effort to reform itself measures at any moment the health of its muscle tone (*tonus vital*)."[4] I have argued the muscle tone of Methodism grows healthier as it moves to and from the margins, which, in turn, strengthens its contribution to reforming the whole body of Christ.

In this concluding essay, I build on the work of the preceding chapters to call for a rediscovery of the heart of Methodism. The rediscovery is not for the sake of restoring Methodism to its glory days but for the sake of missional renewal. Methodism's founding commission remains relevant: "What may we reasonably believe to be God's design in raising up the preachers called 'Methodists'? To reform the nation, and in particular the Church, to spread scriptural holiness over the land."[5] Methodism does not exist for itself. It was raised to renew the church's doctrine, worship, and mission by proclaiming Christian holiness across the land, starting

3. See Pew Research Center, "About Three-in-Ten U.S. Adults Are Now Religiously Unaffiliated" (Dec. 14, 2021), https://www.pewforum.org/2021/12/14/about-three-in-ten-u-s-adults-are-now-religiously-unaffiliated/; Lovett H. Weems, Jr., "The Coming Death Tsunami," *Ministry Matters* (Oct. 5, 2011), https://www.ministrymatters.com/all/entry/1868/the-coming-death-tsunami; Weems, *Focus: The Real Challenges that Face the United Methodist Church* (Nashville, TN: Abingdon, 2012).

4. Yves Congar, *True and False Reform in the Church* (Collegeville, MN: Liturgical, 2011), 21.

5. John Wesley, "The 'Large' Minutes, A and B (1753, 1763)," Q.4, *Works* 10:845.

from the peripheries. One way of rediscovering the heart of Methodism is by learning how to read Wesley in Spanish. In this chapter, I apply the practice of reading in Spanish to the three rises of Methodism in Oxford, Savannah, and Aldersgate before going south to the future and dreaming in Spanish of mañana.

Reading Wesley in Spanish

In an essay titled "Can Wesley Be Read in Spanish?," Justo González chronicles Wesley's journey with mystics such as Miguel de Molinos and Gregorio López, whom Wesley read in their original language.[6] For González, reading Wesley in Spanish means attending to the Spanish—and even Latin American—roots of Wesley's theological vision. It also means reading Wesley with eyes and ears formed in Hispanic and Latin American social and ecclesial locations.

If I may be autobiographical for a moment, when I first read Wesley in English as a seminarian, I was not attracted by what I saw. The eighteenth-century language and cultural context appeared far removed from my experience. Two factors transformed my receptivity to Wesley. First, immediately after I graduated from divinity school, I was appointed to plant a new church among the Hispanic population in Durham, North Carolina. Second, as I began this church, I was asked to become the official indexer for a fourteen-volume translation of John Wesley's works into Spanish. The combination of reading Wesley in a missionary context and in my own native tongue opened my eyes to the richness of the Wesleyan tradition, casting it in a new light. The translation brought the language closer to my vernacular. The ministry context highlighted the ongoing vitality of the stories, sermons, and practices of the early Methodists.

Reading in Spanish is not primarily about reading Wesley's texts in the language of Cervantes; rather, it is more about allowing one's Christian imagination to be translated by immersion in a missional context where the gospel makes a life-and-death difference. Wesley himself encountered

---

6. Justo L. González, "Can Wesley Be Read in Spanish?" *Rethinking Wesley's Theology for Contemporary Methodism*, ed. Randy L. Maddox (Nashville, TN: Abingdon, 1998), 161–68.

such missional contexts and identified three as the rises of Methodism—namely, Oxford, Savannah, and Aldersgate, which birthed and rebirthed the theological vision of the people called Methodists. In what follows, I read Oxford, Savannah, and Aldersgate in Spanish to rediscover the heart of Methodism with the people called metodista and to open our imaginations to dreaming of a future that goes south.

Reading Oxford in Spanish

Today we think of Oxford as a world-class university; in the eighteenth century, it was chiefly a seminary for the Church of England. The curriculum included lectures on the New Testament, instruction in divinity, and mandatory chapel attendance. As Henry Rack explains, Oxford was "the trustee of orthodoxy in the church: it trained the clergy and defended the church intellectually against the subversive religious and political opinions of Roman Catholics and Dissenters."[7] This role as defender of the faith was accompanied by a reputation for lax morals and theological latitudinarianism. Oxford was a place where the Articles of Religion of the Church of England were "signed more than read, and read by more than believe them."[8] In this place of contradictions, John Wesley rediscovered primitive Christianity.

John Wesley was a student at Oxford's Christ Church College from 1721 to 1724. While at Oxford, "the providence of God" led him to pursue holiness in every aspect of his life.[9] Ordinations as deacon, priest, and curate at Epworth and Wroot soon followed. In 1729, Charles Wesley began a small gathering of students at Oxford. When John returned to

---

7. Henry D. Rack, *Reasonable Enthusiast: John Wesley and the Rise of Methodism* (London: Epworth, 2002), 62.

8. Rack, *Reasonable Enthusiast*, 62. Rack cites words from Edward Gibbon that present a bleak and no doubt exaggerated view of the culture of Oxford: "The fellows or monks of my time were decent easy men who supinely enjoyed the gifts of the founder; their days were filled by a series of uniform employments: the chapel, the hall, the coffee house and the common room, till they retired, weary and well-satisfied, to a long slumber. From the tasks of reading, and thinking or writing, they had absolved their consciences" (61).

9. John Wesley, May 24, 1738, *Journals and Diaries I, Works* 18:243–44.

Oxford that year to resume his duties as fellow of Lincoln College, he became this group's leader. The group was young, with an average age of 17, and consisted mostly of students along with some tutors. They were influenced by the writings of nonjurors who emphasized strict adherence to primitive models of Christian life. They combined study (reading the Scriptures and church fathers in the original languages) with works of piety (journaling, prayers, biweekly fasts, frequent Eucharists) and works of mercy (visiting the poor and the imprisoned). As might be expected, the unusual nature of these practices drew attention and epithets. They were called Bible moths, sacramentarians, the Holy Club, and Methodists.

Reading the rise of Methodism in Oxford in Spanish requires cultivating new habits of seeing, of reading through Hispanic eyes. This means, as González explains, adopting "the perspective of those who claim their Hispanic identity as part of their hermeneutical baggage, and who also read the Scripture within the context of a commitment to the Latino struggle to become all that God wants us and all of the world to be—in other words, the struggle for salvation/liberation."[10] When speaking of a Wesleyan approach to education, Methodists often quote Charles Wesley's verse: "Unite the pair so long disjoined, Knowledge and vital piety."[11] Reading Oxford in Spanish calls for expanding the pair to a trio: knowledge, piety, and poverty.

Reading Oxford in Spanish requires reforming the Christian idea of the university. Reflecting on the witness unto death of Ignacio Ellacuría, rector of the University of Central America in San Salvador, J. Matthew Ashley offers an account of the university that can help us read Oxford with the people called *metodista*.[12] On this reading, the university, as a place dedicated to the search for knowledge, has God at its center, a God whose wisdom is always greater (*semper major*), always new (*semper*

---

10. Justo L. González, *Santa Biblia: The Bible through Hispanic Eyes* (Nashville, TN: Abingdon, 1996), 28f.

11. Charles Wesley, Hymn 461, *A Collection of Hymns for the Use of the People Called Methodists, 1780*, *Works* 7:644.

12. J. Matthew Ashley, "The University as an Instrument of Consolation in the Modern World," *The Way* 49.2 (2010): 21–36.

novus), and inexhaustible.[13] The habits of critical thinking cultivated in a university have as their ground and goal the finding of God in all things while rejecting all substitutes. Seeing through Hispanic eyes also means seeing from a trinitarian perspective defined "by the immense compassion with which the divine persons see and respond to this world."[14] By implication, a university's engagement with the world around it, particularly with its places of suffering, is "not a distraction or even an addition to the university's proper role, but integral to its academic-intellectual mission."[15] Thus, the university has a Samaritan mission. Its scholarship orients toward the ditches of society, where violence and indifference leave human beings for dead.[16]

Rediscovering the heart of Methodism requires reclaiming a vision of education in general and theological education in particular that engages the experience of the margins of society. At Oxford, Methodism rose as a school for contemplatives in action, persons who were instruments of consolation in the world because they found the God of all consolation in all places and circumstances. By reading Oxford in Spanish, we are reminded that universities have historically been places of revival and can play this role again. By engaging in ministries of consolation, the university cultivates new ways of seeing the beauty and woundedness of the world, leading to works of compassion and mercy. This formation happens in libraries and laboratories, lecture halls and dining halls—in *lo cotidiano*—the quotidian, ordinary existence of the university community, particularly as this community engages places of exclusion on and off campus.

---

13. Ashley, "The University as an Instrument," 23.

14. Ashley, "The University as an Instrument," 29.

15. Ashley, "The University as an Instrument," 29.

16. Ashley expands this point in precise terms: "If our universities are not instruments of consolation then, whatever other worthy tasks they fulfil, they will not be places in which God becomes present to the ones acting (at least acting as contributors to the university). If they can, in whatever small measure, give others—the poor above all—cause for consolation, cause to hope and to act in the conviction that sin and death do not have the final word in history, then they become instruments of consolation, which means they become places where God is experienced." Ashley, "The University as an Instrument of Consolation in the Modern World," 36.

Reading Savannah in Spanish

On February 6, 1736, John Wesley landed in Georgia full of dreams and hopes. In a letter to his friend John Burton, he explains his motives for leaving England and crossing the Atlantic: "My chief motive, to which all the rest are subordinate, is the hope of saving my own soul. I hope to learn the true sense of the gospel of Christ by preaching it to the heathens."[17] His dream was to save his soul and to reestablish primitive Christianity in a new world. For this reason, he published *A Collection of Psalms and Hymns*, the first hymnbook published in what would become the United States. Wesley ministered to the Indigenous people; he learned Spanish in order to read the life of Gregory López and to facilitate communication with Indigenous people who had learned Spanish from previous contacts with conquistadors. Less than two years after landing in Georgia, Wesley left despondent over his lack of genuine faith: "I went to America to convert the Indians; but Oh! who shall convert me?"[18] Wesley's sorrow at not finding Christ in the wilderness was compounded by his frustrated romance with Sophy Hopkey and his troubles with the local magistrate. He arrived by day as a preacher of the gospel and left by night as a fugitive of the law. John Wesley's time in Savannah was marked by missional failure.

Five years before his death, in his "Thoughts upon Methodism," Wesley said, "I am not afraid that the people called Methodists should ever cease to exist either in Europe or America. But I am afraid lest they should only exist as a dead sect, having the form of religion without the power."[19] In his 1789 sermon "Causes of the Inefficacy of Christianity," he wonders, "What a mystery is this! That Christianity should have done so little good in the world!"[20] Noting how in many of the cities where John Wesley preached church buildings now serve as stores and nightclubs, the

---

17.   John Wesley, Letter to Revd. John Burton (Oct. 10, 1735), *Letters I, Works* 25:439.

18.   John Wesley, January 24, 1738, *Journals and Diaries I, Works* 18:211.

19.   John Wesley, "Thoughts upon Methodism," ¶1, *Works* 9:527.

20.   John Wesley, Sermon 122, "Causes of the Inefficacy of Christianity," §3, *Works* 4:87.

missiologist Andrew Walls states: "It is as though there is some inherent fragility, some built-in vulnerability, in Christianity."[21]

Reading Savannah in Spanish opens our imagination to reinterpreting our history in a new way. Justo González describes Hispanic and Latin American history as "noninnocent."[22] Failure should not scandalize Christians. Christianity was born from a failure. The followers of Jesus had hoped "that he was the one to redeem Israel" (Luke 24:21). Then Jesus was crucified. The resurrection vindicated the hopes of God's people. Even so, the cross is not discarded as an unfortunate tragic event that is now over. Paul is clear on this point: "We proclaim Christ crucified" (1 Cor 1:23). There is wisdom to be found in stories of failure. The mystery of iniquity is powerful and patent through sins and infirmities, even among God's saints. It is the Lenten wisdom that leads us to repent of our sins and learn from our mistakes. It is the Lenten wisdom of knowing that we are dust and that whatever we build is also dust and that God has the power to redeem dust. If we are to rediscover the heart of Methodism, we need a theology of failure to purify our theology of hope.

Reading Savannah in Spanish helps us interpret the congenital weakness and failure that afflicts the heart of Methodism. Wesley offers a way of understanding failure and fragility rooted in the connection between the way of salvation and a theology of history. Seen theologically, history charts the progress of God's pilgrim people toward the new creation. It is a journey of grace upon grace (prevenient grace, convicting grace, justifying grace, sanctifying grace, glorifying grace), mediated through means of grace (instituted and prudential). It is a journey where backsliding is both a persistent possibility and a historical fact. Methodism abounds in accounts of personal and corporate backslidings. Even when doing our best to avoid evil, do good, and attend to all the ordinances of grace, we can still get it wrong. Indeed, even when we get it right, our accomplishments remain corruptible and liable to decay. Take, for example, nineteenth-

---

21. Andrew Walls, *The Cross-Cultural Process in Christian History* (Maryknoll, NY: Orbis, 2002), 29. Walls contrasts this fragility with the tenaciousness of the spread of Islam, which has only rarely experienced the territorial and demographic reversals common in church history.

22. Justo L. González, *Mañana: Christian Theology from a Hispanic Perspective* (Nashville, TN: Abingdon, 1990), 38–41, 40.

century Methodism. Arguably, the nineteenth century was the Methodist century. Alfred Hough composed a hymn expressing Methodism's missionary spirit, and the first stanza reads:

> The infidels, a motley band,
> in council met, and said:
> "The churches die all through the land,
> The last will soon be dead."
> When suddenly a message came,
> it filled them with dismay:
> "All hail the power of Jesus' name!
> We're building two a day."[23]

"Two a day" or even "three a day" was the Methodist refrain. At the same time, this golden age of Methodism was also the time of genocide and chattel slavery. There are good theological reasons for Methodist confidence, like our belief in free grace and our conviction that God has a special purpose for the Methodist people. There are also good theological reasons for Methodist humility. By rejecting "once saved, always saved" theologies, Wesley also rejects "once strong, always strong" and "once right, always right." Failure is at the heart of the story of Methodism, just as it lies at the core of the broader story of Christianity.

Reading Savannah in Spanish helps metodistas and Methodists approach the story of Methodism—even its most challenging chapters—with honesty and boldness. Failure can be a school where we learn to see again and see differently. The historian Reinhart Koselleck says it well: "If history is made in the short run by the victors, historical gains in knowledge stem in the long run from the vanquished."[24] In retrospect, Wesley learned to see his time in Georgia as the second rise of Methodism. Savannah was not a failed chapter in Wesley's life but a new movement in the

---

23. Alfred J. Hough, "We're Building Two a Day!" in *One Hundred Choice Selections, Number 25: A Repository of Readings, Recitations, and Plays Comprising Eloquence and Sentiment; Pathos and Humor; Dialect and Impersonations, Etc.*, ed. Phineas Garrett (Philadelphia: Penn, 1906), 143.

24. Reinhart Koselleck, *The Practice of Conceptual History: Timing History, Spacing Concepts* (Stanford, CA: Stanford University Press, 2002), 76.

drama of the rise of Methodism. The struggles in Savannah helped Wesley grow in his understanding of biblical Christianity by disabusing him of romanticized notions of the early church and deepening his understanding of sin and grace. The hardships he experienced were occasions for growing in what he termed "the passive virtues"[25] or what we today might call resilience.

This is counterintuitive. One might think failure instead teaches us to play it safe. Once bitten, twice shy. To avoid backsliding, don't walk. This was not Wesley's experience. At the cross, the vision of the vanquished became the vision of God. Wesley's short stay in Savannah prevented him from fully learning its lessons. To avoid backsliding while dreaming big, one must learn to see and walk with and as the Indigenous and marginalized. That said, he did not return to England to settle into a curate at Epworth or a professorship at Oxford. Instead, he dreamed not just of starting primitive Christianity in a colonial outpost but of reforming England and its Church and of spreading biblical Christianity everywhere.

Reading Aldersgate in Spanish

On May 24, 1738, John Wesley reluctantly travelled to a society meeting in Aldersgate. The day began with a sense of expectation. As he recorded in his journal, "I think it was about five this morning that I opened my Testament on those words . . . 'There are given unto us exceeding great and precious promises, even that ye should be partakers of the divine nature' [2 Pet 1:4]. Just as I went out I opened it again on those words, 'Thou art not far from the kingdom of God' [Mark 12:34]." By afternoon, hope had dimmed to lament. Wesley visited St. Paul's Cathedral, where the anthem was Psalm 130: "Out of the deep have I called unto thee, O Lord. Lord, hear my voice." By evening, lament soured to complaint: "In the evening I went very unwillingly to a society in Aldersgate Street, where one was reading Luther's preface to the Epistle to the Romans." While Luther described how God changes the heart through faith in Christ, Wesley experienced the grace of God in a fresh and powerful way and recorded

---

25. John Wesley, Sermon 59, "God's Love to Fallen Man," II.11, *Works* 2:432.

the experience, and this account became proverbial among Methodists: "I felt my heart strangely warmed. I felt I did trust in Christ, Christ alone for salvation, and an assurance was given me that he had taken away *my* sins, even *mine*, and saved *me* from the law of sin and death."[26]

Methodists often point to Aldersgate as a landmark—if not *the* landmark—in Wesley's biography. Even so, interpretations of the event are so diverse as to verge on incoherence.[27] For a long period of Methodist history, Aldersgate marked John Wesley's conversion away from a works-righteousness, high church Anglicanism to biblical Christianity. More recent readings have looked to Aldersgate as a mirror that reflects and warrants viewers' theological commitments and ecclesial locations. Liberal theologians saw in Aldersgate validation of the central role of experience in Christian life. Revivalist preachers saw in Aldersgate the model for conversion; the Holiness movement saw an example of entire sanctification; Pentecostals saw baptism in the Holy Spirit. That May 24 evening, which marked an ecumenically facilitated encounter with Christ's forgiving love, has become disputed ground.[28] Some scholarly factions call for Aldersgate to be reconsidered,[29] while others resolutely reject any downplaying of its significance.[30]

The United Methodist Book of Worship includes an entry for celebrating "Aldersgate Day or Sunday."[31] The entry is bare-boned, with a few recommended hymns, suggested readings from those Wesley heard on May 24, 1738, and a prayer of thanksgiving for the Wesley brothers. However, in my experience, the ritual is relatively foreign among English-speaking

26. John Wesley, May 24, 1738, *Journals and Diaries*, ¶¶13–14, 18:249–50 (emphasis original).

27. Randy L. Maddox, "Aldersgate: A Tradition History," in *Aldersgate Reconsidered*, ed. Randy L. Maddox (Nashville, TN: Abingdon/Kingswood, 1990), 133–46.

28. See Lyle Dabney, "What has Aldersgate to do with Wittenberg?" *Lutheran Forum* 43 (2008): 47–50.

29. Randy L. Maddox, ed., *Aldersgate Reconsidered* (Nashville, TN: Abingdon/Kingswood, 1990).

30. William J. Abraham, *Aldersgate and Athens: John Wesley and the Foundations of Christian Belief* (Waco: Baylor University Press, 2010), 2.

31. #439 in *The United Methodist Book of Worship: Regular Edition, Black* (Nashville, TN: United Methodist Publishing House, 2016), 346.

Methodists in the US.[32] If Aldersgate has suffered from neglect among some branches of the Methodist family, that is not true of many metodistas. Some Methodist churches in Latin America refer to May as "Methodism month" in honor of Aldersgate. May 24 is referred to as the day of the "corazón ardiente" (the burning heart) because the Spanish translation of Wesley's journal entry reads, "sentí un extraño ardor en mi corazón" (I felt a strange burning in my heart).[33]

The translation of Aldersgate to Latin America increased the temperature of the experience from warm to hot, aligning it both with the more charismatic experiences of Latin American and Hispanic Methodists as well as connecting with significant moments in the biblical story. The "corazón ardiente" recalls the condition of the disciples on the road to Emmaus when Jesus opened the Scriptures to them (Luke 24:32). The fiery heart also evokes the imagery of Pentecost when, Wesley says, God touched "their tongues as it were (together with their hearts) with Divine fire: his giving them such words as were active and penetrating, even as flaming fire."[34] It also resonates with the words of Jeremiah, who felt an ardent fire within him (Jer 20:9). In a sense, translating Aldersgate opens the door to rediscovering parts of the Methodist House otherwise lost to Wesley's heirs. Early Methodists were called Montanists, referring to a second-century sect that followed Montanus, a man who claimed the Holy Spirit moved him in extraordinary ways.[35] Rather than be too troubled by the charges, Wesley wore this epithet as a badge of honor—they must be doing something right to earn such rebuke.

---

32. Not to say Aldersgate Day is never celebrated in the US. E.g., a blog post from a Michigan pastor on Aldersgate Day in 2019 answers "What on Earth is Aldersgate Day?"—which at once suggests this Methodist community marked the occasion while also implying it is not well known. See Jeff Nelson (May 24, 2019), https://www.rofum.org/aldersgate-day/.

33. John Wesley, *Obras de Wesley, Tomo 11: Diarios I*, ed. Justo L. González (Franklin, TN: Providence House, 1998), 11:64.

34. John Wesley, *NT Notes*, Acts 2:3, 2:3.

35. E.g., James Clark, *Montanus Redivivus: Or, Montanism Revived, in the Principles and Disciplines of the Methodists* (Dublin: H. Saunders, 1760). For discussion, see Randy L. Maddox, *Responsible Grace: John Wesley's Practical Theology* (Nashville, TN: Abingdon/Kingswood, 1994),134–35.

Reading Aldersgate in Spanish calls for opening Methodism to charismatic and Pentecostal expressions of Christianity. The first Pentecostals in Latin America were Chilean Methodists.[36] When a charismatic revival swept through a congregation in Valparaiso, more traditional Methodists rejected and ultimately expelled their Spirit-baptized siblings. While retaining much of the Methodist doctrine and discipline, the Methodist Pentecostal Church has far outgrown the non-Pentecostal Methodist Church of Chile. A similar phenomenon has occurred throughout Latin American Methodism, with charismatic *metodistas* significantly outpacing their mainline counterparts, numerically speaking. True, the story of Methodism cannot be reduced to membership numbers; moreover, even when charismatic revivals have not resulted in schisms (like the schism in Chile), the Pentecostalization of Methodist churches is not without its ambiguities. Many Pentecostal Methodists uncritically embraced Augusto Pinochet's dictatorial policies while more mainline Latin American Methodists were championing human rights and paying dearly for their advocacy. The *corazón ardiente* of Aldersgate set afire by revivals has cooled Wesley's catholic love. The reasons Brazilian Methodists withdrew from the World Council of Churches and Cuban Methodists separated from the ecumenical seminary in Matanzas are doubtless complex. Even so, these actions are emblematic of challenges facing all *metodistas* and Methodists.[37]

John Wesley rode (and rides still) through many places in Latin America and among Latinx communities as an "enthusiast," a charismatic preacher who emphasizes private revelations, miraculous gifts, and moral purity. In other places, Wesley rode (and rides still) as an enlightened reformer no longer surprised by God's work in the world. The first Wesley still rides among "Methocostal" churches that are Methodist in name but Pentecostal in fact. The second Wesley still rides among mainline

---

36. Allan H. Anderson, *An Introduction to Pentecostalism: Global Charismatic Christianity* (New York: Cambridge University Press, 2004), 64–67. See also this volume's introduction, pages 9–11.

37. Pablo Andiñach, "Methodism in Latin America," *The Oxford Handbook of Methodist Studies* (New York: Oxford University Press, 2009), 53.

expressions of Methodism that are sometimes labeled "muertodistas."[38] The twentieth-century renewal of Methodist theology depended in large measure on rediscovering John Wesley and, concurrently, early English Methodism. The twenty-first century renewal of Methodism requires more than a new synthesis of Wesley as a "reasonable enthusiast"[39]; it demands a fresh reading of Aldersgate in Spanish and a new translation of Wesley's "strangely warmed heart."

The Future of Methodism Goes South

In this book, I have argued the renewal of Christian doctrine, worship, and mission can be advanced by rediscovering the heart of Methodism from the margins. Such rediscovery requires revisiting the sources and wellsprings of the people called Methodists.[40] We honor our mothers and fathers and acknowledge the wisdom of the past. In the process, we must beware the risks of looking to the past with nostalgia and of framing rediscovery as mere repetition. To mitigate these risks and open new paths for renewal, we have listened to the witness of the people called metodista. Methodism began in the North, but the future of Methodism goes South.

In common American English, "going south" has a negative connotation. Things go south when they go wrong. The origin of this phrase may

---

38. *Muerto* means dead; *muertodistas* loosely translates to Deathodists.

39. Referring to Henry Rack's *Reasonable Enthusiast: John Wesley and the Rise of Methodism* (London: Epworth, 1989).

40. The Brazilian theologian Rubem Alves once said, "The historian is someone who recovers forgotten memories and disseminates them as a sacrament to those who have lost the memory. Indeed, what finer community sacrament is there than the memories of a common past, punctuated by the existence of pain, of sacrifice and hope? To recover in order to disseminate. The historian is not an archaeologist of memories. He is a sower of visions and of hopes." Rubem Alves, "Las ideas teológicas y sus caminos por los surcos institucionales del protestantismo brasileño," in *Materiales para una historia de la teología en América Latina*, ed. Enrique Dussel (San José, Costa Rica: Departamento de Estudios Ecuménicos, 1980), 363–64. Cited in José Míguez Bonino, *Faces of Latin American Protestantism*, 107.

well lie with the common orientation of maps that place north as up and south as down. This cartographical convention tacitly reinforces a worldview where the north is on top culturally, economically, and politically. In this social convention, the north and the west stand for Christianity and civilization, whereas the south and the east stand for what is different and deficient. There is an expression in Spanish that captures the disorientation many metodistas experience when in diaspora in the United States: "norteado." It means being disoriented like a spinning compass unable to find its true north. Going south is a way to recalibrate and recover our bearing; it means going to the peripheries of the North, the borders and the barrios. From the peripheries, from the South, we learn to see anew and to dream again.

Dreams are often dismissed as illusions. In Wesley's sermon "Human Life a Dream," Wesley compares life without God to a dreamlike state that is only a simulacrum of real life. As he explains, "A dream therefore is a kind of digression from our real life. It seems to be a sort of echo of what was said or done a little when we were awake. Or, may we say, a dream is a fragment of life, broken off at both ends, not connected either with the part that goes before or with that which follows after?"[41] However, Wesley also believes that, as on the day of Pentecost, dreams can come from God.[42]

The people called metodista have a commission for the church as a whole. "To dream for those who do not dream, until the day when hope becomes reality."[43] In his book *Let Us Dream: The Path to a Better Future*,

---

41.   John Wesley, Sermon 124, "Human Life a Dream," §5, *Works* 4:111.

42.   John Wesley, *NT Notes*, Acts 2:17, 2:192–93. Wesley here distinguishes the visions of the young from the dreams of the old as modes of divine revelation suited to the physical condition of each: "I will pour out of my Spirit—Not on the Day of Pentecost only, *upon all flesh*—On persons of every Age, Sex, and Rank. *And your young men shall see visions*—In young Men the outward Senses are most vigorous, and the bodily Strength is entire, whereby they are best qualified to sustain the Shock which usually attends the Visions of God. In *old men* the internal Senses are most vigorous, suited to Divine *Dreams*. Not that the Old are wholly excluded from the former, nor the Young from the latter." Emphases original.

43.   Justo L. González, The Hispanic Creed, *Fiesta cristiana: Recursos para adoración (Resources for Worship)*, ed. Raquel M. Martínez (Nashville, TN: Abingdon, 2003), 270.

Pope Francis names a principle he believes to be fundamental for our current moment: "ideas are debated, but reality is discerned."[44] This does not downplay the importance of ideas; instead, ideas only get us so far. The problems we face in our world will not be solved by good ideas alone. What the church most desperately needs is not more debaters or apologists. It needs people who have unlearned the wisdom of this world and have received the wisdom of God, people who can therefore see what is really going on in the light of the cross. The church needs young people with Christ-shaped visions, and old people who still dream world-changing dreams. Reflecting on the prophesies from Joel fulfilled on Pentecost, Pope Francis declares, "The future will be born from the conjunction of the young and the old."[45] The dreams of the old keep the visions of the young root in history, and the visions of the young keep the dreams of the old from falling into nostalgia. "If we journey together, young and old, we can be firmly rooted in the present, and from here, revisit the past and look to the future. To revisit the past in order to learn from history and heal old wounds that at times still trouble us. To look to the future in order to nourish our enthusiasm, cause dreams to emerge, awaken prophecies and enable hope to blossom."[46]

Rediscovering the heart of Methodism calls for dreaming in Spanish. It is an odd experience when, after studying a new language, one begins to dream in this new language and actually understand it. Dreaming in Spanish pertains not so much to language as to location, to desiring and wishing new things as a "new we." Dreaming, like hope, has a social dimension: it is not only imagining *that* something might be different but imagining *with* someone else about that difference. The social is requisite to hope because the object of hope, on account of its arduousness, requires

---

44. Pope Francis with Austen Ivereigh, *Let Us Dream: The Path to a Better Future* (New York: Simon & Shuster, 2020), 54.

45. Pope Francis, *Let Us Dream*, 58.

46. Pope Francis, *Christus Vivit*, Post-synodal Apostolic Exhortation at Loreto (March 25, 2019), 199, https://www.vatican.va/content/francesco/en/apost_exhortations/documents/papa-francesco_esortazione-ap_20190325_christus-vivit.html.

help.[47] The story of the people called metodista has found this help from the margins.

A beautiful ritual characterizes a Methodist church I visited in Tulyehualco, a community on the outskirts of Mexico City. When they celebrate the anniversary of the church's founding, the whole community gathers outside the church building, where, after words of welcome and prayer, the assembly processes into the building from eldest to youngest. Only when all were inside did the worship really begin. It embodied and enacted Psalm 148:12-13, which proclaims: "Young men and women alike, old and young together! Let them praise the name of the Lord." In Tulyehualco, the prayer of the Psalmist and Pope Francis's Pentecost dreams took on flesh. The young and the old are signs of our times and interpreters of the work of the Spirit.

The church as the people of God is on a pilgrimage to mañana (tomorrow).[48] Mañana interrogates the present. It is a word of judgment on the manner in which the world is constituted today. Mañana begins not with prudent projections and strategic plans but with dreams— dreams not of winning the lottery but of Christ's coming mañana. We anticipate the end of this pilgrimage by how we journey on the way. Even now, Christians need to adopt and practice the language of God's reign, to speak "Reignese." According to Justo González, herein lies the problem with a number of the solutions intended to address the church's decline and spiritual malaise: "Instead of trying to develop practices and structures on the basis of the grammar of Reignese, we try to emulate 'successful' organizations of 'this world,' and to apply their grammar."[49] For many Latin American and Hispanic Christians, it was our abuelitas, our grandmothers, who instructed us in the grammar of mañana by teaching us how to pray for God's kingdom to come. From the wisdom of the

---

47. In the words of William Lynch, "Hope cannot be achieved alone. It must in some way or other be an act of community, whether the community be a church or a nation or just two people struggling together to produce liberation in each other." William F. Lynch, *Images of Hope: Imagination as Healer of the Hopeless* (Notre Dame, IN: University of Notre Dame Press, 1965), 24.

48. González, *Mañana*, 164.

49. González, *Mañana*, 167.

dreams of our grandparents and the passion of the visions of the young, God is preparing the church for renewal for sake of new creation. Federico Pagura's hymn "Hemos cubierto la tierra" ("We have covered the earth") voices these Pentecost dreams of a new mañana:

> Fulfill, Lord, your promise,
> Your kingdom of love come,
> And may the son of your justice
> Shine on us again, Lord.
> Cleanse, Jesus, your church
> From all its corruption;
> And may your earth be renewed
> By your presence and love.[50]

---

50. Federico Pagura, "Hemos cubierto la tierra," *Un cántico nuevo*, ed. Jorge Maldonado (Quito, Ecuador: Eirene, 1989), 192. See also https://himnosycanciones.com/acordes/hemos-cubierto-la-tierra/.

Index

Romero, St. Óscar, 28, 66, 194–204
Rodríguez, Rubén Rosario, 117n45, 124

saints, 41, 55, 65n42, 66, 113, 126–27, 133–34, 137, 140–43, 146, 178n53, 185, 195, 199, 205–06, 214
  see also Christian perfection
  see also holiness
Sobrino, Jon, 25–26, 32, 37–39, 46n59, 58
social creed, see creeds
solidarity, 22, 24n73, 27, 40, 48, 58, 76, 79, 83, 89, 110–11, 113, 121, 148, 180, 196
Souza, José Carlos de, 35–36, 47–48, 179
speculative divinity (a.k.a. speculative theology), 12, 15, 32–34, 104

Tamez, Elsa, 25–26, 32, 40–47, 64–65, 172, 194
tempers, 46–47, 54, 76n18, 181
  see also habits
tradition, in general, 12, 13n41, 27, 36–37, 39, 44–45, 46n59, 47–48, 56, 79, 82, 87n50, 97–100, 110, 113, 124, 128, 129n26, 130–32, 136, 195
Wesleyan tradition, *passim.*, *see esp.* 10–22, 27, 32, 35, 40–41, 45, 99–100, 106, 110, 128, 219

transfiguration, 26, 66–67, 167
translation, 2, 19, 25, 27, 51, 55, 59–60, 67–68, 74, 76, 113, 126n14, 145–46, 151–59, 181, 209, 218, 220
Trinity, 13–15, 21, 44, 45n52, 47–48, 63, 67, 114, 142, 171, 187, 191n10, 193, 195, 202, 205–06, 212

via salutis, *see* way of salvation
Vatican II, 26, 74–80, 84, 95–98

Wagner, Peter, 90–95
way of salvation, 15, 32, 34–36, 40–45, 48, 118, 120, 135, 143, 147–48, 172, 214
Wesley, John, passim.
  origins and mission of Methodism, 3–4, 5, 15–19, 162–66, 175, 182–84, 190
  ressourcement of, 21, 99–100, 208–220
  see also Methodist House
Wesley, Charles, 1, 13–14, 27, 35, 46n56, 53–54, 67, 101, 142–43, chapter 6 (145–60), 210–11
works of mercy and works of piety, 44–45, 211
  see also means of grace